HEMINGWAY AND GELLHORN

The Untold Story of Two Writers, Espionage, War, and the Great Depression

Jerome Tuccille

WinklerMedia Publishing Group, Baltimore, MD

To Marie, for all the right reasons

TABLE OF CONTENTS

PART ONE

HEMINGWAY

Chapter One

Ernest Hemingway had been a fresh water fisherman all his life, pulling trout and other fish from the streams and rivers of the Midwest and Europe. When he and Pauline had first visited Key West, Ernest quickly discovered the special challenges of salt water fishing, which required a different set of skills entirely to land the huge, sharp-toothed denizens of the ocean depths. At first he tried his luck casting off bridges east of Key West.

On a warm sunny day typical of the area when the weather is good, the prosecuting attorney for Monroe County, George Brooks, was waiting for the ferry to take him over from Lower Matecumbe Key. He looked across and spotted a rough-hewn character whom he didn't recognize dressed in a fish-stained shirt, a long-billed cap, dirty tennis shoes, and wrinkled canvas shorts. The man was casting into the Gulf from the nearby bridge. He was big, scars visible around his right kneecap, and a half-moon scar above his eye. The stranger looked suspicious to the prosecutor's well-trained eye. He looked more like a bootlegger or a rum-runner than a fisherman. George sauntered over and struck up a conversation with the burly stranger.

"Stranger to these parts?" George asked casually.

"Yeah."

"What brought you down here?"

"Time for a change. I'm a writer. Been living in Paris most of the past ten years and figured it was time to leave. This strikes me as a good place to write my books and catch some fish."

Ernest introduced himself, but George remained skeptical. He had never heard of the self-proclaimed author or the titles of his books. George would check out his story later. But something about the man's open demeanor put him at ease. He decided to take the stranger at face value.

"Do you know anybody with a boat who would be willing to share fishing expenses?" the author asked him.

"Go down to the Thompson Hardware Store on Caroline Street and ask for Charlie Thompson. He likes to fish as well as any man I know. He'll take you out. Just tell him George Brooks sent you by."

Charlie Thompson was one of the wealthiest men in Key West. The hardware store was only the tip of the iceberg of his family's business interests. They owned large tracts of land and numerous commercial interests in the heart of town. Charlie was behind the counter when Ernest walked in. The two men took an immediate liking to each other. By the time Ernest left the store, he and Charlie had made arrangements to go out fishing the next afternoon. After Charlie closed up that evening, he walked a few blocks to his home at 1029 Fleming Street.

"George Brooks sent this guy by," Charlie said to his wife Lorine. "Says his name's Hemingway. Says George told him I like to fish and might take him out. Says he's written a couple of books."

*   *   *

The next day the two men set off in Charlie's eighteen-foot powerboat following the channel that cut through Key West Bight into the Gulf of Mexico. The Gulf Stream flowed fast and green and sometimes blue a few miles out in the Gulf off the southern rim of Key West. Ernest was mesmerized by the look and smell of the warm salt water as he and Charlie plowed across its depths. Charlie fixed mackerel for bait, passing the hooks through their mouths, out the gills, slitting the sides and pushing the hooks through the other sides and out, tying their mouths shut on the wire leader, then tying the hooks tight so they couldn't come out and the bait would troll smoothly without slipping.

"They're a funny fish," Charlie said to Ernest. "They aren't here until they come. But when they come there's plenty of them.

10

And they've always come. There's a good stream and we're going to have a good breeze."

"So you think today's a good day?" Ernest asked.

"I hope so."

The "funny fish" Charlie was referring to were big tarpon, fighting game fish also known as the silver king. Ernest had never seen fish like this up close before. They were truly regal monsters that grew up to eight feet long and weighed in at a hundred pounds or more. They were sleek and powerful-looking at home in their element. What a thrill it would be to hook into one of these creatures and wrestle him aboard. It was a good day, as Charlie suspected. By the time the sun was setting down over the western horizon, Ernest and Charlie had hooked four tarpon and were cruising back to shore. The fish were not the only creatures hooked that day. Ernest was hooked himself—hooked on Key West and game-fishing.

Charlie and Lorine invited Ernest and Pauline over to their house for dinner a few days later. Ernest brought the Thompsons a couple of gifts—signed copies of his books—to prove he really was a writer of note and not a rum-runner as George Brooks had first suspected. Ernest and Pauline sat down to their first real Key West dinner, prepared by the Thompsons' Bahamian cook Phoebe. She cooked up black beans and yellow rice with green turtle steaks. The turtle came from one of Charlie's factories that processed turtle meat from the local waters. As a side dish, Phoebe made a raw conch salad with crusty Cuban bread. After watching Ernest wolf down her food with obvious delight, Phoebe later said, "That mon Hemenway is one fine eater."

Ernest and Charlie had hit it off well right from the start, and it was a relief for the men to discover that their wives were equally compatible. Both had been reared in rural Southern communities, Pauline in Piggott, Arkansas, and Lorine in Decatur, Georgia. Pauline had been a fashion writer for *Vogue* when she met Ernest, and Lorine had worked as a social science teacher before she married Charlie. After dinner the men sipped a couple of scotches before going out for a walk along tree-lined Fleming Street to talk about hunting and fishing.

11

The women sat beside each other on the porch discussing interests of their own. They formed a bond that night that would last throughout their lives—although Ernest almost severed it a few years later when he left Pauline for Martha Gellhorn, an ambitious young writer who was destined to become wife number three. Had Pauline known at the time that her husband would find a replacement for her in Key West, she would never have agreed to move there. But it really didn't matter where they lived; Ernest would have found his third wife *somewhere*. For better or worse. Mostly worse as it turned out. It was Lorine who helped Pauline find the house on Whitehead Street, which they eventually bought when Ernest said he was serious about making Key West his home.

One of the first things Pauline did to Ernest's great annoyance—and to the extreme discomfort of their many guests—was take down all the ceiling fans and replace them with chandeliers. The chandeliers looked elegant, but they had no utilitarian value when the weather was hot and humid. After removing the fans, Pauline eliminated the time-tested method of circulating the heavy tropical air that poured into Key West homes and gave Ernest one more excuse to trek down to Sloppy Joe's for some liquid refreshment.

*   *   *

Ernest was already famous by the time he and Pauline moved to Key West. He had finished correcting the galleys for *Men Without Women* on August 17, 1927, and mailed them the same day from Paris to his editor at Scribner's, Max Perkins. The book was published on October 14, the same month that Pauline discovered she was pregnant with their first child. When things are going well, it seems, they all go well together. Not that the book of stories met with universal approval from the literary mafia, who were waiting with daggers drawn to eviscerate Ernest's follow-up offering to his novel *The Sun Also Rises* published a year earlier. Dorothy Parker and the reviewer for *Time* magazine loved the latest book, but others were less kind. Joseph Wood Krutch, an influential critic of the period, sniffed that Ernest wrote "sordid little catastrophes in the lives of very vulgar people."

Virginia Woolf wrote that Ernest was "self-consciously virile," and his stories were "a little dry and sterile." None of their barbs could stop the sale of the book, though, which caught on quickly with the same readers who gobbled up *The Sun Also Rises*. By early December, sales had already topped thirteen thousand copies. But Ernest was stung by the negative reviews nonetheless.

He wrote to F. Scott Fitzgerald saying, "These goddamn reviews are sent to me by my 'friends,' any review saying the stuff is a pile of shit I get at least 2000 copies of."

Early the next year, Pauline started to pack up for a trip back to the States. Her baby was due in June and she wanted him or her to be born on American soil. Pauline's family had yet to meet Ernest, and now that his writing career had taken off she was anxious to trot him around back home. It was different than in the beginning when he was penniless, virtually unknown, about to leave his wife for another woman (her), and had little to show for his efforts except some short stories and a first novel in progress. Now she had a real story to tell and a rising literary star to put on exhibit.

Pauline thought that they could not get out of Paris fast enough. Not only had she inherited Hadley's husband when she married him, but Pauline inherited his social baggage as well. The list of the walking wounded whom Ernest left scattered over the literary battlefield as a result of his writing included just about everyone he knew. The list was long and impressive: Harold Loeb, Ford Madox Ford, Gertrude Stein, Robert McAlmon, Sherwood Anderson, Lewis Galantiere, Duff Twysden—the roster was endless. Pauline wanted to leave town before Ernest started in on *her* friends now that he had turned his own into road kill. But before she could get him out of Gay Paree, the roof quite literally fell in on him. The *Herald* reported the accident in March.

"Mr. Ernest Hemingway, author who was wounded about the head when a skylight crashed on him at his home Sunday morning, yesterday was recovering, according to officials at the American Hospital at Neuilly. Mr. Hemingway's wound, which required three stitches inside and six outside, is healing and he was able to pursue his usual life."

"I was there shortly after a skylight fell on his head," said writer Archibald MacLeish, another of Ernest's benefactors. "I think he'd probably had a good deal to drink and pulled the wrong rope in the can. I was the first one called. Someone dug up a taxi at about half past two in the morning and I went around and picked him up and took him to the hospital. He'd lost a lot of blood by that time so that he babbled a good deal on the way to the hospital. He took a great many stitches with just a local anesthetic and he sat through the whole thing talking to the doctor, telling him the story of his life."

The look and smell of his own blood put Ernest back in World War I when a mortar blast turned his right knee into jelly. The war injury left Ernest with a slight limp, and the skylight accident would leave him scarred for many years afterward, but it turned out to be fortuitous in a significant way. For some time now he had been searching for a viable subject for his next novel, and now he had it. Not since he was a youth in the war had he seen so much of his own body flayed open like raw meat on a butcher's block. The war had been the most telling and traumatic experience of his life to date. Against Pauline's protests that he should heal first and then get ready for their trip, Ernest sat down and wrote the opening pages of a new novel. He didn't have his title yet, but it would come to him soon enough. It seemed almost inevitable that he would call it *A Farewell to Arms*.

And finally they left—but not immediately to Arkansas where Pauline's parents were anxiously waiting to greet their daughter and son-in-law. Ernest had always wondered if he could ever live back in the States again after immersing himself in the sights, smells, and wonders of Paris for several years. He had his answer as soon as he cast his eyes on Key West. Ernest and Pauline had gone there to pick up a new Ford given to them by Pauline's rich Uncle Gus, who managed her trust account.

Key West was the closest thing to a foreign country that Ernest had seen inside the country of his birth. On the surface the town was shabby and down on its heels at the time. But the flowering jacaranda trees, the explosion of scarlet bougainvillea, yellow cassia, and red-orange flame trees more than made up for the sun- and salt-blasted fishermen's shacks with weather-dulled paint peeling off like layers of old, parched skin. The local sponge beds were blighted, the cigar factories had been boarded up, and the naval base deactivated. But the local honky-tonk bars were lively and the streets were filled with men who spoke everything from English to Caribbean Creole to Cuban Spanish and chose to ignore the infamous Prohibition laws. Key West was an outlaw town populated by rebels, and the Feds chose to ignore their open rebelliousness for fear of igniting an insurrection by men who would fight to the death to preserve their lifestyle.

Ernest fell in love with Key West at first sight. When the local inhabitants weren't drinking they were fishing, and when they weren't fishing they were drinking. Here was a place where he could write, fish, drink, and live life to the fullest if he ever chose to do so. Key West was made for him. The pregnant Pauline looked around somewhat aghast at first. This was not exactly what she envisioned coming home to. But Ernest was in pig heaven.

A Farewell to Arms was published at the end of September 1929 and exploded out of the gate. Within a month the book sold thirty-three thousand copies. At the end of the year sales were up to fifty thousand, and on January 8, 1930, Max wrote to Ernest to tell him that sales were up over seventy thousand copies and climbing. The reviews were almost universally euphoric from the leading literary movers and shakers, including Malcolm Cowley, Clifton Fadiman, J.B. Priestley, Arnold Bennett, and countless others. A rave review by Dorothy Parker pushed Ernest over the top, from mere famous author to a legend in his own time—even if some people in Key West had never heard of the author and his books before.

*   *   *

15

The Gulf Stream sweeps out of the west across the southern rim of the country. It snakes eastward between Cuba and the Florida Keys, running fast and warm from the Gulf of Mexico through the Strait of Florida where it accelerates before turning north in the Atlantic along the eastern rim of the United States. It is a relentless force of nature, powerful and inexorable, in turn peaceful and violent as it flows past the Bahamas and Bermuda. The stream sweeps farther north into the icy waters of the North Atlantic, brushing past Iceland, Greenland, and the British Isles. But it is not those northern islands that people think of when they talk about the Gulf Stream. They think mostly about Key West and Cuba, sometimes Bimini and Dry Tortuga. And it is only Cuba that is truly tropical, sitting big and majestic south of the Tropic of Cancer. But Key West is tropical enough, dotted with palm trees and surrounded by warm aquamarine water teeming with some of the biggest fish that patrol the ocean depths. Catching those gargantuan creatures requires more than skill. Also required are strength, endurance, and knowledge of how the fish behave and how to outsmart them in one of the most challenging sports dreamed up by man.

Chapter Two

Cayo Hueso sits forty-five miles north of the Tropic of Cancer, ninety miles north of Cuba and one hundred and fifty miles south of Miami. *Cayo Hueso*—Bone Island or Island of Bones. Whose bones the Spanish were referring to when they christened the island *Cayo Hueso* remains a mystery. Was the island actually covered with bones? If so, whose bones were they? They could have been the remains of the Caloosa Indians who may have buried their dead there. No one knows for sure, but by the 1700s the English translated *Cayo Hueso* into Key West, and the misnomer has survived the centuries. The local economy had always been marginal, depending on exotic trades like shrimping, fishing, smuggling, and wreck-diving to bring in the money. But by the 1930s even those volatile occupations were gone.

The land itself that Key West rests on is not exactly terra firma. The firma keeps getting rearranged, reconfigured, or wiped away by hurricanes and tropical storms. In 1846 a monster hurricane blasted the Island of Bones and pushed a pile of sand up along the shoreline, so that a small graveyard that had previously been on the water's edge was now a few blocks inland. The lighthouse, too, looked as though it had been physically moved and suddenly became the most landlocked lighthouse in the country. The beacon from the lighthouse, located near Ernest's house, guided him home from his late-night drinking sprees at Sloppy Joe's.

"As long as I can see that beacon," Ernest said, "I'll always be able to find my way home."

Pirates were terrorizing the island in 1822 when an exasperated Spaniard named Juan Salas sold Key West to John Simonton, a businessman from Mobile, Alabama, for two thousand dollars. To celebrate the transfer of the island to an American, Lieutenant Matthew Perry sailed down to raise the American flag over what is now Mallory Square. He declared before a motley crew of sweating sailors and Cuban fisherman that the new U.S. possession had one of the largest deepwater anchorages in the country. Once the military significance of Key West had been established, Navy Commodore David Porter followed Perry's wake from the mainland with a squadron of ships to wage war against the pirates. Porter's "Mosquito Fleet," as the natives were quick to call it, took a bit longer to rid the waters of pirates than Porter had anticipated, but by 1830 he had succeeded in chasing them down to Cuba and east over to Puerto Rico.

It didn't take the locals long to decide that they preferred the pirates to Porter, who seized the locals' livestock, buildings, and strategic supplies to wage his war. At least they had a fighting chance against the pirates, who made no claims about representing the interests of the federal government. When the government court-martialed Porter for overstepping his authority, he resigned in a huff and joined the Mexican Navy as Chief of Naval Operations. The Mexicans didn't like him much either—indeed, General Santa Ana tried to assassinate him twice—so he embarked to Turkey, where he tried to impose his special brand of leadership on the Middle Eastern infidels. Death finally caught up with him in 1843 when he died a bitter old man.

"A retrospect of the history of my life seems a highly-colored romance, which I should be very loath to live over again," was the way he assessed his own life.

Half of Key West didn't even exist until real estate developer William Whitehead surveyed the town and carved it up into tiny plots. Ships' carpenters built most of the houses on those plots without paying much attention to architectural style or positioning. The result was a jumble of small ramshackle houses sitting alongside paths and alleys that came in off the main roads at odd angles. Ava Moore Parks described the Key West of the period in her book *The Forgotten Frontier*: "There was nothing else like it; a city crowded on a small island in the middle of nowhere…This was it—civilization began and ended here."

An anonymous observer summed up Key West as "densely settled, and about as un-American as possible, bearing a strong resemblance to a West Indian town. The houses are of wood, plainly built, and, with few exceptions, painted white. The houses are of all sizes, jumbled up in the oddest way…The interior of each block is filled up with one-story shanties."

Ernest and other writers found a special charm in the Island of Bones, but Mark Twain was not one of them. Traveling through Key West from Nicaragua in 1867, Twain entered in his diary: "If I have got Key West summed up right, they would receive War, Famine, Pestilence, and Death without a question, call them all by some fancy name and then rope in the survivors and sell them good cigars and brandies at easy prices and horrible dinners at infamous rates. They wouldn't quarantine anybody; they'd say 'come' and say it gladly, if you brought destruction and hell in your wake."

The famous author's vision almost came true when a great fire swept across the island on April Fools' Day 1886. It flared up in the Cuban Patriotic Club on Duval Street and quickly swept across the island. The island's only fire engine had been shipped to New York City for repairs, so there was nothing to contain the conflagration as it roared down Fleming Street from Whitehead to Bahama. The locals tried to fight the inferno by blowing up houses in its path with gunpowder, but the blaze continued to rage for twelve hours straight, wiping out fifty acres of Key West and dozens of its inhabitants.

Finally it spent its fury and died out on its own.

The indomitable locals were not defeated, working around the clock as they cleared out the burnt-out areas. They rebuilt their homes and public buildings quickly. Stubborn to a fault, they replaced what had been incinerated with new houses built of wood. The wealthier among them built new houses larger than the ones they had lost. Key West remained a mostly wooden town, except for a handful of military installations and public facilities made of rusticated stone—concrete blocks formed in a mold. In short order the trees, vines, flowers, and plants grew back, the termites returned and feasted on the wooden porches as they had before, and a casual observer would never know that the look, feel, and pace of the town had gone through a cataclysm just a short time back.

Henry Flagler looked at Key West and formed a different opinion of the place than Mark Twain did. Flagler was a visionary and a businessman first and foremost, and unlike Twain, a successful speculator as well. After the turn of the twentieth century he recognized the value of Key West as a port for goods flowing to and from Cuba and South America. Flagler bought one hundred and thirty-four acres of land on Trumbo Point to serve as a terminus for a railroad connecting the Keys to the mainland. When his engineers informed him that there wasn't enough dry land to erect the terminus, Flagler characteristically said,

"Then make some."

Times were good once again on the Island of Bones. And they remained so for a while longer. Key West had become the richest town per capita in the United States in the aftermath of the fire, thanks to its deepwater port that made it a center of trade with Cuba and South America. The fishing, sponge, and cigar industries flourished. But, inevitably it seemed, Key West was destined to be plagued by a new blight—this one economic and more difficult to overcome. Prohibition had destroyed most of the legitimate commercial activity on the island, and the Crash of '29 drove the final nail into the town's economic coffin. The jobs fled, the population declined by two-thirds, and per capita income had sunk to the lowest in the nation. Henry Flagler's train from the mainland chugged through the Keys "carrying nothing, nowhere, for nobody," as he put it.

*   *   *

The hard times hit the Island of Bones worse than almost anyplace else in the country. The Island of Bones found itself five million dollars in debt with eighty percent of its twelve thousand inhabitants on welfare. David Sholtz, the governor of Florida, was so distraught that he turned the administration of the town over to the federal government. President Franklin Delano Roosevelt

20

responded by appointing an autocratic character named Julius F. Stone as the dictator of Key West in all but name. Ernest and Julius detested each other on first sight. They were both cut from the same mold—haughty, egotistical, domineering sons of the Midwest. Ernest hailed from Oak Park, Illinois, and Julius from Columbus, Ohio. It was inconceivable that a town the size of Key West could host two outsized egos like theirs. The problem for Ernest was that Julius had the power, the full force and power of the federal government behind him. Ernest was not the only writer to take a unique disliking to the imperious Mr. Stone. The eminent American poet Robert Frost was equally disenchanted with him.

"Here in Key West," Frost wrote, "we have a national rehabilitation project running everything. I am dragged by the house-renting clerk before the Rehabilitator in Chief to see if I will do, that is to say, measure up to his idea of what the new citizenry must look like as it thought, felt and acted under God and the President in Washington. The Rehabilitator is a rich young man in shorts with hairy legs named Stone…It is a very, very dead place because it has died several times. It died as a resort of pirates, then as a house of smugglers and wreckers, then as a cigar manufactury…This town has been nationalized to rescue it from its own speculative excesses. The personal interest of Roosevelt in his second coming has been invoked and both mayor and governor have abdicated till we see what absolute authority can do to restore the prices of the speculators' graveyard plots and make Key West equal to Miami…[Key West] has a million dollars worth of concrete sidewalks with no houses on them."

*   *   *

Ernest was equal parts a man of action and a man of letters. In October 1933, the man of action finally got a chance to act out one of his most cherished fantasies thanks to a twenty-five-thousand-dollar gift from Pauline's Uncle Gus. Ernest had long dreamed of going to Africa to hunt wild game in the company of his closest friends. But as the Great Depression bit deeper, the list of

21

Ernest's drinking and shooting companions grew shorter because of a shortage of money. The only ones who could afford to go off with Ernest on such an expensive adventure were Charlie Thompson and, of course, Pauline whose uncle was financing the entire trip in the hope that Ernest would get another major book out of it.

They arrived in Paris on October 26, the day before Ernest's latest effort, a book of short stories called *Winner Take Nothing*, was published to mixed reviews. His friends in the literary world found good things to say about the book, but most of the others were negative. Max Perkins wrote to tell Ernest that the reviews were "unsatisfactory and a good many are absolutely enraging." Most thought Ernest was mining old ground while events had moved on and left him in the dust. The *New York Times* summed up the thoughts of most mainstream reviewers with its comment, "The dialogue is admirable…The way of life is caught and conveyed without a hitch…It is not that the life they portray isn't worth exploring. But Hemingway has explored it beyond its worth." A year earlier Ernest had published his book about bullfighting, *Death in the Afternoon*, which would eventually be regarded as the best book on the sport by a non-Spaniard. But at the time the literary world regarded it as too much effort expended on a trivial subject while the world was slowly starving.

The public saw it differently, however. While the literary intelligentsia wanted Ernest to engage himself more with the political and economic travails of the era, Ernest's readers were happy to find an escape from the misery that beset them every day. Other books sold fewer than five thousand copies in the throes of the Great Depression, but Ernest's latest opus pushed above eleven thousand within weeks of publication. Max Perkins wired Ernest that Scribner's was happy with sales and expected the book to become a long-term success.

Ernest, Pauline, and Charlie sailed from Marseilles on November 22 aboard the *General Metzinger* bound for Africa. Seventeen days later they arrived in Mombasa, Pauline wearing a pristine white dress, Charlie a white suit and tie, and Ernest a safari shirt with the sleeves rolled up. "Pauline and I looked like missionaries," Charlie said, "while Ernest had the distinct look of a whiskey drummer." The next day they boarded the Kenya and Uganda Railway bound for Nairobi.

There, in the heart of darkest Africa, they met up with legendary Great White Hunter Philip Percival who had once guided Ernest's hero Teddy Roosevelt on a safari through the bush. Ernest had followed Teddy's adventures with great interest as a boy in Illinois, and he had wanted to travel in the great man's footsteps ever since. Now it was Ernest's turn to turn the heavy guns on the biggest game of all, the life-threatening game of killing your prey before it kills you. The trip was a great success for Ernest from every standpoint except one—Charlie outhunted him. He bagged his animals before Ernest bagged his, and when they both killed a rhino, Charlie's measured six inches longer across the horns than Ernest's did. It was a measure of their affection for each other that their friendship endured. Ernest was competitive to a fault, having attacked his literary rivals with great ferocity, including those who had gone out of their way to help him in the early days when he was having trouble getting published. If Charlie had been a writer, it might have been different. But Ernest shrugged it off, lifted his glass in a toast to Charlie, and they all returned home with more than enough trophies to hang on their walls for the rest of their lives.

On April 11, 1934, a jazz band greeted them in Key West with all the locals turning out to celebrate their arrival. Word of their great African adventure had preceded them, reported in minute detail in the nation's leading newspapers. Ernest lost no time in getting back to work. The safari had stimulated his creative juices, as Uncle Gus had anticipated, and Ernest started work almost immediately on *Green Hills of Africa*. Ernest finished the first draft by the end of the year, and Scriber's brought it out in October 1935. The reviewers were no kinder to his book about big-game hunting than they had been to the bullfighting book and the last book of short stories. Even Ernest's old buddy F. Scott Fitzgerald weighed in against it, but part of his motivation may have been due to Ernest's blasting *his* last effort, *Tender is the Night*, for having "no true writing" in it. No matter though. Sales were good to say the least. Better than Scott's and better than Ernest's other competitors.

And success is the best revenge of all, Ernest thought.

Chapter Three

Ernest was a literary superstar by the time Julius Stone descended on Key West like a provincial governor on the outskirts of the Roman Empire. Julius cast his gaze wide and far across his domain. He took in the abandoned cigar factories, collapsed piers, and dilapidated houses that had clearly seen better days. His hairy legs, as Frost remarked, were very much on display since he introduced Bermuda shorts to an area that preferred fish-stained trousers or cut-off shorts tied around the waist with a length of rope. The Conchs—or native-born locals—made fun of him walking around in public in what looked like "his underwear." Some took to wearing flowery undershorts themselves, both to spoof him and also to show that they could get away with anything he could. But their taunts were lost on Imperator Stone. Julius was lord and master of all that he surveyed. He had the power as southeastern director of FERA, the Federal Emergency Relief Administration, and they would all knuckle under his rule if they knew what was good for them. Every state had a FERA administrator with almost absolute authority, and in Florida the man whose word was law was Julius Stone.

"Your city is bankrupt," he told the locals, "your streets are littered and filthy, your homes are rundown, and your industry is gone."

Emperor Julius rarely smiled. He stood tall and thin and unyielding. At first he thought of shutting down the island altogether and moving the inhabitants north, perhaps to Tampa, were they might find work in the cigar factories that had relocated there— whether the locals wanted to go or not. That would have been an early American version of the Pol Pot solution in Cambodia a few decades later: ship an entire population off to an area where they might do something useful with their lives. But that seemed too drastic an option, even for the imperious provincial governor.

Finally Julius hit on a solution that he thought would work. There was one solution to the town's problems, as he saw it, and the ragtag Conchs would have nothing to say about it. The abandoned buildings and houses, the rotting piers, the garbage-strewn streets offended Julius's Midwestern sensibilities. He would rip down the homes, such as they were, and rebuild the entire island into a *tourist* Mecca—a new Bermuda in the Gulf Stream. Beyond the blighted wasteland lay dazzling blue-green water teeming with giant fish, some of the most spectacular sunsets on earth, bougainvillea in bloom on the water's edge, great breezes rustling through stately palm trees. Julius literally drafted the town's welfare recipients into the Key West Volunteer Group and put them to work. No work, no relief checks for you. He would feed them and give them shelter in return for their stoop labor. Their options were limited. That's how the pyramids got built, and that's how Key West would be transformed into a haven for tourists with big boats to tie up in the harbor and pots of legal tender to spend in the island's restaurants, bars, and hotels.

And so began one of the most far-reaching rehabilitation projects in the nation's history. Julius looked on as the locals scurried about, so many dung beetles on a putrefying mound of decay. He permitted some of them to retain title to their houses but charged them rent, which they paid with their relief money until the cost of renovating their houses had been paid back. In doing so he overstepped his authority. Nowhere in the federal guidelines did it say that Stone had a right to attach private property and charge the owners rent for it.

"I got away with it because we were so far off no one knew what we were doing," Julius crowed, giddy with absolute power. "With a scratch of my pen I started this work in Key West, and with a scratch of my pen I can stop it—just like that."

Over a whirlwind five-month period, from July to December 1935, Julius Stone's four thousand conscripted minions labored long and hard for a million and a half hours collectively. They fixed up more than two hundred houses; erected cabanas with thatched-roof huts on the beaches; renovated bars, restaurants, and hotels; planted

26

trees along the streets; and put up an aquarium at Mallory Square. And still they were not finished. Their toil was far from over. Stone started a school for maids, enticing the few remaining wealthy dowagers in town to teach the unwashed local girls how to clean, launder, and otherwise serve the needs of the visiting tourists. He drafted unemployed fishermen as fishing guides to teach the moneyed classes how to haul in the giant billfish that lived in the blue-green waters. He conscripted out-of-work musicians into a Hospitality Band to greet wealthy tourists arriving by boat and train. He turned the abandoned submarine base into a private yacht basin. And Emperor Julius admonished the visitors themselves about just how long it would take them to fully appreciate his renovated fiefdom.

"To appreciate Key West with its indigenous architecture, its lanes and byways, its friendly people and general picturesqueness, the visitor must spend at least a few days in the city…Unless a visitor is prepared to spend at least three full days here, the Key West Administration would rather he did not come."

Julius incurred Ernest's unmitigated fury when he drafted Key West's most celebrated literary icon into serving as a tourist attraction without checking first with the author. There it was—the Whitehead Street house that belonged to Papa, as he started to call himself even in his thirties, listed number eighteen on a list of forty-eight places tourists should plan to visit on the Island of Bones.

It is not clear what infuriated Papa more: being included on the list in the first place, or being placed so far down on Stone's roster of attractions. Shouldn't the Heavyweight Champion of American Writers, the man who had knocked Turgenev, de Maupassant, and Stendhal on their asses in the literary ring, have been number one if he was mentioned at all?

"I started out very quiet and I beat Mr. Turgenev," Ernest had written. "Then I trained hard and I beat Mr. de Maupassant. I've fought two draws with Mr. Stendhal, and I think I had an edge in the last one. But nobody's going to get me in any ring with Mr. Tolstoy unless I'm crazy or I keep getting better."

Ernest responded with a characteristic curse and a threat to flatten Julius the next time he saw the dictator, and he even took a shot at Julius's wife: "Anyone would have to be a FERA man to have a wife like that." In a calmer mood, Ernest had a fence built around his property to keep Julius's nosy tourists from peering at him in his skivvies as he sauntered at dawn across a catwalk to his second-story office in the adjoining tower. Then again, how many rich tourists got up before dawn to see any writer, even one as famous as Ernest, commuting to his lair to put words on paper?

The *Florida Grower*, a newspaper published in Orlando, also had a dark view of Emperor Stone and his efforts in Key West. "FERA rule is the rule of fear," it claimed. "No American city is more completely ruled by one man than is this small island city."

Another newspaper called Julius "the king of a tight little empire…Call it a 'dictatorship,' a 'kingdom within a republic,' or anything you choose."

Most galling to all of Julius's critics was that his heavy-handed tactics succeeded in creating the tourist Mecca he envisioned. The tourists arrived by boat and train, some by airplane from the mainland. They craved food, drink, shelter, and entertainment to satisfy their desires. The restaurants, bars, hotels, and fishing excursions began to thrive once again. Indeed, many residents turned themselves into entrepreneurs, moving out of their renovated homes to accommodate the invasion and charging exorbitant rents for them. Suddenly, all was well on the Island of Bones while the rest of America struggled to free itself from the relentless stranglehold of the Great Depression. The tourists arrived and saved Key West from drowning under the sea that attacked its shoreline on all sides—figuratively if not literally. The Conchs hated the tourists but had no problem turning their houses over to them in return for sorely needed cash. They despised the tourists but welcomed them as benefactors.

Chapter Four

You know how it was early in the morning in Key West back then. The rummies were still asleep on the sidewalk with their backs propped against the building outside Sloppy Joe's. By the time Ernest walked down from his house, the rummies were mostly gone, except for one or two inside the bar working off their hangovers by sipping slowly from frosted glasses of beer. Ernest had already put in a day's work on his typewriter, rising around six a.m. and writing for four or five hours before sitting down to a hearty meal. Now it was almost noon and Ernest was ready to have his first drink and go out fishing with his cronies. This had been his pattern since he had moved to Key West with Pauline after spending most of the past ten years in Paris, in the beginning with his first wife Hadley, and then with Pauline after he divorced Hadley.

"Hey, Hem," Josie Russell greeted Ernest when he walked in, mopping off a place on the bar near Papa's favorite spot. "You goin' out to try your luck today?"

"Hell yes. A day like this was made for fishing, right? You want to come? I'm going out with Charlie later."

"Can't do it, Hem. I'm legit now. Got to tend to business now that the legal trade is back."

Josie Russell had run a speakeasy during Prohibition, then opened up a legal joint on Greene Street that he called Sloppy Joe's when Prohibition ended. Josie Russell had done a lot of things when booze was illegal in the U.S., running rum from Cuba to the States, carrying human cargo from Cuba—mainly Chinese—who wanted to enter the U.S. illegally, running guns from Key West to Cuba. You name it, Josie had done it. It was better not to know too much about all the things Josie had done during that benighted decade when the government thought it could change human behavior just by making some things illegal.

29

Ernest was at the peak of his abilities physically and mentally. An inch or so over six feet tall, his weight was trim at one eighty-five. A neat black mustache and his long dark hair gave him the look of the actor Clark Gable who was two years younger than he was. The writing was going well. The horrors, the deep depression that plagued him and other members of his family from time to time, the dark side of the soul that prompted his father to end his own life with a pistol in 1928, had not tormented Ernest for some time now. They never did when the writing was good, the creative juices were flowing, and he maintained a good balance between his literary life and his love of sport.

Ernest's friend and fellow writer, John Dos Passos, had said it best: "Key West is just the place for Ole Hem to dry out his bones." After the cold, damp Paris winters, Key West was the ideal tonic for him. Even the name of the place resonated well with Ernest. *Cayo Hueso,* "The Saint Tropez of the Poor," Ernest had labeled the town when he first set eyes on it.

*   *   *

A neatly dressed American tourist and his half-drunk, overweight wife occupied the stools on Ernest's left. The man was tall and thin, very tan, with a trimmed blond mustache. She looked like a wrestler and was dressed in shorts that barely contained her thunder thighs. On the other side of them sat a down-at-the-heels Conch drinking coffee laced with Cuban rum. Ernest had seen him before at Sloppy Joe's and knew him from around town. He was a rough-and-ready character with a foul mouth and a tendency to get in fights after his third or fourth drink. Ernest liked him.

"Nerts to you," the lady wrestler said to her husband. "Nerts, double nerts to you."

"Don't mind her," the tall tourist said to the Conch. "She's my wife."

"Oh nerts to him too," the fat lady said. "Double nerts to him."

30

"I got to talk to you," the Conch said to Josie. "Can we talk alone?"

"Go right ahead and say anything you want," the lady wrestler said.

The Conch looked her over long and hard. "Okay, lady. Shut up, you whore," he said. Then to Josie, "Let's go in the back, Josie. I got a favor to ask. Hem can talk to the whore a couple minutes."

Josie flinched, then waved the Conch off to the back. "Listen," Josie said. "You can't call my trade names like that. You can't call a woman a whore in my joint."

"Did you hear what she said to me? 'Nerts to you,' she said."

"I don't like them tourists any more than you do. Just don't call her a whore to her face here, that's all I'm sayin'."

"That man insulted me," the fat lady said to Ernest when the other two disappeared.

"He talks like that," Ernest said. "That's just his way."

"I'll speak to him when he comes back," said her husband.

Ernest chuckled to himself, taking it all in with great amusement. A fat lot of good talking to a Conch about insulting your wife was going to do.

"Listen here," the thin man said when the Conch and Josie came back. "What's the idea of talking to my wife like that?"

"What's the lady drinking?" the Conch asked Josie.

"A Cuba Libre," Josie said.

"Figures. Give me a straight whiskey then," said the Conch.

The Conch downed his drink in a single gulp and headed toward the street.

"I should have hit him," the tall man said. "What do you think, dear?"

"I wish I was a man," she said. "He was cute though. I'd like to get to know him better."

"Let's get out of here," the thin man said. "Everybody here is either insulting or nuts."

"This is a strange place," Ernest said. "They call it Singapore West or the Gibraltar of America. It's closer to Cuba than it is to

31

Miami. It's actually three hundred and seventy-five miles south of Cairo, Egypt."

"You know, I like you too," the fat lady said to Ernest. "What's your name?"

"I like you too, darling," Ernest said. "But I've got to go out fishing now before my chums leave without me."

"Wish I could go with you guys, Hem," Josie said. "But I got to tend to business now that everything's legit."

* * *

The wind and rain blew in hard off the water and kicked up a chop at the edge of the shore. The weather was relentless—horizontal rain, shuddering wind, dark gray sky—a terrible tempest blasting the people inching down Duval Street toward the dock at the end of the street. The weather was even worse on the islands farther east, particularly on Windley and Matecumbe Keys where the land was flat, the trees spindly, and the structures unfit to withstand little more than a stiff tropical breeze. The population was sparse throughout the Keys east and north of Key West. They were mostly local Conchs who fished the waters for whatever they could pull out of the sparkling blue depths, and a ragtag contingent of World War I vets living in makeshift camps erected during the Great Depression. No sooner had Julius Stone transformed Key West into his cherished tourist Mecca than FDR sent the vets to the Keys to get them out of the nation's capital where they were an embarrassment to the federal government.

The vets had started agitating for a special bonus for their service during the First World War to end all wars. The survivors returned from the blood-stained battlefields of Europe to an America that shunted them aside as the good times rolled on and those who didn't serve had money to burn in nightclubs and dancehalls across the length and breadth of the nation. The country was too busy enjoying its prosperity during the Roaring '20s to pay much attention to battle-scarred men who had fallen between the economic cracks. They were men with limited skills and not enough education to compete with the college grads and skilled laborers who had taken their jobs while they were thousands of miles away, fighting a war no one cared to think about. Everyone, it seemed, was earning enough money to feed their families and enjoy a night out on the town, except for the vets who had put their lives at risk in foreign lands. Four million of them had been displaced. As they raised their voices in protest, Congress prodded itself out of its usual stupor when times are good and voted the vets a retroactive bonus to compensate for the meager one dollar a day they had been paid on active duty.

President Calvin Coolidge, Silent Cal as he was called, vetoed the bill, saying, "Patriotism which is bought and paid for is not patriotism."

Maybe not, but veterans had been receiving bonuses for their service since the beginning of time. Two thousand years earlier, the Romans rewarded their own returning legions with land grants and gifts of cash. The question of patriotism, whether it is measured in blood or money, is moot when citizens are prospering at home while men who fought for their freedom are out of work and destitute. Congress overrode Silent Cal's veto in 1924, but then rubbed salt in the vets' wounds by awarding them a bonus that was not payable until 1945, more than twenty years later. The vets were incensed, and when the Stock Market Crash of 1929 gave way to the Great Depression of the 1930s, their mood turned ugly, bordering on the very edge of revolution.

*   *   *

By 1932 more than half of the nation's outstanding mortgages were in default. Three thousand banks had failed during the past twelve months alone. In May of that year, three hundred angry vets hopped aboard railway cars heading out of Portland, Oregon, heading east across the great American mountains, forests, and plains toward the nation's capital. Along the way they picked up other vets and sympathizers, unemployed legions of disgruntled workers determined to extract a measure of justice from their elected

33

representatives in Washington. They maintained military discipline on their long journey east, playing reveille every morning, sounding taps at night, shunning panhandling, violence, and extremist rhetoric within their ranks. By June their numbers had grown to fifteen thousand rebels and patriots, including more than one thousand wives and children. The press hopped aboard the bandwagon and published stories about this great "Bonus Expeditionary Force" that was about to invade the very citadel of government.

The angry legions set up squalid camps along the Anacostia Flats across the river from the Capitol. They built their shelters with materials scavenged from junk piles—rotting lumber, packing boxes, scrap tin—and covered their shacks with roofs of thatched straw. The veterans had one demand: the immediate payment of the bonus Congress had promised them. Their ramshackle camps spilled over to other encampments around the city while the Bonus Army, as the public had now dubbed them, waited patiently for the government to respond.

Discipline in the camp was good, despite the fears of D.C. residents who spread stories about the "Red Scare" in their midst. The veterans laid out pathways linking their various campsites, dug latrines, and held daily formations to maintain their military discipline. They required newcomers entering the camps to register and prove they were bona fide veterans rather than rabble rousers looking to stir up revolutionary fervor.

"We're here for the duration and we're not going to starve," said the leader of the vets, Retired Sergeant Walter Waters. "We're going to keep ourselves a simon-pure veterans' organization. If the Bonus is paid it will relieve to a large extent the deplorable economic conditions."

To help their families survive, battle-hardened young men pummeled each other for nickels in an ongoing boxing marathon. Salvation Army volunteers organized a library inside muddy tents. The faces of hunger and deprivation haunted a wealthy socialite, Evalyn McLean, the owner of the Hope Diamond, to such a degree that she burst into a greasy-spoon diner to demand sandwiches for the vets and their families.

"I want a thousand, and a thousand packs of cigarettes," she demanded.

Roy Wilkins, a reporter who later became the head of the NAACP, walked among the tents and shocked his readers with accounts of "black toes and white toes sticking out side by side." The veterans had created a truly interracial community at a time when Jim Crow segregation reigned supreme. Tourists flocked in to see the spectacle first-hand, thrilled and mostly sympathetic to the veterans' plight. Another reporter labeled the tent city a milestone for Western culture, "the first large scale attempt to mimic Mahatma Gandhi's passive resistance."

J. Edgar Hoover, the young head of the FBI, was less than impressed. He reacted with claims that "misfit radicals were plotting to blow up the White House." General Douglas MacArthur, the Army chief of staff, viewed the Bonus Army as a "cancerous threat from pacifism and its bedfellow, communism." MacArthur's deputy for intelligence called the destitute veterans proof of "objectionable blood in our breed of human beings." A less-than-sympathetic reporter demanded protection "from the criminal fringe of the invaders." *The Washington Post*, owned by Evalyn McLean's husband, conjured images of "demagogues manipulating servile hordes." Senator James Lewis of Illinois spurned fellow veterans who came politely to solicit his vote. "Go to hell!" he told them.

Chapter Five

More than six thousand vets blanketed Capitol Hill on the night of June 17, 1932, the year before Ernest had left on his safari. A local newspaper described the event as "the tensest day in the capital since the war." Two days earlier, the House of Representatives had passed a bill offering veterans $2.4 million in cash for their 1924 bonus certificates. The debate had been contentious, with one congressman dying of a heart attack during the proceedings. The Senate then commenced its own debate on the bill, whether or not to immediately give the vets their bonus money. Senator Hiram Johnson of California warned colleagues that "it would not be difficult for a real revolution to start in this country." By dusk the Bonus Army crowded the Capitol grounds awaiting the outcome. When messengers emerged with news that the Senate had defeated the bill, reporters envisioned furious veterans storming the Congress. Waters took his place at the head of the crowd and reported the bad news: The U.S. Senate had voted against the bill 62 to 18. The legions stood mute, crushed into stunned silence.

"Sing 'America' and go back to your billets," Waters instructed the vets, who began a silent "Death March" that started in front of the Capitol and lasted until July 17, when Congress adjourned.

On July 28, the federal government ordered the evacuation of the veterans from all government property. As the police moved in, shots rang out and two veterans fell dead with gunshot wounds. At that point President Herbert Hoover ordered the army to clear out the veterans. Even opponents of the bonus bill fumed that stern measures kept backfiring with the public. The public display of haggard old soldiers silently trudging along in their Death March until they dropped only whipped up more support for the veterans. Waters enthralled the press with stories about how he and his wife had been fired from a cannery after serving their country in wartime.

36

President Hoover, whose popularity was sagging by the hour in an election year because of the deepening depression, found his patience tested to the limits. Hoover dug his heels in and refused to meet with Waters or anyone else associated with the vets. At the end of July, Hoover sent the *current* army in to put down the insurrection mounted by the *old* army—Americans going to war against Americans for the first time since the Civil War. By 4:45 p.m. General MacArthur's troops were massed on Pennsylvania Avenue below the Capitol. Thousands of Civil Service employees poured out of their cubicles and lined the streets to watch. The veterans cheered, assuming the military display was in their honor. Suddenly MacArthur's troops turned on them and charged. "Shame, Shame" the spectators cried. Soldiers with fixed bayonets followed, hurling tear gas into the crowd. By nightfall the Bonus Army had retreated across the Anacostia River where Hoover ordered MacArthur to call a stop to the charge.

But MacArthur refused to be deterred. He continued his assault with tanks, tear gas, and fixed bayonets, flagrantly exceeding his orders to contain the bonus marchers within their mudflats away from public buildings and monuments. "Instead," wrote historian David M. Kennedy, "MacArthur's troops proceeded to Anacostia and drove the marchers out of the camp with tear gas." By early morning all its inhabitants had been routed. Major George Patton relished the mounted charge on the Bonus Army with an almost sexual joy as "sabers rose and fell with a comforting smack," according to one account. He gleefully sent his cavalry to rout the bewildered inhabitants and torch their flimsy huts in a giant bonfire. Two more veterans died of gunshots, two infants suffocated from gas, and several hundred people fell injured. Nearby hospitals were overwhelmed with casualties. Major Dwight D. Eisenhower reacted more humanely, writing later, "The whole scene was pitiful. The veterans were ragged, ill-fed, and felt themselves badly abused. To suddenly see the whole encampment going up in flames just added to the pity."

MacArthur grandly claimed that he saved the republic from insurrection, and President Hoover refused to rebuke his general. He issued a terse statement that "a challenge to the authority of the United States Government has been met, swiftly and firmly."

But the public saw things differently. "The Bonus Army episode," David Kennedy observed, "came to symbolize Hoover's supposed insensitivity to the plight of the unemployed."

*   *   *

Franklin Delano Roosevelt rose from bed in his pajamas the next morning at Hyde Park. "There would hardly be any need to campaign against the incumbent president once readers saw the news," he remarked to Eleanor. His assessment was prescient as he swept to victory in November. After his inauguration in 1933, his advisers diverted a returning caravan of homeless veterans beyond the Potomac River to an isolated military camp in Virginia, where First Lady Eleanor Roosevelt placated them with a visit.

"Hoover sent the army," said one veteran. "Roosevelt sent his wife."

Roosevelt enjoyed his victory throughout his first one hundred days in office, but the lingering plight of the veterans posed a problem as the depression deepened. The patience of unemployed Americans wore thin as the vets pressed the government for special benefits while the rest of the nation plunged deeper into despair. "Opposition to the bonus," historian Arthur Schlesinger Jr. recalled, "was one of the virtuous issues of the day." Roosevelt read the shifting polls and did an about-face. He spoke before a giant American Legion convention in October 1933 and announced that he would reject any payout for World War I veterans as fiscally irresponsible and unfair to the rest of the nation.

"No person because he wore a uniform must therefore be placed in a special class of beneficiaries," he told the legionnaires.

When both houses of Congress passed a new bonus bill in 1935, Roosevelt delivered his veto personally to a joint session of Congress for the first time in history. By a narrow margin, the Senate upheld the president's veto. Roosevelt and his advisors then devised a plan to *relocate* the "veteran problem" far away from Washington, D.C. Any place would do as long as it was remote and off the beaten track, away from the cameras and microphones of nosy reporters. Roosevelt would set up work camps in the Florida Keys, just up along the spit of land from where Ernest lived, and enlist the vets in a jobs program modeled on the WPA, or Works Progress Administration.

Early that year, federal administrators began the removal of seven hundred bonus marchers into Veterans Rehabilitation Camps south of Miami, where road crews were building a highway to connect the Keys all the way through to the Island of Bones. *Time* magazine latched onto the story and labeled the work camps "playgrounds for derelicts." The *New York Times* embarked on a campaign to shut them down, branding the grizzled veterans "shell-shocked, whisky-shocked and depression-shocked."

The federal government erected a total of eleven work camps in Florida, three of them in the Keys. Camp 1 was put up on Upper Windley Key, the first one to be built. Camp 3 was situated on the lower end of Lower Matecumbe Key, the place from which the unfinished highway would continue. The third work camp, Camp 5, was located on the upper end of Lower Matecumbe Key. The veterans who moved there were a cross-section of America at the time—aging war-torn vets, many of them alcoholics; roustabouts; tradesmen when they had any work at all; poison gas victims; others with serious wounds; some not incapacitated at all. They were a miserable lot, depressed, battered, and hungry for any work they could get, including building a road for a dollar a day along a godforsaken stretch of sand hundreds of miles off the mainland. They posed a stark contrast to the wealthy tourists flocking down to

Key West to check out the sunsets and test their skills hauling giant fish from the surrounding waters.

*   *   *

Game fishing had its cultish mystique just like any major sport, and Ernest quickly graduated into the big leagues when he learned the rules of the game. A small circle of men who lusted to land the greatest fish that prowled the ocean depths held sway within the ranks of the truly initiated. Billfish came in several varieties— sailfish, swordfish, and various species of marlin. And the giant blue marlin was the biggest catch of all. The giant blue marlin was more than the big leagues; it was the World Series and the Super Bowl combined. Those who discovered it hunted it to the exclusion of every other fish that lived. One *aficionado* called fishing for giant blue marlin "an expensive form of mental illness." The tarpon Ernest had caught when he first went out with Charlie Thompson were one thing, but giant blue marlins were an entirely different dimension of aquatic life. Ernest quickly became addicted.

His birthday fell on July 21, and on that special day in 1935 he landed a 540-pound marlin in the waters off Cuba, the largest fish he had ever caught. After posing for photographs alongside his giant catch on the dock in Havana, Ernest gave the meat away to the locals.

"Killing fish for no useful purpose, or allowing their meat to waste wantonly, should be an offense punishable by law," Ernest wrote in one of his articles for *Esquire*.

A few weeks later, Ernest crossed the Gulf Stream from Cuba in his new boat, which he named *Pilar*. Pilar had been Pauline's code name when he conducted an affair with her in Paris while still married to his first wife Hadley. The hull of the boat was painted pirate-black with its name emblazoned in bright white letters on the stern. The crossing to Key West took twenty-six hours in calm seas and near-perfect weather. The mood on board was celebratory with Ernest and his crew whooping it up, enjoying the lingering glow of a fishing season that had gone well so far, better than expected by all accounts. The rum and wine flowed freely, the Conch chowder was fragrant and spicy, and the men were no worse for wear as they maneuvered *Pilar* into the Navy yard marina in Key West.

Ernest planned to spend a short time answering mail and dashing another article off for *Esquire* before making a return trip to Cuba for the rest of the fishing season. But *Pilar* had developed some problems during the crossing from Cuba. The boat was burning too much oil and needed to have its piston rings replaced. As luck would have it, the replacement rings were en route somewhere between Detroit and Key West, and when they finally did arrive the local mechanic was on vacation. By the time he returned a storm took shape out in the Atlantic, churning the sea into a milky gray cauldron as it chugged westward. The rest of the Cuban fishing season was now a lost cause, so Ernest settled in for the duration planning to get back to some serious work. On August 20 an advisory reached Key West, warning that the tropical storm was now roiling the ocean just east of Bermuda. The lines of communication were fragile back then, relying on wireless reports from shipping stations scattered throughout the islands. The news was getting worse by the hour, and as the Labor Day weekend approached, the tropical storm had evolved into a full-scale hurricane making a serious run toward the Florida Keys—even though the *Miami Herald* still identified it as a "tropical disturbance."

Ernest studied his charts showing the paths of forty September hurricanes since the turn of the century. Always the meticulous researcher and chronicler of important data—including daily readings on his weight, temperature, and blood pressure—Ernest estimated that the hurricane would roar into Key West around noon on Monday. On Monday morning Ernest walked over to the marina at the Navy base where he kept *Pilar*, only to find a line of boat-owners ahead of him waiting to have their own boats hauled out of the water onto dry dock. He had to settle for a heavy hawser to secure *Pilar* in an area that he thought would provide the greatest safety during the storm. He returned home to bring in outdoor furniture and board up the windows on his house, then went back to the boatyard where he discovered that the Coast Guard had tied up a confiscated "rum boat" with contraband booze right next to *Pilar*.

"For Christ's sake!" he yelled at the sailor on duty. "You know those lousy ringbolts will pull out of her stem and then she'll come down on us. What's the use of letting a piece of junk like that sink a good boat?"

The marina—the entire town—was in chaos, with people rushing in all directions to secure their boats, their homes, and everything that wasn't nailed down from the encroaching hurricane. Ernest double-checked his barometer reading and recalculated that the hurricane would strike at midnight. Sleep was out of the question as he prepared himself, Pauline, and their staff to gear up for the worst. By midnight the barometric reading had dropped to 29.50 and was sinking rapidly. Ernest figured the lights would blow as the wind picked up. Soon it was rattling the windows, the shutters, the very walls and foundation of his house. Ernest was sick to his stomach thinking about *Pilar* and the rum boat berthed next to it. He dressed and went outside to get in his car and drive to the marina, but the engine wires were saturated by the windblown rain whipping in hard off the water. He had no choice but to push his way through the howling tempest and go down on foot. On the way the batteries in his flashlight shorted out and he was forced to fight his way against the wind in zero visibility. Sure enough, his worst fears materialized when he reached the Navy yard and saw the rum boat rocking wildly with the ringbolts pulled out. But this time he was lucky. Before it could slam into his boat, a Spanish sailor named Jose Rodriguez had stepped aboard and maneuvered the rum boat away from *Pilar*. Ernest never loved the Spanish and the Cubans more than he did at that moment.

"You feel like hell," he wrote later. "You figure if we get the hurricane from there…you will lose the boat and you will never have enough money to get another."

And then a miracle took place. At two in the morning the wind subsided, the rain let up, and the worst of the hurricane passed. Three hours later the barometer held steady and the pressure began to rise. The hurricane, bad as it was, had struck Key West only a glancing blow. When Ernest returned to his house later in the morning he noticed only minimal damage. Some branches had fallen and trees were uprooted in his yard, but the house was intact. Ernest, *Pilar*, and Key West had made it through one of the most powerful hurricanes to slam the Island of Bones in its long turbulent history.

"We got only the outside edge," Ernest wrote in a letter to his editor Max Perkins on September 7. "It was due for midnight and I went to bed at ten to get a couple of hours sleep if possible having made everything as safe as possible with the boat. Went with the barometer on a chair by the bed and a flashlight to use when the lights should go. At midnight the barometer had fallen to 29.50 and the wind was coming very high and in gusts of great strength tearing down trees, branches etc. Car drowned out and got down to boat afoot and stood by until 5 a.m. when the wind shifting into the west we knew the storm had crossed to the north and was going away."

Chapter Six

The Keys further east were not nearly as lucky. The hurricane was small in size, only ten miles across the eye at the center, but it was the most violent one ever to hit the Keys with wind gusts soaring to two hundred and fifty miles an hour. The barometric reading on Windley and Matecumbe Keys, where the vets were housed in their flimsy work camps, plummeted to 26.35, the lowest ever recorded. The hurricane made a direct hit on the work camps, pushing a wall of water eighteen feet high across the narrow strip of sand. The vets and Conchs had nowhere to go, nothing to hang onto.

The government had ample warning that the work camps in the Keys were a disaster waiting to happen. Five months earlier, Fred Ghent, who was in charge of the Florida camps, wrote to FERA in Washington saying, "This area is subject to hurricanes and it is our duty…to furnish a safe refuge during a storm." He specifically recommended building a solid two-story warehouse where the vets could congregate when a hurricane was imminent.

He received no reply.

When the monster storm struck, a seventeen-year-old fisherman named Bernard Russell, no relation to Josie, felt his sister's hand pull out of his grip in the pitch-black night as the ferocious winds and towering waves pummeled their bodies.

"You went wherever the waves pushed you and wherever the winds pushed you," he said after the storm. "It was so dark you couldn't see what was going on and maybe that was good."

He never saw his sister again, nor his mother and two other sisters. They were somewhere out there, lost in the sea. He survived when he was tossed on top of a trash pile. "There were sixty-one in the Russell family and fifty of them died that night," he said. The official death toll came to four hundred and twenty-three, two hundred and fifty-nine of them veterans whose camps had been torn away and flung out into the Gulf as though they never existed.

"There were so many dead people and no place to take them," Russell elaborated. "They stacked them up and burned them." The ones they could find in the horrific aftermath that is.

Another survivor recalled that "there was a big wall of water—fifteen feet high, twenty maybe. It swept over those shacks and messed them up like they were match boxes."

Someone else remembered that the roof of the canteen was ripped away. "We all started away in the same direction and the roof came down on us. It must have hit every one of us. After the roof fell all I could hear was the grunting and groaning of the boys. I never saw any of them after that."

"Bodies were lying all over the roadway and lumber piled on them and some of them had holes in their heads," read another account. "I saw bodies with tree stumps smashed through their chests—heads blown off—twisted arms and legs torn off by flying timber that cut like big knives."

The 1935 storm was a Category Five hurricane, the first of two to hammer the United States since the government started to keep records. It took out thirty-five miles of Henry Flagler's railroad and wiped every tree and every structure off Windley and Matecumbe Keys. With *Pilar* now seaworthy once again, Ernest set out a couple of days later to survey the carnage.

"All the next day the winds were too high to get out and there was no communication with the keys," he wrote to Max Perkins. "Telephone, cable and telegraph all down, too rough for boats to leave. The next day we got across and found things in a terrible shape…The foliage absolutely stripped as though by fire for forty miles and the land looking like the abandoned bed of a river. Not a building of any sort standing…Max, you can't imagine it, two women, naked, tossed up into trees by the water, swollen and stinking, their breasts as big as balloons, flies between their legs. Then, by figuring, you locate where it is and recognize them as the two very nice girls who ran a sandwich place and a filling station three miles from the ferry…Harry Hopkins and Roosevelt who sent those poor bonus march guys down here to get rid of them got rid of them all right."

Up to this point Ernest had not been overtly political. His politics, such as he had thought about politics at all, could best be described as passively anarchistic. He distrusted authority of any sort and was instinctively individualistic. He wanted to be left alone to do his writing the way he saw fit and not have his language censored by bureaucrats always on the hunt for obscenities. And he preferred to keep most of the money he earned and not turn big chunks of it over to tax collectors. But the plight of the vets on the Keys pushed him into a more revolutionary frame of mind. He was no fan of the New Deal and viewed the intrusions of civil authorities as a misguided attempt to improve the lot of working people. Leave people alone and they will find a way to make things better on their own, he believed. In some ways he wandered further to the left of New Deal administrators, but a later generation might have put him further to the right of traditional conservatives into the realm of individual anarchism. Ernest had become a rebel. He was so infuriated by the death of the vets that he took time out from his regular writing to pen a diatribe, which he called "Who Murdered the Vets?" *The New Masses*, a publication of the American Communist Party, asked him to write his version of what happened. Ernest had no use for communists or their literature, but he was happy to have an outlet for his fury. The article was published on September 17, 1935.

"Whom did they annoy and to whom was their possible presence a political danger?" he wrote. "Who sent them down to the Florida Keys and left them there in hurricane months? Who is responsible for their deaths?" Ernest answered his own questions at the end of the piece and put the blame squarely in the lap of the Roosevelt administration.

"Who sent them down there? I hope he reads this—and how does he feel? He will die too, himself, perhaps even without a hurricane warning, but maybe it will be an easy death, that's the best you get, so that you do not have to hang onto something until you can't hang on, until your fingers won't hang on, and it is dark...You're dead now, brother, but who left you there in the hurricane months on the Keys where a thousand men died before you when they were building the road that's now washed out? Who left you there? And what's the punishment for manslaughter now?"

*   *   *

The vets who survived descended on the Island of Bones like a plague of locusts, a horde of hollow-eyed warriors with little left to live for except to scavenge drinks in waterfront bars and take their anger out on fellow vets when they drank too much. They discovered Sloppy Joe's and other bars scattered like weeds along the waterfront. A crowd of them were in Sloppy Joe's one night, men in dungarees, some bareheaded and others in caps, all of them pressed three-deep around the bar, jamming the place out to the sidewalk. As Ernest walked in, two men flew out through the doorway, one on top of the other. The one on top grabbed the other guy's hair and banged his head against the cement. The town sheriff pulled up in his car and pried the two of them apart.

"Cut it out," he said. "Get up off him."

"For Christ's sake! Can't you mind your own business?" asked the man who had been on top.

"Leave my buddy alone," the battered man said. He had blood in his hair, more blood trickling out of his ear and down his face. He squared off as if to throw a punch at the sheriff. "What's the matter? Don't you think I can take it?"

"He can take it. Give me a buck," the man who had been on top said to the sheriff.

"No."

"Go to hell then." He fastened his eyes on Ernest. "What about it, pal?"

"I'll buy you a drink," said Ernest.

The three of them pushed their way through the crowd up to the bar. Josie was there as he always was, along with Al Skinner, his three-hundred-pound black bartender who doubled as a bouncer. They kept a bat behind the bar just in case the crowd got out of hand inside the joint. Josie said "Skinner was as strong as a mule, could

47

drink like a horse." He made a good "hatchet man if there was anything or anyone to take care of," said one of Josie's regulars.

Later that night, Ernest wandered alone through the streets. The moon was high in the night sky with the stars twinkling sharply. The trees were dark shapes against the sky as Ernest passed frame houses with narrow yards, faint lights escaping through shuttered windows. He headed back home past unpaved alleys with double rows of houses; Cuban bolito houses with open doors where you could see rough men gambling inside; the pressed-stone Catholic church with sharp, ugly triangles for steeples; the black-domed convent; a filling station; a closed sandwich shop alongside an empty lot that had once been a miniature golf course; a pool parlor; and a barber shop. Pauline would be waiting for him in bed when he got home, awake, unhappy with his drinking and his late-night hours, but nonetheless patient with him and his routine that didn't include her.

But Ernest was not thinking about Pauline at the moment. He was thinking about other women, including the gorgeous Jane Mason with whom he had a heated affair two years earlier. Jane Mason—a blonde goddess with a body to match her face. Jane not only collected the books of well-known writers. She collected the writers themselves.

"You reek of that woman!" Pauline had shrieked at him when he returned from one of his trysts with her.

"What are you talking about?"

"Don't deny it, you liar! You phony! You change your women like you change your politics. Whatever suits you at the time."

Women had thrown themselves at him right from the beginning. He was big and handsome, and he was now a famous writer too. Hadn't Pauline set her sights on him when he was still a penurious young writer in Paris married to Hadley? His affair with Jane Mason had taken place near his favorite fishing haunt in the waters off Havana. When he was not with Pauline, his usual companion on the trips across to Cuba was the luscious Jane with her wavy blonde hair and curvaceous body. When they were not on

Ernest's boat, they shared a room at the Ambos Mundos hotel in the heart of Havana.

"Jane Mason not only drank a bit but was one of the wildest, hairiest, most drinking, wenching, sexy superwomen in the world when she was in her twenties, thirties, and early forties," a friend of Ernest who preferred to remain anonymous described her. "She was proud of being the model for the Macomber woman in 'The Short Happy Life of Francis Macomber,'" one of Ernest's best-known short stories.

"She was in love with Ernest at various times," said another friend.

Her face was a study in white and gold, and her husband Grant, a top executive with Pan American, regarded her as an invaluable business asset. They lived part of the time in a Cuban mansion set high up on the hills above the Jaimanitas Golf Course. Their parties were legendary, attracting the wealthiest members of the Anglo-Cuban community and celebrities from around the globe. Grant was well aware of his wife's attraction to other men, as well as her numerous infidelities, and was said to pardon them as long as she let him watch once in a while. Ernest regarded him as nothing but a "wealthy twerp" who ignored her when she seriously injured herself a couple of times, once in a car accident, and another time during an attempted suicide leap from the balcony of their home in Cuba.

Beautiful and athletic, she loved to fish and hunt with Ernest and his cronies and held her own with all of them. But she wanted to be remembered for something more than her physical allure. The inscription she wrote for her tombstone summed up her own self-image better than anything else written about her: "Talents too many, not enough of any."

Chapter Seven

Every other Friday was fight night on the Island of Bones. They staged the matches in an arena on the corner of Thomas and Petronia Streets that also doubled as a whorehouse. Ernest liked to sample the trade, referee the fights, and occasionally get in the ring himself and mix it up with the boxers when the matches were over. A few hundred boxing fans usually showed up, paying a buck and a quarter for general admission and three dollars for ringside seats. The fighters got a cut of the purse that amounted to twenty-five or thirty dollars apiece. Most of the fighters were professionals, aging guys on their way down and young ones on their way up.

"Hemingway looked like an ordinary hippie," James "Iron Baby" Roberts told *Sports Illustrated* years later. At the time he met Ernest, Roberts was a teenage light-heavyweight. "I always tell people that it was the first time I saw a hippie, because he used to dress that way. He had a long beard, and he needed a haircut, and he was wearing shorts and an old shirt, just like a common person. You'd never have guessed that he was the big writer he was. He carried right on like ordinary people. That's the way he lived here."

One Friday night Ernest refereed a bout between a black fighter named Alfred "Black Pie" Colebrooks and a Cuban who went by the name Joe Mills. In Colebrooks's corner was his handler, a lightweight boxer called "Shine," whose ring name was Kermit "Battling Geech" Forbes. It was clear from the first bell that Colebrooks was outclassed. Mills charged across the ring and belted Colebrooks onto the canvas. Black Pie got up, and Mills knocked him down again. After the eighth knockdown, with Black Pie gamely struggling to his feet, Shine threw in the towel, signaling the fight was over. His fighter had taken enough punishment.

Ernest picked up the towel and threw it back. He figured as long as a fighter was game, he had a right to keep on trying until he couldn't fight any longer. Shine tossed the towel back at Ernest, and once again it flew back into the corner. After Ernest had thrown the towel back the third time, Shine lost his cool. He charged into the ring and took a swing at Ernest, who stood a foot taller than the corner man. The blow fell short, and Ernest grabbed Shine's ears and shook him back and forth until a local cop ran into the ring and pulled Shine away.

"No, don't arrest him," Ernest told the cop. "Anytime a man's got guts enough to take a punch at me, he's all right."

Shine later said that he didn't know who Ernest was. "I thought he was some bum trying to pick up a dollar" refereeing fights.

The next day Ernest invited Shine over to his house to spar with him in a ring he set up in his backyard. "He had two speed-punching bags and one heavy bag and three kinds of gloves—eight, ten, and sixteen ounces," said Shine. "At one time or another, all the local fighters sparred with him at fifty cents a round."

"We all took it easy on Mr. Ernest," Iron Baby, the light heavyweight, recalled. "We'd go about three or four rounds with him. I was the only one he was kind of leery of, on account of my weight." The light heavyweights came in at about one seventy-five compared with Ernest's one eighty-five when he was in shape. As he got older, Ernest tipped the scales at over two hundred pounds most of the time, sometimes ballooning up to two-fifty. "We were pretty young then, and Hemingway was older than us, but he'd give us a tussle."

"He liked to box and so did I," said novelist Harry Sylvester. "I think we both had glorified notions of what we were. He was still very badly slowed down by his World War I war wounds. But he gave off a great feeling of energy. You got the feeling—an intelligent bear is here."

Iron Baby went on to become a ranking light heavyweight, while Shine was a ranking lightweight in the Army. "The average person in Key West didn't believe in this segregation stuff with black and white," said Iron Baby. "We all lived next door to each other. We didn't know anything about white sections and black

51

sections. I was raised with white guys. Hemingway was friendly with black people. But the whole town was that way."

*   *   *

From the deck of *Pilar*, and from the balcony of their room in the Ambos Mundos, they could hear the big guns in the distance. Cuba was in turmoil throughout the 1930s as the revolution to topple Gerardo Machado y Morales became more deadly. Machado had been the youngest Cuban general in the war of independence that ended with the U.S. occupation in 1898, when he was twenty-seven. During the occupation he was mayor of Santa Clara, the town where he was born. Shortly after taking office, a mysterious fire incinerated the records of his criminal past; before the war, and before the Americans arrived, Machado and his father had served time as cattle robbers. The three fingers remaining on his left hand bore testimony to a life devoted to butchery—butchery in a meat shop in his home town, and in the way he dispatched his political enemies.

Machado ran a losing race for governor of Las Villas but then went on to serve in various posts in the government of Jose Miguel Gomez. He was also a businessman who ran a sugar mill and an electricity company that controlled most of Havana's utilities. He married his cousin and had three daughters with her. In 1924 he ran successfully for president, defeating Mario G. Menocal and becoming the fifth democratically elected Cuban president.

In the beginning, Machado was popular with his countrymen. He adopted a nationalistic agenda, imposing heavy taxes on American investments in his nation. At the same time, he began the construction of a seven-hundred-mile central highway and promoted investments in tourism, industry, and mining. His balancing act worked—in the beginning at least—as he combined a support for U.S. interests while defending the idea of Cuban sovereignty. Wilfredo Fernandez, leader of the opposition Conservative Party, paid Machado the ultimate compliment, saying Machado's programs were so "full of patriotism" that to oppose them would be "unpatriotic." But the honeymoon quickly ended. In the late 1920s the Cuban economy took a nosedive, opposition to Machado's policies gained traction, and his instincts as the butcher he once was resurfaced. Those who criticized him felt the full brunt of his arrogance and brutality.

By April 1928, university students demonstrated against his "dictatorial tendencies." Machado responded in typical fashion, ordering the University Council made up of teachers and administrators to convene disciplinary tribunals and expel the student leaders. Using a combination of threats and bribes, Machado positioned himself as the *only* candidate of the *only* legal political parties he allowed to operate: the Liberal, Conservative, and Popular parties, all of which he controlled with a steel grip. He had Cuba's constitution amended to permit a six-year term, which he won in November 1928 as an unopposed candidate.

And then Machado orchestrated the murders of his most vocal opponents. Exiled student leader Julio Antonio Mella was assassinated in Mexico in 1929. Others were dispatched in quick order. Machado's main critics met secretly to consolidate their forces. Opposition to Machado and his policies grew rapidly as the economy deteriorated and the price of sugar— Cuba's main commodity—plunged. Machado reacted with even harsher, more violent measures than before. His secret police, the Porra, served as a Death Squad, relentlessly pursuing and killing Machado's main opponents. Once more his opponents regrouped. Student groups, organized labor, and middle class professionals armed themselves in 1931 and staged an open revolt. Machado had nothing but contempt for their efforts and announced that he would stay in office until May 20, 1935, "not a minute more or a minute less."

"By the end of 1932," wrote Jules R. Benjamin in *The Hispanic American Historical Review*, "the militant response of the Cuban proletariat to both the depression and the dictatorship had become one of the major threats to the regime." The U.S. took a stand in favor of political reform in Cuba, trumpeting the New Deal shaping up under FDR as the ideal model for Cuba. A year later, Cuba was in a state of all-out war. President Roosevelt sent Ambassador Sumner Welles to Cuba to monitor conditions on the island-nation. In July 1933 Welles insisted that Machado reinstate the constitution that he threw out two years earlier or face the full wrath and fury of the United States. Machado was as disdainful of FDR and his minions as he was of his home-grown opponents. "The reestablishment of the guarantees is a prerogative of the President of Cuba and will be done when the President considers it necessary," he said.

Revolution burst out across the length and breadth of the country, with the guns booming in the distance as Ernest and his "mob," as he called them, fished for giant blue marlin in the waters off Havana. The end for Machado was more clearly in view. His coalition of thugs fell apart, and he began to look for an opportunity to leave his country under conditions favorable to himself. In typical fashion, the U.S. negotiated a deal with Machado amounting to a payoff if he agreed to leave the country under safe passage to Miami. Machado accepted the bribe and allowed the U.S. to install a new provisional president, Carlos Manuel de Cespedes, as his temporary successor. As soon as Welles left the scene, proclaiming that all was well in Cuba once more, the guns began to boom again in the hills around Havana. An army sergeant named Fulgencio Batista was not as taken with the U.S. puppet president as Sumner Wells was. Batista led a revolution of his own, one that would go down in history as the "Revolt of the Sergeants."

And so, in its inimitable and predictable fashion, U.S. intervention on the turbulent island just ninety miles off America's southernmost shore ushered in a new dictatorship. This one was led by an ex-sergeant named Batista, who imposed his own reign of terror for the next twenty-five years, until a bearded communist named Fidel Castro knocked him out of the catbird seat. Batista was a quick study; in no time at all he learned how to do business with American interests in his country. He allowed the Mafia to run the Havana gambling casinos and American corporations to control the country's sugar monopoly, while lining his own pockets at the same time.

*   *   *

The big guns were silent now. No longer could Ernest hear them as his crew fired up *Pilar* for the return trip to Key West. The revolution in Cuba was over, and the fishing was done for the season. Ernest was a student of war, having served in Italy during World War I and covering other conflicts as a journalist. What was going on in Cuba intrigued him at the time, but not enough to keep him there any longer. A bigger conflict was boiling over in Spain, a revolution in the making that would occupy a larger canvas. It was a revolution that would involve all of Europe and the U.S. over the next few years. The Cuban revolution by comparison was a tempest in a teapot as far as the world at large was concerned. It was a provincial matter, an event of interest only to Cubans and the giant nation that viewed Cuba as its playground—a playground with opportunities for American corporations to make some money.

For the moment, it was time for Ernest to go home and get back to work, back to the manuscript that had been sitting on his desk waiting idly for him for a long time now, for far too long while he enjoyed his pleasures in Cuba.

PART TWO

GELLHORN

Chapter Eight

She was tall and blonde with long sensuous legs that seemed to begin just under her armpits. For as long as she could remember she had wanted to be a writer. And the writer she admired most, the one whom she tried not to imitate too closely lest he overshadow her own creative efforts, was the most successful and famous writer of his generation. His photograph had adorned her dormitory wall in college. Indeed, she was not the only student of literature who had pinned a picture of Ernest on her wall, who had quoted frequently from his work, who read every one of his books as soon as they came out and admitted that her writing style had been affected by his. She was not the only one seduced by the clarity and economy of his prose, every line of which rejected the cant and stylized rhetoric of writers who had come before him. But Martha Gellhorn may well have been the most talented

Martha Gellhorn was a daughter of the Midwest, born in St. Louis, Missouri, on November 8, 1908. Her father was a half-Jewish gynecologist named George Gellhorn, and her mother was a half-Jewish suffragette whose birth name was Edna Fischel. They were Ethical Humanists who put those principles to work in their own home. One of Martha's earliest memories was sitting around the dining room table with black folks from town. The Gellhorns were one of the few white families in St. Louis who regularly hosted black people in their home at 4366 McPherson Avenue, comfortably located on a wide shady street, and reached out to them in other ways. Both of Martha's parents were way over on the political left and believed in progressive education and social equality for everyone. George, in particular, was a physical fitness buff who pushed Martha and her siblings to exercise regularly and eat sparingly.

After graduating from the John Burroughs School, Martha enrolled in her mother's alma mater, Bryn Mawr in Philadelphia. But college life was not for her. At the end of her junior year she announced that "a college degree would only qualify me for precisely the kind of job I would never want." The picture of Ernest on her dormitory wall reminded her every day of her true calling, her obsession to become a writer.

"I'll get something, somehow," she told her mother. "And I'll use it as a stepping stone to get a job abroad. Oh Gosh! How I ache to get over there."

After quitting Bryn Mawr, she landed a less-than-romantic job as a reporter for the *Albany Times Union*, covering the police beat including the local morgue with cold, stiff corpses laid out on slabs. "I found myself growing cold and shaking," she said. "I wanted to scream that it was all too ghoulish to be true." When Martha was not writing about the recently departed with their "grey, marcelled bobs" and "narrow shoulders," she was fighting off the advances of the hard-drinking city editor who had taken a fancy to her long slender legs and elegant good looks. One of her fellow reporters observed the newspaper's only female reporter with a good measure of amusement and nicknamed her the "blonde peril" because of the effect she had on men.

She put her time in Albany to good use, turning the stories she covered into fiction that she would eventually use in her novels. Her mother, who had disapproved of her decision to abandon college for a life of letters, took pity on Martha and sent her enough money for a train ticket to New York City. Edna understood that New York would be simply a way station for her daughter before she found a way to support herself in Europe, but she decided not to stand in Martha's way.

Martha landed in Paris in the spring of 1930, just as Ernest was departing the City of Lights with his second wife to make a new life for himself in Key West. She had devoured all his short stories, his first major novel *The Sun Also Rises* about life in Paris and the bullfights in Spain, and *A Farewell to Arms*, which came out to great acclaim the previous fall and was scheduled to become a movie starring Gary Cooper. Martha was enraptured by Ernest's vivid, yet economical descriptions of European life, and she was determined to experience it all firsthand. But first she needed a job. The seventy-five dollars she had squirreled away in her suitcase would not last very long. Other than that and a few changes of clothes, she had her typewriter and her gritty, plucky determination to succeed in her chosen career.

She showed up early one morning at the offices of the *New York Times* and asked to speak to the bureau chief. The gentleman, startled to hear that some cheeky young woman had shown up without an appointment demanding to see him, came out to find out what her visit was all about. He took in her tall good looks, cloaked in a tweed skirt, her old college coat, and her unfashionable brogues, and asked her what she wanted.

"I'm highly experienced," she said, citing her time on the Albany newspaper and two articles she had written for the *New Republic*. "I can start work immediately as a foreign correspondent."

The editor was at first taken aback by her aggressive approach, but he then burst out laughing when he realized that her effrontery was nothing more than a cover for her *naïveté*. His amusement quickly turned to pity. For one thing, the venerable newspaper only hired reporters with far more experience than she had. And second, no major publication employed women as journalists. When she told him where she was living, he informed her that her hotel was a *maison de passage,* a brothel, which accounted for the low rate she was paying. The proprietor no doubt hoped to entice her to become one of his "girls" for hire. The editor suggested that she move out immediately and look for something on the Left Bank, where she might also find employment as an assistant in a beauty shop. Martha found a room in a building on the Rue de l'Universite that cost only six dollars a week. There were flowers in a vase in the hall and a grand piano for romantic young men to play pieces by Chopin and other masters. She was the only female in the place, which was well-known as a refuge for homosexual men. But no matter. It was better than living in a whorehouse, and she felt safe there.

Martha did indeed find a berth in a beauty salon, which lasted about two weeks before she landed a job writing advertising copy for a bubble bath product. Finally, when she thought she could stand her plight no longer, United Press International agreed to give her a shot transcribing stories sent in by far-flung reporters scattered around the globe. She jumped at the opportunity. "I want to go everywhere and see everything and I meant to write my way."

*   *   *

Martha was picky about the men she got involved with. She liked tall men, intelligent men, men who were not intimidated by strong women with minds of their own. She hooked up with a young American lawyer named Campbell Beckett who had an adventurous streak equal to hers. Campbell was a friend of the French military governor of Tunisia and his countess wife, who invited the lawyer to visit them in their house in Tunis. He asked Martha if she would like to come along with him, and she accepted. It was only later that she realized what a spectacle she made of herself. There she was in the old Arabic part of the city, attending formal functions with the only clothes she had brought with her—a pair of sneakers and a housedress adorned with purple flowers and ruffles. She drank too much one evening and passed out in her bathtub, oblivious to being carried naked from the tub to her bedroom by two Senegalese man servants.

The countess was "horrified by the brazen unworldliness of the arrangement," Martha wrote later, "and had catalogued me as a girl who would come to a deservedly bad end."

Shortly after returning to Paris, a South American business tycoon with ties to her employer escorted her home from a company function one evening in a taxi, where he made an unwanted pass at her. Martha was indignant enough to complain to her immediate boss, who was further down in the pecking order at UPI. The next day she was fired. "No money. Jobs hard to get. What the hell," she wrote. With the little money she had managed to save, she moved down to the Mediterranean coast to see for herself the fishing villages, sandy coves, and umbrella pines described by Ernest in one of his books. She found herself exhilarated by the spicy air scented with wild herbs. It was a place for siestas and making love, as the writer Colette had described it. Martha found cheap accommodations in a pension along the coast, sat down at her typewriter, and waited for inspiration to strike her.

And she waited. Then she waited some more. The inspiration she sought failed to materialize. So she went for a long hike, high up the pass leading into Andorra until she could walk no longer. The badly fitting boots that she hoped would serve her well throughout the twelve-hour climb over the pass resulted in blisters and swollen ankles. At the same time a red rash appeared across her chest, convincing Martha that she had contracted syphilis—perhaps a byproduct of her sojourn in Tunisia. Twenty-one years old, nearly destitute, and now panicked over the sprawling stamp of venereal disease emblazoned on her breasts, Martha went to a clinic in Marseilles where she waited in a long line with French and Arab longshoremen to see the doctor. The doctor took one look at her flaming chest and burst out laughing. Her visit was for nothing, he informed her. She did not have syphilis. She had prickly heat.

Chapter Nine

The next man who entered Martha's life—the life of the "blonde peril" who was living up to that soubriquet with unintended exuberance—would play a critical role there for the next few years. In the journal she had begun to keep, she noted the key events that took place from the time she first set foot in Paris. In July 1930 she wrote, "July 14 (circa): met Bertrand."

Bertrand de Jouvenal was one of France's most successful young journalists, the son of a father who was a politician and magazine editor and a socialite mother who ran a salon. Bertrand was half-Jewish like Martha and Roman Catholic on the other side of his family. At twenty-six he was five years older than she and he tilted toward the left side of the political spectrum, an area where Martha felt most comfortable. Bertrand was also married to a woman twelve years older than him named Marcelle. At sixteen years of age, he had been famously seduced by Colette, his father's second wife who was forty-six at the time. Bertrand's birth mother had inadvertently set up the tryst by asking her son to convince his father to let her retain the name de Jouvenal after their divorce. Monsieur de Jouvenal had insisted that she drop it since he found her political activism an embarrassing impediment to his career. Colette was home when Bertrand arrived and his father was off on some last-minute business.

Colette was "small, stocky, quick," the sixteen-year-old observed. Her high forehead and almond-shaped eyes, accentuated with thick lines of antimony sulfide, conveyed a look of power rather than age. At the time she was at the peak of her literary fame. The boy never got to see his father that day, but he did get to know his stepmother a bit more intimately than he had ever anticipated.

She was decidedly overweight, so much so that she refused to let him see her naked, but she was brimming with sexuality. Bertrand submitted to her immediately, without a moment's hesitation. After the seduction, she grew quite fond of him, calling him her "little leopard" and a "great whippet of a boy."

When Martha met Bertrand she was taken in by his slim body, his fine features, his high prominent cheekbones, and his startling eyes that shone with green or gray intensity, depending on the quality of the light. For his part, Bertrand was mesmerized by the tall blonde American with legs that just went on and on. He kept "staring at me," Gellhorn wrote later, "reaching for me, almost maddening me with his love." He kissed her "like a starved man with food."

"You deliciously overturn everything that you lay hands on," he wrote to her, "while I force myself, small-mindedly, to rearrange things that look to me untidy."

Martha tried to escape from Bertrand's intensity at first, but she couldn't put him out of her mind for very long. He left his wife, he told Martha, to spend more time with her. They traveled together to Mussolini's Italy so he could report on the political situation there and she could work on her fiction. "My beloved, I am so happy," he wrote when he was away on assignment. "We have such a marvelous life—your work—my work—our car—our Sundays—our nights—our friends—we're independent—we're free—we're proud—we're young—we're in love—we stand out from all others…Oh my love." Martha was his "rabbit" and Bertrand was her "Smuf."

But the real world intruded on their idyllic life together. Under fascism, Italy's economy was in tatters. Unemployment soared, food became scarce as little children scrounged for tomatoes, bread, and olive oil wherever they could find them. And Bertrand's love for Martha began to weigh on her. She found his love to be a "wild will to possess" her. She was truly fond of him, perhaps even in love herself, but she had no interest in being tied down to one man by marriage. To make matters even more complicated, Bertrand's wife announced that she was pregnant and begged him to return, and Martha also got pregnant as the year drew to a close. "I was stuck with a lot of maddening emotional problems which I did not want," she wrote later. "I began to feel like a plaything of destiny which made me at once gloomy, angry, and confused." Not knowing what to do, to have an abortion or not to have an abortion, Martha was close to despair. She felt "in every way trapped."

She had to get free of the trap, which meant freeing herself from the man who had entrapped her. Her family in St. Louis would be furious with her and her predicament, she knew, but she saw no other alternative except to return home and face her father's wrath. When he set eyes on her after her lengthy absence, Dr. Gellhorn told Martha that she was nothing but "selfish scum." And Bertrand? The man was beneath contempt. It was just as well that Bertrand had not accompanied Martha to America. Doctor Gellhorn might have thrashed the Frenchman on sight, despite his pacifist convictions. He sent his pregnant daughter off to see a colleague of his in Chicago, a man who could be trusted to abort in the safest way possible this child from hell inhabiting Martha's womb.

*   *   *

She worked on her writing, starting a novel and selling stories to the *Post-Dispatch* so that she could once again save up enough money to leave St. Louis and the stultifying middle-class existence that entrapped her there. She traveled by train through the west, observing and writing about an America that struck her as "vast, beautiful, and empty." She made stops in Texas, Nevada, New

67

Mexico, California, dipped south into Mexico, interviewed union leaders, other writers, and boxers including Jack Dempsey for her newspaper stories, which served as material for her novels. Men fell in love with her along the way, some of whom she took a brief interest in, but most of whose advances she deflected. In rejecting a would-be suitor, Martha was fond of quoting Ernest who wrote in *A Farewell to Arms*, "You're brave. Nothing ever happens to the brave." She longed for more and more travel, a "need of the far lands" as the "only thing besides writing which is worth the sweat."

But Bertrand would not go away. He had lived in Paris since her abrupt departure, publishing a biography of Emile Zola in the spring of 1931 and contributing to several left-wing magazines. All the while he missed his "rabbit" until he could no longer stand being separated from her. Bertrand crossed the Atlantic, ostensibly to cover the Great Depression in the U.S. for the French magazines, but mostly to be close to the woman he loved in her own country. In September 1931 Martha met him as he debarked from the *Ile de France* in New York City, eager to see if she could rekindle the affection she felt for him the year before. They bought a beat-up Dodge jalopy for twenty-five dollars and set off on a trip through rural America to observe the impact the Great Depression was having on her fellow citizens. As it turned out, the two lovers saw a bit more than they bargained for.

Their Dodge broke down along a godforsaken road in the boondocks outside Columbia, Mississippi. They waited beside the car in the pitch black night, smoking cigarettes furiously for several hours in an unsuccessful attempt to chase away swarms of hungry mosquitoes. Finally a pickup truck appeared out of the darkness. The driver slowed down, then brought his vehicle to a stop. A local redneck who was visibly drunk stared at them through his open window, sizing up this elegant blonde and skinny Frenchman who might as well have descended from a distant planet. In his unintelligible accent, the driver offered them a lift. Wearily they accepted, wondering what kind of special hell they had gotten themselves into.

As they climbed aboard, the driver informed them that he was on his way to take part in the lynching of a nineteen-year-old black boy accused of raping a white woman in her fifties. Martha and Bertrand sat stone-still beside the driver as he chugged down the road and came to a stop in a field beneath some trees. A crowd had gathered there, and the driver got out to help the others slip a noose around the black boy's neck. Martha and Bertrand tried not to watch as the crowd pulled the rope taut across a thick tree limb. But it was impossible not to watch, any more than they could keep their eyes averted from a freak show in the circus. From the corner of their eyes they could see the boy swinging from the end of the rope, the boy and tree silhouetted against the star-lit sky. When it was over the driver came back and told them God's will had been done. That little nigger would never rape another white woman again. They drove on in silence.

"We did not speak to each other," Martha wrote later. "I have a memory of trying not to be sick and trying not to believe any of this. We had heard children's voices too."

Chapter Ten

The lovers took a sojourn from each other in California, Bertrand attending to business of his own in Hollywood while Martha traveled north to Carmel to work on her novel. The absence suited Martha more than it did Bertrand, who wrote to her every day describing the pain he was in. For her part, she felt guilty about not missing him more. "You've given me everything," she wrote from her rented two-room cottage overlooking the ocean, "and I've given you in exchange faint, grudging thanks, so little warmth. My dear, forgive me." She even encouraged him to have an affair. "Please be a conqueror for a bit; forget me. I'm a shit face."

Bertrand could stand Martha's coldness no longer. His career had suffered since his departure from France, and his love for her had clearly become one-sided. In April 1932 he returned to Paris, where his wife Marcelle frantically waited for him. Unlike Martha, she had decided to keep her baby rather than abort it, and she hoped the cute blond boy she had given birth to would entice Bertrand to become a more steadfast husband and father. Marcelle refused to divorce him on any account, refused to make it easier for him to leave her for good. But his mind was elsewhere.

"I want you," he wrote Martha. "Find out for yourself whether you want me. I think you do." She hoped to find some solace in St. Louis, but her father was as unyielding as ever. "There are two kinds of women," he told her, "and you're the other kind." Well, if that was the case, Martha reasoned, she might as well enjoy her role of being the other kind of woman. Rejected once more by her father, she turned back to Bertrand. "Ah my beloved," she wrote him. "I've missed you so…I'm coming, I'm coming, I'm coming."

And so she went back once again to the man she had all but told to take a hike the last time they were together. Her emotional swings back and forth from coolness and indifference to romantic infatuation with the *same man* were positively breathtaking. One envisions her coming and going with reckless speed, passing herself in transit from one emotional extreme to the other. More cynical folks might see a measure of opportunism in her behavior, but who could blame a talented and attractive young woman doing what she had to do to survive in a man's profession set against the backdrop of a man's world at the time?

Bertrand was there to greet her when she stepped off the boat in Le Havre in July 1932, with plans to take her to Germany to cover the Reichstag elections. But the Martha who debarked was literally a pale and gaunt version of the woman he last saw. She looked ill, as indeed she was. At first Bertrand thought she had come down with tuberculosis, but a German doctor diagnosed her condition as an ear infection that she likely had contracted aboard ship. After he lanced her abscess and gave her morphine, she told Bertrand that the doctor had all but tortured her. He was undoubtedly a Nazi, she told Bertrand. "I am terribly tired. I would like to die." The medicine she prescribed for herself was to leave Bertrand behind yet again, this time in Germany, and travel south to France—to Hemingway country along the coast—where she stayed by herself for several months. Bertrand was exasperated, beside himself with longing and grief. "I can't live a monk's life," he wrote to her, ignoring the fact that he had a doting wife and children at home. "I shall be driven to leading a dissolute life, to taking a succession of mistresses. This displeases me."

Really? What was Martha if not an on-again, off-again mistress?

"You haven't got a clarity of vision because you don't want to have it," Bertrand continued in his letter. And Martha? She felt like an animal sneaking away to get well, as she described herself.

71

"Don't come to see me," she wrote. Why would she be jealous of a man who threatened to have mistresses, the *same man* she told to have some affairs when they were separated in California? Bertrand may have been lovesick, but Martha was just being Martha again. Bertrand loved his Martha, but she and his love for her were driving him to the brink of madness.

Martha knew exactly who *she* was. "I know there are two people in me," she wrote. "But the least strong, the least demanding, is the one that attaches itself to another human being…Since I was a child people have wanted to possess me. And because our life is so badly managed, I turn upon you, with resentment and bitterness, because you bring it into neither order nor tranquility, because you do not make the best of it, either materially or morally, because your discontent is ever present, like a restless dog wandering through the room."

Bertrand responded to that vitriolic broadside by traveling south to be with her. And he gave her badly needed money to help her pay her bills and pursue her dream of writing until her ear infection cleared and she could return to…to wherever suited her fancy next. Her fancy took her to Paris where she found a job as a general factotum for *Vogue*—ironically enough, the former employer of Ernest's second wife, whom Martha would eventually displace. She hoped to parlay that meager job into a bona fide assignment as a journalist. She had packed on a few extra pounds in the South of France and dyed her hair an even lighter shade of blonde, giving her the appearance of the *madchen* she had seen in Germany.

In Paris she grew friendly with kindred spirits on the left, young socialists, communists, and anti-fascist radicals who attended political salons affiliated with Leon Blum's *Front Populaire Francaise*. Gellhorn also met Colette, her lover's aging seductress, who gave her unwanted advice on writing and her personal appearance. Colette told Martha to paint her face with antimony sulfide or kohl, as Colette was fond of doing. Martha obeyed until a friend informed her that Colette had turned her into a freak, probably to render her unattractive to Colette's favorite little leopard, her now middle-aged great whippet of a boy.

*   *   *

Martha found herself pregnant once again, with no more intention to give birth to this one than she did the first. She paid for her own abortion this time with money she earned at *Vogue*, a situation she found wildly amusing. After recovering from her second abortion, she traveled with Bertrand to Germany again, where she got a close look at Hitler, his evil but mesmerizing rhetoric, and the horrifying hordes of goose-stepping Hitler Youth, which already boasted more than a hundred thousand members. Sick to her stomach with fear and loathing, she and Bertrand returned to Paris more convinced than ever that any hope of *rapprochement* with the growing Nazi menace was little more than a naïve pipedream.

Bertrand, surprisingly, was on the political fence at first. Hitler terrified him, but he did speak up ostensibly for the underdogs in society. And Bertrand had "such a feeling for underdogs," as Martha wrote, "that he managed to be in every movement while it was a failure and to leave it the minute it looked as if it were succeeding." Timing is everything in politics, it seemed, both then and now.

France hardly offered a viable alternative to the surging Nazi menace. On February 6, 1934, the new Prime Minister, Edouard Dedalier, rose to address the French Chamber of Deputies only to be greeted with shouts, insults, and fistfights breaking out among the deputies. Across the Seine, ragtag hordes of extremists reflecting every political stripe formed an unlikely coalition. For a brief spell they put their disagreements with one another aside and united against the police and other representatives of civil authority. They threw paving stones, bricks, anything of substance they could pry loose, forcing the *gendarmes* to cower behind their vans. Paris, if not all of France it seemed, was on the threshold of a new revolution.

But it quickly fizzled, like most popular insurgencies. It is one thing to talk of anarchy in cafes and throw rocks when half-drunk on wine and absinthe, and quite another to risk everything in pursuit of an ideal. So they, along with Bertrand and Martha, started a new magazine instead, *La Lutte des Jeunes*, to campaign for greater freedoms for students—hardly a movement designed to prod the middle class to take up arms against the government. This venture, too, came to naught when one of their colleagues quite seriously advocated joining with the Nazis in a temporary struggle to bring capitalism to its knees. After that goal was attained, the left would then wrest power from their so-called allies on the right. Bertrand was more amenable to the concept than Martha was. She had developed a good bullshit-detector by now, as Ernest had advised everyone to do when he was a struggling writer living in Paris with wife number one. Martha kept her distance, contributing articles to *Vogue* by day while writing incendiary pieces for the political magazine by night.

But she was growing bored. Bored with all the dead-end rhetoric and bored once more with Bertrand. She was bored as well with the radicals whom she increasingly found to be "ugly—and mostly so bloody stupid." They were the kind of people "who go mad, or drift into gutters or suicide, from broken hearts." She longed for a place outside the city in the countryside, where one could feel the "wind on one's face." Bertrand, too, was interested in getting away from Paris, largely because his wife and family were there impatiently waiting for him to come home. But Martha was not quite sure she wanted Bertrand to get away from Paris, at least not with her this time. For one thing, she found sex with him to be less than inspiring.

"Physically, for me, it was nothing, ever." What a cruel assessment to lay on a Frenchman! At the same time she felt guilty about not being able to give him "complete joy in sexual love." Many years later, Martha would say much the same about Ernest, prompting his critics to say that he was more adept with a fishing rod than he was with the one he was born with. But the critics were far off the mark. They either overlooked or deliberately ignored Martha's own comments on the subject. By her admission she "practiced" sex but never totally enjoyed it. "I accompanied men and was accompanied in action," she wrote. "That seemed to be their delight and all I got was a pleasure of being wanted, I suppose, and the tenderness (not nearly enough) that a man gives when he is satisfied. I daresay I was the worst bed partner in five continents."

She even consulted a series of doctors about her low libido and the pain she experienced from repeated intercourse.

Bertrand got even though. True Frenchman that he was, he had an affair with somebody else, a woman named Suzanne whom he also got pregnant.

Chapter Eleven

Martha finished her novel, which she would entitle *What Mad Pursuit*. Four publishers turned it down at first on the grounds—you can't escape the irony—that it contained too much explicit sex. She slashed, rewrote, and slashed some more. I've been busy "slashing out sex right and left," she said, obliterating abortion scenes and tossing "syphilis into the wastepaper basket." Soon, the publishers would be able to "use it as a text in Sunday schools."

She made her final revisions, and her publisher Frederick A. Stokes brought the book out early in 1934. The book was met with tepid reviews, with most critics unimpressed by her story of three college girls searching for something to believe in as they drank too much and exposed themselves to venereal disease and unwanted pregnancies. The *Buffalo Evening News* called the novel "hectic," and the *New York Times* said it was "crude…It would be more likable if Miss Gellhorn were not so enamored of her own heroine, and if she did not dabble so ineffectually with questions of social justice." Martha's hometown newspaper, the *St. Louis Post-Dispatch*, referred to her as one of the city's outstanding local women—along with actress Betty Grable, not the best company from Martha's point of view. She would have preferred a literary allusion. Martha herself was later embarrassed by her novel and refused to bring it back into print after it disappeared from view shortly after it was published.

In June 1934, Martha's mother Edna came to France for a visit, the first time mother and daughter had seen each other in more than a year. They vacationed together in the Midi, along the coast in the South of France north of the Spanish border. While they were in the Midi, repairing their old bond, enjoying the sunshine and the breaking surf, Bertrand sulked in Paris. Finally he came to his senses. No longer able to put up with Martha's ambivalence without completely losing his mind, he decided that a final break was in order. "My beloved, you do not love me," he wrote her. "You told me once that I was standing in your sun, keeping its light from you. I remove myself from it, dear love. The world is limited with me, so wide open, so limitless if you're alone. Take this chance, my little one. Escape." Return to America with your mother, he advised her. Just go and find other hearts to break, he seemed to be saying. You've left mine in pieces.

But Martha was never one to do as she was told. She reacted to his entreaty by telling a friend, "He is so weak, that it is like having cancer; it is an incurable and killing sickness."

Martha hung around France by herself for a while after Edna departed for home, and then returned to the country of her birth in her own sweet time, Martha time, in the fall of the year. Bertrand had hoped that his letter offering to free her of him would reverberate to his own advantage, make her see that she truly loved him after all. But his strategy backfired. After sorting out her own feelings, Martha left for America in October 1934. "Great God!" she wrote. "What an eagerness and energy I have to live; how much living I can stand and must have." She was not Bertrand's rabbit any longer; she was a bird flying free of its cage.

*　　*　　*

Her life was her own now. She was free to live and do as she pleased. After debarking from the *Normandie* in New York City, she contacted a well-known journalist named Marquis Childs who covered the Roosevelt administration for the *St. Louis Post-*

Dispatch. Martha told him she wanted to get involved in the president's programs to repair the economic ills afflicting the nation. Childs introduced Martha to Harry Hopkins, FDR's point man in the New Deal. Within weeks of landing in the States, she had a new job, traveling the country for Hopkins and other New Deal administrators to observe first-hand the horrific human toll the economic collapse had taken on America's working class.

Martha was horrified by what she observed out there in the nation's heartland, in rural America as well as in its smelly, overcrowded cities. The spirit of the nation was broken, with steel mills shut down, coal mines idle, women garment workers earning five cents an hour in sweatshops, banks shuttered in the vast majority of states, hordes of unsupervised children roaming through the streets fighting over whatever scraps they could find in garbage bins, KKK racists lynching black people with impunity, seventeen million laborers without any purpose in their lives, and well over twenty-five percent of the entire population without any work whatsoever. Martha was shaken to the core. Her entire sense of justice and wellbeing had been turned upside down. She came to despise her boss Henry Hopkins, whom she regarded as an arrogant, disheveled young man who smoked too many cigarettes and drank too much coffee.

Martha found a writing voice of her own on the road, a uniquely political voice that was more socially engaged and more ideological than that of her idol Hemingway. As she traveled by train through the South and Midwest, subsisting on her vouchers allowing her five dollars a day for food and hotels, Martha wrote of the dispossessed, the victims of stupidity and brutality, the hungry and homeless, the hollow-eyed vagrants in slums, and other human wreckage strewn across the towns, villages, and cities of America like flotsam on the beach. It was a theme that would distinguish her writing for the rest of her life. She thought she had been radicalized before, but now she was not just intellectually committed; she was passionately engaged in a calling that took root in her soul and characterized everything she wrote from that point onward.

When she returned to Washington, D.C., she burst into Hopkins' office uninvited and delivered a diatribe about the ineffectiveness of FERA and Hopkins' shortcomings as the head of the agency. She threatened to resign and write exposes about what she had seen during her travels. The young man was unruffled, unflappable as ever. He studied her clinically, as though she were another problem that needed to be dealt with dispassionately. His detachment infuriated Martha even more. She regarded him as a lifeless bureaucrat, a cold technocrat with a brain but no heart, no warm blood coursing through his veins.

"I've sent your reports to Mrs. Roosevelt," he said. "Why don't you discuss it all with her?"

Edna Gellhorn had become friends with Eleanor Roosevelt at Bryn Mawr and arranged a dinner invitation for Martha at the White House. Martha found a new heroine there, a role model to emulate. The president's wife was an ungainly fifty-year-old woman with protruding eyes, no chin, and boundless reserves of energy. Martha and Eleanor bonded instantly and would remain lifelong friends. But her first moments in the presence of FDR and Eleanor were awkward at best. Martha was offended by the opulence on display, the gold-and-white porcelain china, the crystal goblets, the fine wine and generous portions of food. Eleanor was hard of hearing, which forced Martha to raise her voice to an embarrassing decibel level to make herself understood. The president sat at the far end of the long dining-room table taking everything in with a measure of amusement. Martha described in intense detail what she had witnessed in her travels. Finally, Eleanor turned her head and all but screamed at her husband, as though he were the one who was half-deaf.

"Franklin, talk to this girl! She says all the unemployed have pellagra and syphilis!"

Martha thought she had been caught up in a bad dream. Eleanor's comment was met with a long heavy silence by the president, who tried not to smile at his wife's clumsiness. Martha filled the void by describing to FDR what she had already explained in great detail to his wife—an explanation that he had undoubtedly heard loud and clear the first time. FDR listened attentively, and when she was finished he asked her to come back and tell him more at a later time. Both FDR and Eleanor encouraged Martha to keep her job despite her misgivings about FERA's ineffectiveness.

"You can do far more for the unemployed by staying there," Eleanor told Martha as she left after dinner. She later said to a friend, "She must learn patience and not have a critical attitude toward what others do. She must remember that to them it is just as important as her dreams are to her."

Eleanor "gave off light," Martha wrote years later. "I cannot explain it better."

*　　*　　*

Another writer who visited the White House at this time was the well-known novelist H.G. Wells, who described it as a comfortable private house transformed by the Roosevelts from a "queer, ramshackle place like a nest of waiting rooms with hat stands everywhere."

Wells was already an old man of sixty-eight at this stage of his life. Along with Jules Verne he had been dubbed one of the

"Fathers of Science Fiction," the author of genre classics such as *The War of the Worlds* and *The Time Machine*. He was an outspoken socialist and pacifist who wrote about other things, including history and social problems, which resonated with Martha far more than his science fiction did. Wells was also a notorious womanizer with an eye that never ceased to wander. While married first to his cousin, then later to one of his former students, he conducted a series of affairs with many well-known women. They included birth-control activist Margaret Sanger and novelist Rebecca West, who was twenty-six years younger than him and bore him a son out of wedlock—Anthony West, who would go on to become a famous writer in his own right. In the White House, Wells' eyes fastened on the youthful Martha and liked what they observed.

How could they not? The man was an aging lecher, but his libido remained intact. Martha's youth, her intelligence and physical allure were the perfect aphrodisiac for an old man approaching the seventh century of his life.

Chapter Twelve

Martha's friendship with Eleanor Roosevelt deepened. They enjoyed taking long walks together to discuss pressing issues of the day, although Martha was terrified of Eleanor's ill-tempered dogs. They snarled and lunged at everyone they passed, especially children, and barely tolerated Martha who was not overly fond of dogs in the first place. But Eleanor refused to give them up until they drew blood from the legs of a diplomat and a high-ranking U.S. senator. At that point she reluctantly agreed to part with them—after a bit of prodding from her husband who was eager to keep his political relationships on firm footing, so to speak. Eleanor trusted Martha well enough to confide in her, revealing intimate details about her life with the president with whom she had not shared a bedroom for more than twenty years, ever since FDR had begun an affair with his wife's social secretary.

"I have the memory of an elephant," Eleanor said. "I can forgive but I can never forget."

Martha was anxious to begin a new book about the Great Depression, and she needed a quiet place to work free from daily pressures. She moved into a vacation home in Hartford, Connecticut, owned by China expert W.F. Field. Martha decided to present the book as a novel, as fiction, although the line between Martha's nonfiction and fiction often blurred to the point of obscurity. Later on she received a lot of criticism for that from reviewers, but she was in good company since Ernest, the master himself, admitted that his nonfiction books could be read as either fiction or nonfiction. He was incapable of writing raw truth without embellishing it, and Martha was no different in that regard.

Her father had made it clear that he was not a fan of her first book and did not consider her to be a serious writer. She tried to repair their damaged relationship, but he wrote her a letter at this time excoriating her for her "affair with that little French runt that gave you so much 'valuable experience' and us so much real pain." George Gellhorn was vicious and unyielding, accusing her of "capitalizing on your yellow hair and your lively, spicy conversation." She should, he continued, "have the pride of wanting to *show* the world that you can hold your place with anybody else, not only while you are young and attractive to men, but at any time."

They were harsh words, indeed, for any father to direct at his daughter; he all but accused her of whoring herself to achieve her literary goals rather than relying on her talent. And his words were all the more painful coming as they did in the last year of his life. Martha finished her book in a mad burst of creative energy and sent the manuscript off to St. Louis for her father's approval. This time he softened, reading her vivid descriptions of human suffering during the depression "without stopping and with breathless interest."

Sadly, he took to his bed with stomach pains while scrutinizing her latest literary effort. Martha raced home to be at his side, then returned to Connecticut when it appeared he was out of danger. Shortly afterward, he unexpectedly died following surgery to remove the growth in his stomach. Martha went back home for the funeral, which was attended by many down-and-out local people whom the Gellhorns had helped, including most of the black citizens in town. She had managed to extract some measure of respect from her father before he passed away, but she would have given anything for more time to convince him that she was the writer he wanted her to be.

Her short novel, *The Trouble I've Seen*, was published first in England thanks to the efforts of H.G. Wells, who not only functioned as her literary agent, lining up the publisher and negotiating her advance, but also contributed a preface in which he talked about Martha's "lucidity and penetration." British novelist Graham Greene chimed in as well, giving her a backhand compliment by saying her novella benefited from its lack of "female voices of unbalanced pity or fictitious violence."

While H.G. Wells talked about Martha's lucidity and penetration, it was penetration of a different sort that occupied his mind. The randy old writer was head-over-heels in lust with his literary protégé. He bombarded her with lovesick letters, calling her "Stooge" and envisioning them together "on a sunny beach, Stooge getting sunburnt, me getting sunburnt, Stooge very much in love with me and me all in love with Stooge, nothing particular ahead except a far off dinner, some moonlight and bed—Stooge's bed."

The Trouble I've Seen finally came out in the U.S., published by Morrow in September 1935. Its American reception was even more encouraging than Great Britain's, with the novella garnering reviews in every major city and publication in the country. The *Saturday Review of Literature* put an endearing photo of the author on its cover, praising her for her "profound and sympathetic understanding." Martha's prose, the reviewer said, appeared to be "woven not out of words but out of the very tissues of human beings."

H.G. Wells continued his frenetic pursuit of the talented and attractive woman he had launched. His letters flew across the Atlantic and grew more and more ardent by the week. Martha was clearly not attracted to the short, round man with his shaggy mustache, who stood six inches shorter than her and smelled constantly of walnuts, according to Rebecca West. But Martha was not beyond encouraging him nonetheless, writing back to him and calling him "Wells darling," a salutation that was calculated to stoke his burning passion for her even more.

"What is liking? What is love?" he asked in one of his missives. "I dunno. I am strongly moved to ask you to pack up and come to England and to bed with me."

When she remained in Connecticut instead of sailing across the ocean to be with him, Wells decided to visit her to continue his entreaties in person. He arrived in Connecticut as snow was falling late in the autumn of 1935—and proceeded to drive her to distraction with his nonstop ranting that kept her from her work. He followed her around the house most of the day, talking constantly, beginning at breakfast with his theories about the ice age and ending at dinner with his thoughts about Henry James and his influence on American and British literature. Martha could stand it no longer. She sent a telegram to the famous comedian Charlie Chaplin, a friend of Wells, encouraging—*begging*—him to invite Wells for an extended visit to Hollywood. Luckily for her, Wells accepted, but not before informing her that she would be sorry when he was dead because she had not taken advantage of the opportunity to learn more about the world and about life from him. But three thousand miles of separation did not deter Wells from his pursuit of her through his letters, any more than that distance mattered when he was on the other side of the Atlantic Ocean.

"Why have I of all men to wander about the world without a responsive Stooge to talk to and sleep with and love?" he wrote. "You weren't given that nice body of yours just to fritter it away?"

Did she actually have sex with Wells at any point along the road they traveled together for a while? The answer depends on whom you believe. The issue remains a matter of conjecture unless there was a fly with the gift of speech on the wall in their bedroom at the time, and so far none has come forward. Wells later wrote that Martha was one of the less important "women I have kissed, solicited, embraced and lived with." About his stay in Connecticut with her, Wells claimed that "We two had a very happy time together for a week, making love, reading, talking over her second book."

Martha was outraged when she heard about his account of their relationship. "Why the hell would I sleep with a little old man when I could have any number of tall beautiful young men?" she asked in a letter to a friend.

The only motivation that makes any sense is career advancement; we've all done less-than-admirable things to get a leg up in the world, and Martha's legs were more lovely than most. But to give her the benefit of the doubt, she may well have been clever enough to present the prize without actually bestowing it.

"I'd have swum the Pacific rather than get involved with him beyond friendship," she wrote separately to Wells's son, who was planning to publish his father's version of their relationship posthumously in an update to his autobiography. "He was my father's age and not, you will agree, physically dazzling...He was fun unless he was bullying intellectually, and I was very fond of him but the rest is rubbish."

She got her way on that point. When Wells's son published the revised edition of his father's book, Martha's name had been reduced to asterisks.

*   *   *

Despite the fifteen minutes of fame that descended on Martha after the publication of her second book, she failed to land assignments she coveted at both *Time* and the *New Yorker* magazines. She did begin a romance, however, with a correspondent for *Time*, a rising young star in the world of journalism named Allen Grover. Allen benefited from being much closer to her age than Wells was, only eight years her senior. He too was raised in St. Louis and was an escapee from its embrace as soon as he was able to set off on his own. He was tall and thin, with straight black hair that he wore in the style of the era—slicked back with hair tonic. Like Bertrand, Allen was also married when Martha took up with him. She fell harder for him than she intended, but then distanced herself quickly when he refused to leave his family.

"The only terms on which to take you are the installment plan ones," she wrote to him, acknowledging that an intermittent fling with him was the only option available.

Martha escaped to Germany, where she found work temporarily in a library and embarked on a series of affairs with handsome blond men who shared her political views. They all "grabbed for my body," she wrote. "The only part I really liked was arms around me and an illusion of tenderness. But I could not make much illusions, and arms didn't last; and the rest happened to someone else (it was always painful) and except for two men I never saw anyone again afterwards." The men she favored more than the others were all married and refused to leave their wives. One of them she called a "monster and a brute." She told her friend Eleanor Roosevelt that she felt "like a canary with a boa constrictor," confiding in her as Eleanor had done with her shortly after they met. But Eleanor was not as sympathetic about her rootless adventures and her serial affairs as Martha would have hoped.

Eleanor wrote a letter to Edna Gellhorn saying that Martha should not be allowed to "get sorry for herself and become just another useless, pretty, broken butterfly. She has too much charm and real ability for that."

On the verge of a nervous breakdown, Martha decided to accept her mother's invitation to return home and take stock of her life. She arrived in St. Louis in December 1936. She was broke, her career was at an impasse, and the men she craved had every intention of remaining married to their existing wives. Martha wanted and needed much more out of life than that. She craved a *real* partner, a man who loved her, a man who understood her ambitions and aspirations, a man who would stay by her side along the less-traveled road to literary achievement and the fight for social justice. The Gellhorns were facing their first Christmas without the family patriarch. Martha suggested to Edna that they head down to Key West with her younger brother Alfred, her favorite sibling, who was home from medical school for the holiday. Martha had never visited Key West, but she was certainly well aware of the storybook town where the sun shone brightly, the water was warm and clear, and the atmosphere was laid back and relaxing.

Yes, Martha wanted very badly to go to Key West. There was a writer who lived there, the most famous writer in America if not the entire world. The writer had inspired her from the time she was a teenager. Hadn't she hung his poster on her dormitory wall and read every book and story he wrote? Hadn't she made a special effort to avoid imitating him too closely so as not to compromise her own individuality as a writer?

He was a big handsome man, a supremely gifted writer, perhaps a literary genius. He was married like the other men she was most attracted to. And Martha knew where he liked to hang out. Everyone knew by now where Ernest hung out after his mornings at the typewriter and afternoons fishing from his boat. She needed a new adventure, a change of direction. And she wanted to go to Key West to find it.

Chapter Thirteen

He was sitting there on his favorite stool in Sloppy Joe's when Martha, Edna, and Alfred walked in. Martha recognized him first and thrilled to the presence of the "large, dirty man in untidy somewhat soiled white shorts and shirt," who was reading his mail, as she wrote later. She had read all of his books, starting with his early short stories, then moving on to his novels, *The Sun Also Rises* and *A Farewell to Arms*. She had read the two quasi-nonfiction books he wrote after moving to Key West with Pauline, *Death in the Afternoon* about bullfighting in Spain, and *Green Hills of Africa* based on his African safari with Pauline and his buddy Charlie Thompson. Ernest had been attacked by critics on the left for writing about bullfighting and big game hunting instead of focusing his talents on the big issues of the day, primarily the fight against fascism that was spreading its poison across the globe. But the public accepted his stories as a welcome escape from their own pressing problems, and his books continued to sell. And there he was in person, reading his mail in the bar that would have remained just one of many Key West watering holes were it not for the famous author who made it his second home.

Martha directed her family to a table in full view of the bar, and she took a seat facing Ernest with her legs crossed while pretending not to notice him. Ernest was an observer before he was a writer. Very little crossed his path that he failed to notice, and Martha could almost feel his eyes drinking her in even though she was careful not to return his stare. From his perspective, Ernest was instantly aware of the elegant blonde with the lovely body and shapely legs. He correctly pegged the older woman as her mother, but he was wrong in assuming that the young man was her husband. Naturally competitive, Ernest resolved to get Martha away from the "young punk," which he estimated would take about three days. His eyes targeted their table as he ignored the stack of mail on the bar while he planned his next move.

Al Skinner, Joe Russell's three-hundred-pound bartender and bouncer, also noticed the young woman who was so atypical of Sloppy Joe's usual clientele. He remembered her wearing a black dress that offset her long legs and her blonde hair piled high on her head. Others who were there at the time described Martha wearing a black cotton sundress and Ernest dressed as usual in a T-shirt and fish-stained Basque shorts held up with a rope instead of a belt. The two of them looked like "the beauty and the beast," said Skinner, a reflection of Ernest's style of dress rather than his muscular good looks. James Joyce, who knew Ernest during his Paris years, described him as "a big powerful peasant, as strong as a buffalo."

"Martha definitely made a play for him," Lorine Thompson remembered. At the time, she, Charlie, and Pauline were at the Hemingway house, waiting for Ernest to return home for dinner. "Martha was a very charming girl, and if I had known her under other circumstances I would have liked her very much. She said she came to see Ernest. She wanted him to read a book she had written, she wanted to know him. There was no question about it. You could see she was making a play for him."

Ernest took the bait. He rose from his barstool, approached their table and introduced himself. He relaxed after he learned that Alfred was Martha's younger brother. He asked Martha about her work, said he would be happy to read what she was currently working on, and offered to take her and her family on a tour of Key West while they were in town. Martha listened intently and found herself charmed by his easy manner. He was "an odd bird, very lovable and full of fire and a marvelous story teller," she wrote later to Eleanor Roosevelt.

The evening wore on agreeably as Ernest poured on the charm that captivated not only Martha, but Edna and Alfred as well.

But at his house on Whitehead Street, Pauline was growing visibly agitated, lingering over cocktails with the Thompsons, wondering when Ernest was going to come home. At seven-thirty, what was left of her patience dissolved in a haze of cigarette smoke. She turned to Charlie and said,

"Oh, Charles, you know where he is. Drag him back here and let's eat."

Charlie Thompson went outside to his yellow Ford sedan and drove straight down to Sloppy Joe's, which was still located on Greene Street. It took only a glance for him to size up what was going on. Ernest waved him off and told him he'd meet them all later. When Charlie got back to the house, he broke the news to Pauline without pulling his punches; Pauline's bullshit detector was as finely honed as Ernest's.

"He's talking to a beautiful blonde in a black dress. Says he'll meet us later at Pena's."

The cook, Miriam Williams, was supposed to serve them all lobsters for dinner, but now that plan had to be aborted. Pauline was more than miffed, but she got in Charlie's car and drove with them to Pena's Garden of Roses, a local beer garden. If Pauline was upset on the way over, she was even more irate a while later when Ernest finally showed up. He had walked Edna and Alfred back to the Colonial Hotel on Duval Street, and then invited Martha to accompany him to Pena's to meet Pauline and his friends. Pauline took one look at Martha and realized that her husband had become infatuated once again, this time with an alluring blonde who was nine years younger than him and thirteen years younger than Pauline.

"Pauline always tried to be very tolerant of Ernest and any of the girls that sort of made a play for him, or that he seemed entranced with," Lorine recalled. "Pauline tried to ignore it. What she felt underneath nobody knew."

Martha and Pauline could hardly have been more different physically. Arnold Samuelson, a writer who knew them at the time, described Pauline "with her black hair brushed back in a boy's haircut. She was built like a boy and wore no makeup. Her face was tanned from being out in the sun and there was nothing you could see she had been doing to make herself beautiful except keeping her weight down." Photos show her to be a small sexy woman in a tomboyish way, with a nice compact figure and shapely legs. It wasn't so much that Martha was more attractive than her that worried Pauline. Some men might have found Pauline more to their taste. Rather it was their *difference* that bothered her. Martha was too much like Jane Mason, the stunning blonde with the angelic face and hyperactive sex life who "collected" books and authors and caused Pauline so much grief.

*   *   *

With the prize she sought in Key West virtually in her grasp, Martha decided to stay on after Edna and Alfred went back to St. Louis. Ernest invited her to his house to meet the "mob," as he referred to the endless stream of writers, editors, painters, and locals who fleshed out his entourage, and join in the festivities. Ernest entertained virtually nonstop, carving out the morning hours for his writing, and then taking whoever happened to be visiting at the time out on the *Pilar* for an afternoon of fishing. Always there were parties in the evening during which the food and drink flowed freely.

Miriam Williams prepared one feast after another for Ernest's guests, but she was appalled by some of the behavior she observed, including her employer's. "Mr. Ernest and Miss Martha would be outside and kissing and carrying on," she said to a friend. "Look at that. The way some people act!" There was something to be said for a man who brought his girlfriends home to meet his wife—but exactly *what* was to be said depended on one's perspective.

Ernest had already started work on his so-called "proletarian" novel, *To Have and Have Not*, which would turn out to be the most political book he had written to date. Perhaps he was more stung than he let on by the reviewers who criticized his lack of social and political engagement. Perhaps he was genuinely moved by the economic conditions that afflicted so many of his countrymen. He also had to be aware that Martha was likely to be impressed by a novel dealing with Prohibition and its impact on the local scene—although it's unlikely that he would have colored his fiction to suit a new paramour. Whatever the case, Ernest pressed on with his latest autobiographical novel that included revealing portrayals of his friends and girlfriends.

Jane Mason became Helene Bradley in the novel, deliciously described by Ernest as a tall lovely blonde who collected writers, painters, and big-game hunters as sexual trophies, along with their works. One of Ernest's characters refers to the real-life author as "the big slob." Ernest wrote an especially vivid scene showing Helene's husband walking in while Jane was making love to the writer who goes limp in mid-performance. Helene flies into a rage, denouncing the writer for being a coward since her husband didn't care as long as he was allowed to watch. Josie Russell took a turn as Freddy who owned Freddy's Bar, a popular watering hole in Key West. Other pals of Ernest quickly recognized themselves in their fictional counterparts, some of them less flattering than they would have liked.

Martha was delighted when Ernest offered to read her own work in progress. He was the master, and honest advice coming from him was invaluable. Don't over-think what you're writing, he told her. Get on with it, take some risks, and have the courage to toss it out and start over when you don't like it. Just go with your gut and don't intellectualize what you feel inside.

Finally, Martha had to leave. She had come to Key West with a goal in mind, and now that she had achieved it she had to return to the real world and let her adventure play out whichever way it would. Ernest made it easy for her. He was more than smitten; he had fallen halfway in love during the past couple of weeks. Martha hitched a ride with someone who was driving up through the Keys on Saturday, January 9, 1937, and Ernest told her to wait for him in Miami where he would join her the next day. He had a friend there, a former heavyweight boxer named Tom Heeney, who had once fought Gene Tunney for the heavyweight championship and lost. Damon Runyon called the New Zealand-born Heeney "the Hard Rock from Down Under." After retiring from the ring, Heeney opened a bar and restaurant in Miami and sometimes went out fishing with Ernest on his trips to Key West.

Ernest told Pauline that he wanted to see Heeney before heading up to New York City to take care of some business with his publisher. Pauline knew Martha had just left town, and Ernest's lame excuse put Pauline's bullshit detector on full marital alert. He boarded the Pan Am seaplane the next afternoon and landed in Miami in time to have dinner with Martha in Heeney's joint on Sunday night. Over steaks and drinks they planned their next move together. Martha wanted to go to Spain to cover the Spanish Civil War, and she intended to go to New York to line up an assignment there. Ernest had been thinking more and more about the war in Spain lately, sorting out his own feelings about which side he favored. He was getting bored with life in Key West and needed a change of pace. He loved Spain more than any country except his own, and he thought it would be a good thing to go back and see for himself what was happening there.

Chapter Fourteen

Ernest and Martha traveled together as far as Jacksonville, at which point Martha boarded a bus for St. Louis and Ernest got on a train to New York City. Martha was clever enough to send Pauline a thank-you letter for her hospitality in Key West. Pauline was less than reassured, however, particularly when Martha referred to Ernest as "Ernestino" and said his books were "pretty hot stuff." She continued, "What I am trying to tell you in my halting way is that you are a fine girl and it was good of you not to mind my becoming a fixture, like a kudu head, in your home." The deception was transparent to a bright woman like Pauline, who had befriended Ernest's first wife Hadley while luring him into her own bed. She didn't want to admit it, but Pauline had a nagging feeling that Martha might be pulling her own version of a "Pauline" on her. Pauline knew Ernest as well as anyone on earth. Hadn't she been coping with his series of extramarital infatuations almost from the day they were married?

Pauline's fears would have boiled over into outright fury had she been privy to the letters Martha sent Ernest from St. Louis. "Please don't disappear…Hemingstein, I am very very fond of you," she wrote, addressing him by one of the many nicknames she found so endearing.

Martha continued to work on her book in her bedroom on the third floor of her childhood home, setting a personal goal of ten pages a day regardless of whether the writing was going well or not. She was the first one to become disillusioned by her latest effort, feeling it was getting bogged down, going nowhere, and she complained about her predicament in a letter to Eleanor Roosevelt. "You do get yourself into a state of jitters," Eleanor wrote back.

"Mr. Hemingway is right. I think you lose the flow of thought by too much rewriting." When Martha's old boyfriend, Allen Grover, told her that her manuscript read more like a political tract than a novel, Martha decided to throw in the towel and abandon it. After a few weeks, she had had enough of St. Louis. She missed her Hemingstein far too much and was badly in need of a dose of his jolly good cheer and optimism. And Ernestino missed his Martha. His letters and phone calls had become more and more frantic, sometimes several in a day, as he nearly begged her to join him in the Big Apple.

*   *   *

New York City was a whirlwind, spinning with far more intensity than Martha expected. Aside from his writing, Ernest did very little that didn't include a coterie of rogues who enjoyed life as much as he did. He wined and dined every night in the Stork Club or "21" with friends and fellow roustabouts, visited Max Perkins, went to the fights to see the heavyweights, and generally immersed himself in boisterous good times and daytime visits to museums and art galleries. His celebrity had grown to movie star proportions, and the press followed his every move, with the flashbulbs popping every time he ventured outside his hotel room. He also found time to help push Martha's career along, showing one of her short stories to Max who arranged for its publication in *Scribner's* magazine.

Martha's time with Ernest in New York was "very dashing— and vulgar," she wrote, thrilling to every minute of it. Wasn't she there in the spotlight with him, basking in the glow of his charisma? "He was intoxicating just to be with," said poet and novelist Stephen Spender. "He was exciting. He was a self-dramatizer, but he was very isolated within his own legend. What was rather surprising to me was that people, Martha Gellhorn particularly, were playing up to him. She talked Hemingwayese to him all the time, calling him 'Hem' and 'Hemingstein,' One of the most unfortunate things about Hemingway is that he invented a style which practically everyone imitated."

"No one who ever met Hemingway ever forgot him," Biographer Michael Reynolds wrote.

Martha hoped to land an assignment to cover the Spanish Civil War for a major magazine or newspaper, but when none was forthcoming she settled for a role as a stringer for *Collier's*. In effect, she was a free lancer writing on speculation; if she sent them anything interesting from the war zone, they might agree to publish it. As if that development were not frustrating enough, Martha was short of money to finance her trip abroad. The only way she could raise enough for her passage was to write an article for *Vogue* about the "Beauty Problems of the Middle-Aged Woman." The topic was a world removed from what was going on in Spain and the rest of Europe. But Martha had little choice but to swallow her pride and write the article—developing a skin rash in the process after trying out an "anti-aging" ointment at her editor's insistence.

"I shall be a great writer and stick to misery, which is my province," she told a friend, "and limit my reforming to the spirit and the hell with the flesh."

To a friend of Edna's in St. Louis, Martha wrote, "I am going to Spain with the boys. I don't know who the boys are, but I am going with them."

Actually, she did know very well who one of the boys was, none other than the writer she had traveled to Key West to meet a short while before. Ernest, too, was all fired up to get back to the country he loved, which was being ripped apart by violence, bloodshed, and atrocities on both sides of the broad political divide.

The North American Newspaper Alliance, known as NANA, was only too happy to sign him up as a correspondent. Martha knew which side of the political divide she stood on, but Ernest was still reserving judgment. Until now, all he had to go on were the unfiltered views of others, which were never reliable enough for him; he needed to see what was going on with his own eyes. As much as he had written about war in the past, he was a gut-level isolationist who once said, "Your own country is the only county worth fighting for."

Martha stayed in New York, finishing up her article for *Vogue* and acquiring the documents she needed for the trip to the war zone, and Ernest returned to Key West to face an anxious Pauline who was starting to feel abandoned by her errant husband. He was leaving for Spain to cover the war, he told her. He intended to write anti-war journalism, he said, to keep America out of the conflict. Pauline said she wanted to go with him, but Ernest was adamant about going alone. It was too dangerous over there for any woman, he said, blithely ignoring the fact that Martha would be joining him. Martha had already sent him a letter saying that she hoped they were "on the same ark when the real deluge begins." In an odd letter to his in-laws, Ernest penned what amounted to a farewell note of sorts.

"I'm very grateful to you for providing Pauline who's made me happier than I've ever been before." The finality of that remark was lost on the Pfeiffers at the time, but in Ernest's mind it appeared that he had already decided his marriage was over.

In a painful missive to Ernest's editor, who had visited them several times in Key West, Pauline revealed her mounting trepidations. She was writing him from "the Widow's Peak," she said. "I am told that when I was a very young baby I could be left alone on a chair and would never fall off. I seem to be still on it."

Nothing she said or did could ever deter Ernest from going wherever and doing whatever he wanted once his mind was made up. This time was no different. Ernest was going to Spain and she was not going with him. Instead, she went on a trip to Mexico City with some friends from Key West. The trip did not offer much in the way of solace, but it was the best Pauline could do. Ernest had given her much pain over the years—as well as a lot of love, cheer, and comfort during the best of times—but this time she could feel her heart breaking inside her breast.

PART THREE

UNCIVIL WAR

Chapter Fifteen

The luxurious French liner the *Paris* left New York Harbor on February 27, 1937, with America's most-celebrated literary star aboard it. Max Perkins was there to see him off, the moment captured in a blaze of flashbulbs by an army of photographers and journalists. Traveling with Ernest were two companions, Sidney Franklin, a flamboyant American bullfighter from Brooklyn, New York—"buoyantly mindless," as some described him—and Evan Shipman, a compulsive gambler who found time to write poetry when he wasn't handicapping horses. Both were perfect Ernest acolytes. They were amusing company for the author who surrounded himself with fun-loving friends, and they were excellent gofers who could do everything from whipping up a good meal to procuring contraband when the circumstances demanded. Noticeably absent out of a sense of discretion was Martha; she would follow her Hemingstein on a different liner shortly afterward.

The *Paris* docked in Le Havre on March 6, and Ernest registered at the posh Hotel Dinard in Paris on March 10. His two traveling companions stayed at a lesser establishment nearby since Ernest was footing the bill for all of them. A few days after he settled into Paris, Ernest met with filmmaker Joris Ivens, a communist who was directing a documentary about the Spanish Civil War, which would eventually be called *The Spanish Earth*. Ivens hoped to enlist Ernest in the anti-fascist cause, but the author was still reserving judgment until he had a chance to observe conditions in Spain firsthand.

"I first met Hemingway in the Deux Magots Cafe in Paris," Ivens recalled, "and asked him what he intended to do in Spain. He said, 'Report the truth about it—that every war is bad.' I said, 'All right, come.'" On Sunday, March 14, Ernest caught the night train to Toulouse with Ivens, and from there the two men flew Air France into Valencia, the provisional capital of Republican Spain.

What happened next is open to interpretation. According to Martha, when she arrived in Paris she was surprised and more than a bit miffed to discover that Ernest had left for Spain without leaving a note for her with instructions on where to meet him. She was no stranger to foreign travel, however, although it was getting increasingly harder to obtain the necessary documentation to cross the border into Spain as the war continued. But Martha was nothing if not resourceful. Dressed in gray flannel trousers and a light windbreaker, carrying a backpack and a duffel bag full of canned food, with the equivalent of only fifty American dollars to her name, she took the train south to the Spanish border. She continued across the mountain pass partway on foot into Spain, and then caught another train headed for Barcelona.

"At seven the snow was falling like petals. By eight the trees were of glass and the fields were white and the snow blew flat over the land," she wrote in a style that was more reminiscent of Ernest than anybody else.

She made it into Barcelona on March 24. Martha observed that the city looked "like an oil boom town." Everywhere there were soldiers with rifles slung over their shoulders, including multitudes of American and British youngsters going off to fight in the war, "looking like hell, and very happy and intense and busy and friendly." After two days in Barcelona, she hitched a ride on a truck that was carrying ammunition to Valencia. There she ran into Ernest's buddy and amanuensis, the buoyant Sidney Franklin. Sidney was traveling to Madrid in a car supplied by the Spanish government, and he told Martha that he was bringing provisions to Ernest's headquarters in Madrid—as though Ernest were a general directing the war from his perch above the action in the streets below. Martha was happy enough to finally be hooking up with her itinerant boyfriend that she consented to share the car not only with Sidney, but with a cornucopia of Spanish hams, coffee, butter, marmalade, oranges, grapefruits, and whiskey, all piled up in the back seat and strapped to the roof.

Ernest, at that moment, was entertaining an armada of adoring reporters, photographers, army officers, and prostitutes— "whores de combat," as he called them—in the basement of a makeshift restaurant near his hotel. They were eating dinner on long wooden planks set up like tables. "One of these days a nice girl whom I know very well," Ernest said, laughing, "a blonde with blue eyes and whose legs start at her shoulders will come here."

Martha made a lasting impression on the group when she walked in. "She was just as Hemingway had described her," said Joris Ivens, adding. "She was a good, conscientious reporter, and she learned from Hemingway the clean, cool work of a good journalist."

Ernest looked up as soon as Martha entered the restaurant. "I knew you'd get here, Daughter," he said, "because I fixed it so you could." He had started calling all women his age and younger "Daughter" a few years earlier. He had had one son with Hadley and two with Pauline and had always wanted a daughter, which would never come to pass. Martha, of course, was still young enough to have a child of her own, but she was not precisely attuned to being a fulltime mom.

The remark about fixing it so she could get to Spain would stay with Martha for the rest of her life. Their romance had barely gotten started, yet here he was boasting about how he had arranged for her to join him in Madrid after she had risked her life getting there on her own. It was the type of comment that Martha would find infuriating as their relationship intensified. But at the time she was inclined to dismiss it as "one of the foibles of genius," Ernest's way of twisting the truth into a "self-congratulatory end."

That's Martha's story.

Sidney Franklin, however, always claimed that Ernest left him behind to meet Martha in Paris, give her money, and help her across the border every step of the way. That has more of the ring of truth to it for the simple reason that it seems unlikely that Ernest would have left his latest paramour in the lurch to fend for herself. Hadn't he practically abandoned Pauline to follow Martha to Miami and insisted that she join him in New York? The other correspondents in Spain remember Martha as always well-dressed in the latest styles, looking as though she had just stepped off the cover of *Vogue*. They joked that she had a knack for dressing in tailored slacks in the midst of a warzone. That's something she could only have done with Ernest's largess, since she had yet to earn a dime writing articles for *Collier's*.

What is certain is that Martha and Sidney Franklin detested each other on sight, and she repeatedly denied his version of what happened after she arrived in Paris. She regarded Sidney as just one of Ernest's flunkies—and, by extension, her own. In her later years she was so bitter about being regarded as little more than Ernest's Third Wife that she refused to be interviewed if his name was mentioned. It appears likely that she invented her own version of the truth—as Ernest constantly did—to establish her independence from him.

* * *

By the time Martha and Ernest joined up in Madrid, the Spanish Civil War had been going on for close to a year. It officially broke out on July 17, 1936, when a claque of army generals attempted a *coup d'état* against Spain's democratically elected coalition government. Paramount among the generals was Francisco Franco, whose forces were an amalgam of nationalists that included monarchists or Carlists, fascists or falangists, Spanish, Algerian, Irish, German, and Italian soldiers of fortune. The unwieldy government coalition comprised a diverse group of anarchists, Stalinists, Trotskyites, syndicalists, various strains of socialists, and a ragtag contingent of international brigades fleshed out by volunteers from all over Europe and North America. Further complicating this ideological stew were a mix of separatists from Cataluna, Navarra, and Galicia, who wanted independence from Spain and self-rule for their own regions. Then there were trade and student unions that splintered into a mind-numbing array of more than forty different factions, each promoting its own political agenda.

When France, Britain, and the U.S. remained neutral and refused to supply arms to Spain's left-wing government, the republicans turned to Russia for support. Franco and his nationalists were backed by Germany and Italy. Figuring out which side to come down on was a devil's choice for most open-minded individuals, with Stalin in one camp and Hitler and Mussolini in the other. For Martha the choice was easy; she had tilted to the left from the time she was old enough to think for herself. The war against fascism was all that mattered to her. If it involved an alliance with Stalin to get the job done, so be it.

But for Ernest, the issue was not so black and white. He was basically apolitical, non-ideological, anarchistic, a gut-level isolationist who thought that all wars were evil despite his mania to write about every one that erupted around the world. "Hemingway said he was neutral because he had friends on both sides," said Welsh author Denis Brian. A major point of contention between

Ernest and Pauline—and her entire family as well—was her staunch support of Franco simply because she was Catholic. All the Pfeiffers were devout Catholics, so when the Catholic Church stamped its Imprimatur on Franco and the nationalists, the Pfeiffers fell in line behind the Church. Ernest had converted to Catholicism when he married Pauline, but in his soul he was essentially a hedonistic pagan.

Ernest had a way of weaseling around the issue when pressed too hard. He loved the pomp and ceremony of the Church and once remarked that Catholicism was the only religion worth taking seriously—assuming that you wanted to take any of them seriously in the first place. Indeed, he had been attracted to the Catholic Church ever since a young priest tended to him on the battlefield in Italy during World War I. Harry Sylvester, a Catholic writer who also claimed to be neutral at the time, remarked that Ernest and Pauline "had a real problem, which I never went into very much with him, about birth control. They seemed happy, but then he was on the verge of breaking up with her. They had separated and he was horsing around with Martha Gellhorn."

In the end, Ernest came down on the side of the republicans. "He called the war a bad war in which nobody was right," said Sylvester, "but said that all that mattered to him was to relieve the suffering of human beings. He said it was neither Christian nor Catholic to kill the wounded in a Toledo hospital with hand grenades, or to bomb the working-class area of Madrid simply to kill poor people."

Ernest acknowledged that both sides were guilty of atrocities and the republicans had slaughtered their fair share of priests and bishops. At the same time he wondered why the Church sided with the oppressors, in this war at least, and not with the oppressed. Ernest wrote that his sympathies were always with exploited workers against absentee landlords, and he believed that Russia had a particularly lousy government, but he added that he didn't like any government that much at all.

Ernest had good company in Winston Churchill, who claimed he would welcome the devil himself as an ally in a righteous cause to defeat his enemy. It should be noted that the full extent of Stalin's crimes against his own people was not yet fully apparent.

Joris Ivens also recalled Ernest's shift on the war. Once in Spain, Ivens said, Ernest weighed one side against the other and decided he was more anti-fascist than anything else. "He saw that most of his friends there, bullfighters and barmen and others he knew before the war, were fighting on the democratic, the republican side, against Franco and the nationalists."

Milton Wolff observed Ernest with a wary eye at first. Wolff was a dedicated leftist who commanded the Lincoln Battalion of the Fifteenth International Brigade and risked his life in the thick of battle. He knew of Ernest's reputation, naturally enough, but worried about whether the renowned author was there on a photo shoot to puff up his own image and ego.

"You had to be there to know what had happened," he said. "Basically, it was a war waged by the army and monarchists led by General Franco to reverse the 1936 election in which a leftist government of several parties was elected. It was called the Popular Front. Franco brought over Moorish mercenaries, a paid army, to destroy the elected government…In the very first weeks of the war, long before Moscow decided to help the Spanish government, the republican side as they were called, Hitler and Mussolini were pouring in stuff to help Franco and the nationalists. The final factor was England putting the arm on France to close the border between France and Spain to cut off military aid to the republicans. And FDR went along."

Wolff wrote an article in which he called Ernest a tourist in Spain, incurring Papa's eternal wrath. "I commanded troops and was wounded before you were dry behind the ears," Ernest shot back.

Wolff then backed off—but not completely, lumping Ernest in with the other correspondents covering the war. "I thought in a sense all war correspondents were tourists in Spain," he explained, "because they could call their shots, visit cathedrals when they wanted. And when I say cathedrals I mean whatever action or inaction they wanted. When they were hungry, they could go to Paris to eat and stock up. And they were warm and dry and didn't have to be in the rain. I thought their attitude should reflect that."

Ernest's attitude was that he was there to participate as well as to write. In almost every conflict he covered for one publication or another, he had a habit of bearing arms and risking his life to get closer to the real story and get it down just right. And he had suffered enough injuries to prove it. In this conflict, he was more than just a journalist and armed combatant. He was also a spy working on behalf of the U.S. government.

Chapter Sixteen

Martha moved in with Ernest in one of the rooms he rented in the Florida Hotel on the Plaza de Callao. Rooms 108 and 109 were situated on the rear corner of the third floor and had balconies overlooking the street. Martha and Ernest occupied one of the rooms, which he thought would be safe from Franco's mortar shells whirring in from encampments just outside of Madrid. The city was constantly under bombardment. Ernest installed Sidney Franklin in the other room to keep an eye on his provisions. As a form of compensation, Ernest moved a Swedish girl who spoke several languages in with Sidney to keep him company.

Madrid was "cold, enormous, and pitch black," said Martha. The city was a "battlefield" with everyone waiting around in the dark. "There was certainly fear in that feeling, and courage. It made you walk carefully and listen hard and it lifted the heart."

Ernest was far and away the best-equipped reporter in Spain. Alvah Bessie, a novelist, journalist, and screenwriter who would later be blacklisted in Hollywood for his communist sympathies, envied Ernest's treasure trove of provisions, which were on display from the day he first arrived in Madrid. Miraculously, it seemed, Ernest had managed to secure a map case, military maps, a compass, and binoculars, none of which were available to loyalist military officers. "I don't know where he got them," Bessie said. Ernest also carried around two letters in his shirt pockets wherever he went. In one breast pocket sat a letter from Franklin Roosevelt, just in case he got captured by the nationalists. The other pocket contained a letter written by the prime minister of Spain, to be unfurled if Ernest got captured by the republicans.

"He had two enormous canteens made to order for him," Bessie remembered, "each of which held about a quart of whiskey."

All of which led to speculation that Ernest was more than a journalist covering the conflict; he was on a spy mission for the U.S. government as well. His fellow journalists believed that Ernest could never have accumulated the things he did, or have had access to some of the places he visited during the war, without help from some well-placed people in Washington.

"I've got a case of Scotch I want you to take up to Milt Wolff," Ernest said to Bessie one day, perhaps in an attempt to get Wolff to soften his opinion of him.

"I'll do it, but it's kind of heavy to carry."

"You're going back in the truck, aren't you?"

"Yeah."

"Well, just be sure nobody swipes it from you."

Despite their envy, the journalists and combatants in the anti-fascist cause were happy enough to have Ernest among them. He was highly regarded as a resourceful man to have around in difficult times. He was a good military strategist as well, who could look over the landscape and instantly glimpse the big picture of what was going on out there—a talent lacking in many top-ranking generals.

Ernest's colleagues marveled at his courage and his grace under fire, even under awkward circumstances. At breakfast one morning in his room at the Florida Hotel, Ernest held court before an audience of generals, politicians, and correspondents. He sought to put everyone at ease as the battle lines got closer to the heart of Madrid. He laid a huge map out on the table, and he explained that it was impossible for Franco's incoming shells to hit their hotel because of the peculiarities of their location. Ernest could speak militaryese as well as any general or grunt in a foxhole. He managed to convince everyone present that they were a distance removed from harm's way.

At that moment, a mortar shell whooshed through the room above Ernest's—the first actually to hit the Florida—and the ceiling fell down onto the breakfast table. To anyone else but Ernest, the event and its timing would have been humiliating. While the assorted dignitaries jumped around the room, pulling plaster out of their hair, Ernest looked slowly around, first at one and then at another. Without missing a beat he said, "How do you like it now, gentlemen?"

For the moment at least, his spontaneous remark conveyed the impression that the bombardment somehow *confirmed* his theory rather than *disproved* it.

Martha went to school on Ernest during the early days of their arrival. To a great extent, she was still in the process of being created by Ernest at this stage of their courtship. Peter Davis, who was making his own documentary film about the war, said that "Spain was the real start of her journalistic career. At the same time, she was overshadowed by Hemingway."

"There was never a secret about Hemingway living with Martha Gellhorn at the Florida Hotel," said author and reporter George Seldes. "When the hotel was shelled, our great fun was to stand at the foot of the stairway to see who was running out of what room with what woman. I don't need to tell you who came out of Hemingway's room. Although I think Hemingway needed one great love affair for each of his four great or near-great books." In that regard Seldes agreed with F. Scott Fitzgerald, who said a decade earlier that Ernest needed a new wife for each book he wrote.

113

New York Times correspondent P.J. Phillip maintained that Martha told him "she was going to get Hemingway come hell or high water."

*   *   *

At this early stage of the war, the republicans had repelled every attempt by the nationalists to capture Madrid. The battle lines seesawed back and forth, with each side winning victories in one area or another. The conflict trapped civilians with varying political persuasions on the wrong side of the lines, resulting in them being pushed up against a wall and summarily shot by whichever side won a particular skirmish. The numbers of the dead mounted steadily through the first year of the war—hundreds, thousands, tens of thousands before Ernest and Martha arrived on the scene.

Ernest liked to leave early in the morning with Joris to one of the many warzones surrounding Madrid. He carried Joris's heavy equipment on his broad shoulders and helped the filmmaker set up shots for his documentary. Ernest walked the battlefield near Guadalajara with commanders, studied their tactics, offered them advice about strategy, and made notes of the dead strewn over the landscape like fallen trees.

"Over the battlefield on the heights above Brihuega," Ernest wrote in one of his dispatches for NANA, "were scattered letters, papers, haversacks, mess kits, entrenching tools and everywhere the dead...They did not look like men but, where a shell burst caught three, like curiously broken toys. One doll had lost its feet and lay with no expression on its waxy stubbled face. Another doll had lost half of its head. The third doll was simply broken as a bar of chocolate breaks in your pocket."

Back in Madrid, the shells rained down on the Florida Hotel with increasing frequency and accuracy. Franco's artillery units had selected it for a target in their sights. Ernest and Martha both pecked away at typewriters in their room with the plaster coming down around them. Through it all, the smell of bacon, ham, and eggs wafted through the corridors, emanating from Sidney Franklin's adjoining room as Ernest shared his food and whiskey with his fellow journalists. While Ernest rode out with Joris to film the action on one front, Martha traveled with other journalists to a different area to cover the violence there. Herb Matthews of the *New York Times* was especially taken with her. Some say he became more than smitten as he accompanied her into a warzone; he had actually fallen in love. Virginia Cowles went with her, covering the war for the Hearst chain. Then there was Sefton Delmer with the *London Daily Express*, Henry Buckley with the *Daily Telegraph*, George Seldes with the *New York Post*, and a host of ink-stained wretches reporting for one venue or another. But Ernest spent most of his days traveling with Joris.

"Hemingway liked to accompany me," said Joris, "because my direct connections with the General Staff of the Republican Army and the International Brigades enabled me to get much closer to the frontlines than other correspondents could. We became good friends. Because he was strong he carried the movie camera. He also contributed to the story line of *The Spanish Earth*, and later in the U.S. he wrote and spoke the commentary for the film."

In Morata outside of Madrid, Ernest, Joris, and his film crew were forced to retreat with their equipment when incoming shells bombarded their position. Ernest had not been that close to actual combat since he had been wounded by a mortar shell as a youth in Italy. A few days later he and Martha toured the republican lines in the Guadarrama Mountains together. Just a few miles away along the Basque coast, German Junker bombers launched a devastating attack on a republican encampment in Guernica, killing or wounding a third of the entire population and leveling almost every building in the village. Guernica would go down as the most infamous battle of the war, immortalized on canvas by Picasso. When Ernest and Martha returned to Madrid, they found "the air still full of granite dust and high explosive smoke," in Ernest's words, "the sidewalks scattered by new round jagged holes with blood trails leading into half the doorways you passed."

Martha contributed her own words on the subject: "Women are standing in line, as they do all over Madrid, quiet women, dressed usually in black, with market baskets on their arms, waiting to buy food. A shell falls across the square. They turn their heads to look, and move a little closer to the house, but no one leaves her place in line…A small piece of twisted steel, hot and very sharp, sprays off from the shell; it takes a little boy by the throat. The old woman stands there, holding the hand of the dead child, looking at him stupidly, not saying anything."

Chapter Seventeen

And then John Dos Passos arrived in Madrid. Ernest and Dos had practically been like brothers during their early days in Paris. Dos was three-and-a-half years older and already a highly regarded novelist when Ernest moved to Paris with Hadley in the early 1920s. Right after World War I, Dos electrified the reading public with his novel, *Three Soldiers*, and reveled at the sight of it peering out at him from the windows of almost every bookstore in America and Europe. Dos and Ernest hit it off immediately when they first met and formed their own mutual admiration society. They recognized each other's talent and vowed to teach themselves all they could learn about writing, starting by reading aloud from the Old Testament.

"We read to each other," Dos said. "Choice passages. The Song of Deborah and Chronicles and Kings were our favorites."

Ernest was just getting started with his short stories as Dos enjoyed his early celebrity. Dos was convinced that Ernest might surpass him one day. He just *knew* that "Hem would become the first great American stylist." Dos was political right from the start, way over on the left while Ernest said he was bored with politics and would rather write about the things he loved, like fishing, hunting, and bullfighting, as well as all the wars he would cover. But the two young men were critical of each other too. Dos, who had developed a crush on Hadley, didn't care for the way Ernest treated his wife.

"Right from the beginning Hem was hard on his women," Dos said. Ernest seemed to have a need to love two women at once. Dos went skiing with them at Schruns in Austria around the same time that Pauline befriended Hadley so she could move in on Ernest.

Dos remembered the good times. "Mealtimes we could hardly eat for laughing," he said. "We ate vast quantities of trout and drank the wines and beers and slept like dormice under the great featherbeds. We were all brothers and sisters when we parted company."

But Dos, as observant as he was, failed to see what was happening beneath the surface—or beneath the blankets, if you will. "It was a real shock to learn a few months later that Ernest was walking out on Hadley."

It was Dos who discovered Key West first. To him it was almost like Spain in America. He wrote to Ernest in 1929, telling him that the place would "suit him to a T." It was like Spain with the palm trees waving in the sea breezes. It was like Provincetown at the tip of Cape Cod, but with much better weather in the winter.

By the time Ernest moved there with Pauline near the turn of the decade, he rivaled his friend, his spiritual brother, in fame and achievement following the publication of his first two major novels, *The Sun Also Rises* and *A Farewell to Arms*. Dos, meanwhile, had come out with his first widely regarded masterpiece, *Manhattan Transfer*, which invigorated the left but infuriated right-wing critics who called it "an explosion in a cesspool." But Ernest loved it. It was "a spiritual Baedeker to New York," he said. Sinclair Lewis thought it was "a novel of the very first importance…the dawn of a whole new school of writing." F. Scott Fitzgerald pronounced it "astonishingly good." Dos followed that book up with *The 42nd Parallel*, the first novel in his U.S.A. trilogy. Ernest, who often resented the success of other writers whom he regarded as serious competitors, remained steadfastly loyal to Dos.

"Trilogies are undoubtedly the thing," he wrote. "You can write so damned well it spooks me that something might happen to you." It was an odd way to phrase his comment. Perhaps Ernest was already thinking of a way to keep Dos from leaping too far ahead of him.

Literary rivals that they were, there was one thing that Ernest excelled at beyond Dos's wildest hopes—indeed, beyond the dreams of any other writer of his generation. Ernest was not only a gifted stylist, he also had a natural genius for being a celebrity. He had a world-class talent for fame that was a function of his natural charisma. Strangers who saw him in a crowd singled him out and remembered him for the rest of their lives. He dominated every gathering with his presence. Dos, on the other hand, could stand on his head in the middle of a room without anyone noticing. He blended into his environment, like an armchair in the corner. In that regard, Dos and Ernest were polar opposites. Women swarmed around Ernest, moths drawn to a flame, while Dos set no one's heart fluttering. Ernest picked up on his friend's loneliness and vowed to do something about it. He introduced Dos to his sister Madeline, who had come down to Key West to recuperate after their father's suicide. But Madeline was less than impressed.

"I was shocked to see a bald man with nervous, jumpy movements," she said. "Ernest had neglected to give me a physical picture of his friend."

There was another woman visiting Key West who saw Dos differently, however. Katy Smith was there as well, Madeline's friend and Ernest's high school girlfriend. She saw in Dos a husky intellectual and brilliant writer who suited her just fine. They were all there together when a box arrived in the mail from Ernest's mother. It was big and nailed shut with a tight row of nails. For some instinctual reason, Ernest didn't want to open it. Pauline was curious, though, and took a hammer to it, clawed off the top, and started to pull out the contents. Oddly enough, the box contained an assortment of Grace Hemingway's paintings and a mess of crushed and moldy brown stuff that had once been a chocolate cake. On the bottom of the gunk was one more item. Pauline pulled it out and laid it on the floor. They all stared at it, speechless. It was the .32 caliber pistol that Clarence Hemingway had used to blow his brains out. Nobody said a word. Ernest just stared at it, horrified.

"Mrs. Hemingway," Dos wrote later, "was a very odd lady indeed. Ernest was terribly upset. Hem was the only man I ever knew who really hated his mother."

Dos and Katy got married in the fall of 1929, and no one was more thrilled about their wedding than Ernest. His best friend marrying his old girlfriend, a friend of his sister, cemented their relationship further. Ernest took them out fishing off Bimini with Charlie Thompson and a few others. There was plenty to eat and drink on board, as there always was on any of Ernest's excursions, including a few bottles of champagne that Ernest set down in the ice that kept the mullet fresh in the bait bucket. They fished into the night, with the silver sheen of tarpon visible in the moonglow on the water when the fished jumped high. When the fish stopped striking, they drank the champagne and ate some conch chowder. Charlie finally yawned and said that he had to open his store at seven in the morning, so he headed back to the dock in Key West.

Shortly afterward, Ernest took Dos and Katy out fishing again in the Gulf Stream. Ernest hooked a tarpon and was attempting to gaff it and haul it on board when he saw the sharks in the water heading for his fish. He cursed at them as they circled around and got closer to his tarpon. Ernest grabbed his rifle and aimed it at the sharks, but just as he pulled the trigger the boat rocked, throwing him off balance. Two rounds from the rifle struck him in the fleshy part of his calf.

"I'm shot!" Ernest yelled out. "Christ! Can you believe I shot myself."

"We had to turn back to take him to the sawbones at the hospital," Dos wrote. "Katy was so mad she would hardly speak to him." She was furious at Ernest for ruining a perfectly good outing for her. Damned Ernest! He always had to be the center of attention. He always did something stupid like trying to shoot a shark and spoil everyone else's fun.

* * *

It seemed inevitable that something would come along and roil the waters for Ernest and Dos. Very few of Ernest's friendships lasted throughout his lifetime. At one point or another, Ernest found a reason to turn on his rivals, particularly those whose success was equal to his own. The turning point for Ernest and Dos was the political drama unfolding in Spain. Dos was thrilled when the Popular Front overthrew the monarchists, and he tried to get his friend to whip up as much enthusiasm for the cause as he had. But Ernest continued to observe Spain with his usual detachment. Everything was fine, he thought, as long as they didn't mess with the *feria*, the bullfights he loved to follow from one season to the next.

"Hem had no stake in any of it," Dos wrote. "His partisanship was in various toreros."

Ernest's lack of involvement weighed on their friendship. Dos invited Ernest to lunch several times to discuss the issue, but Ernest refused to budge. "Those lunches," Dos wrote, "were the last time Hem and I were able to talk about things Spanish without losing our tempers."

Dos had a friend, Jose Robles Pazos, whom he had known since 1916 when Dos was in Spain studying art and architecture at the Centro de Estudios Historicos. Robles's nickname was Pepe, and he and Dos shared many interests in common, including a taste for radical politics and a desire to overthrow the monarchist government of Spain despite Pepe's aristocratic background. Dos and Pepe stayed in touch over the years. Pepe translated Dos's books into Spanish, and they visited each other on frequent trips back and forth

121

across the Atlantic. When the republicans eventually succeeded in ousting the monarchy, Pepe's and Dos's political dream was finally realized. Pepe returned to his native country to serve the government he had helped bring to power. He was immediately made a lieutenant colonel in the republican army, and within weeks after that he was ensconced at the very heart of the government that was fighting for its life against Franco and his nationalists. Pepe was privy to the secret maneuvering taking place behind the scenes, including Stalin's interest not only in supporting the republican government, but in installing a communist regime that would be a puppet of the Soviet Union. Pepe Robles knew a lot about what was going on. Some say he knew too much.

In the spring of 1937, a group of armed men knocked on the door of Pepe's apartment in Valencia. The men refused to identify themselves, but it was apparent that they were connected in some way to the government that Robles served. They pushed their way inside, and without so much as a *con su permiso* they started ripping the place apart. At first they couldn't find what they were looking for, so they demanded that Pepe tell them where his notebook was. What notebook are you looking for? You know very well what notebook we want: the one containing the information you've been compiling about Stalin's plans for republican Spain after the war is over. When the men found what they were looking for, they slapped handcuffs on Pepe and dragged him off while his wife looked on in shock. The armed men held Pepe captive for a short period in Valencia, while their higher-ups assessed the information Pepe had written down in his notebook and its potential damage to the government.

Then they blindfolded Pepe and drove him away to a secret location. The men did not make any inquiries of Pepe, put him on trial, or give him an opportunity to defend himself in any legal proceeding. He was obviously a traitor, a spy, an aristocrat from birth. He had relatives loyal to Franco fighting against republican

Spain. No, the men did not try him. Instead they sat him in a chair, raised a rifle to his head, and splashed his brain against the wall.

Chapter Eighteen

Dos had sailed to France with Katy shortly after Ernest did, on the three-funnel Cunard liner the *Berengaria*. Aboard ship with him were financier Bernard Baruch and Joseph Kennedy, who was crossing with his sons. Dos introduced himself to the dignitaries and engaged them in conversation about his support for republican Spain. Baruch was reasonably cordial, but Kennedy glowered at the novelist whose left-wing sympathies he loathed. He looked Dos up and down and then delivered the most withering putdown he could think of.

"Well you've got some top-notch publicity with Hemingway there. My boys read everything he writes."

Dos resented the remark but he tried not to show it. He had already achieved a landmark victory over Ernest when, in the summer of 1936 after the completion of his U.S.A. trilogy, *Time* magazine honored Dos with a glowing story featuring his photograph on its cover. The caption on the cover read: "Writes to Be Damned, not Saved." Now Ernest had reason to hate Dos even more than he already did. The article about Dos pulled out all the stops, saying Dos deserved a place among the supreme figures in the history of American literature, comparing him to Joyce and Tolstoy—whom Ernest once said he would not get in the ring with. Ernest had seen Dos's uncharacteristically virile image staring out at him, puffing away on a cigar clenched between his teeth. Ernest seethed with unmitigated envy. It would take Ernest more than another year to make *Time*'s cover, after the publication of *To Have and Have Not* in the fall of 1937. Dos was no longer Ernest's closest friend; he was now a "one-eyed Portuguese bastard."

When Dos reached Madrid, he saw that his old buddy was well entrenched at the Florida Hotel with a lovely blonde, a woman he had heard of but had yet to meet. Where was Pauline? What was going on? Ernest was the center of attention, well plugged into the people who were running things and the action in the field. Ernest and Martha, that's all anyone talked about. Dos's arrival was virtually unnoticed. The other journalists knew who he was, but Ernest was their focal point, the man who could get things done. He knew all the generals, the politicians who mattered. Dos knew none of them. And they didn't seem anxious to bring him into their inner circle.

*   *   *

A fidgety, birdlike, tired-looking writer named Josephine Herbst entered Madrid around the same time. She walked into the lobby of the Florida Hotel and dropped her bags on the floor. She wondered who was in charge here. She was told there would be a room for her, but no one was available at the front desk. She had achieved a measure of success so far as a minor novelist, but she was best known for her polemical articles published in obscure left-wing journals that only True Believers had ever heard of. She knew both Ernest and Dos, and both men were genuinely fond of her. Josie and her husband, now deceased, had visited Ernest and Pauline in Key West several times. But when Ernest walked into the lobby of the Florida Hotel, he had another woman by his side, an attractive and energetic blonde named Martha Gellhorn. Josie was just as shocked as Dos was to see Ernest there without Pauline.

125

Ernest greeted Josie warmly, introduced her to Martha, and helped Josie up to her room with her bags. He wondered aloud what Josie was doing in Madrid. She had no money of her own. It didn't take him long to figure out that Josie was there as a paid agent for the Soviet propaganda machine. Josie was so well connected to Stalin's man in Spain, as it turned out, that she was the first one to learn what happened to Pepe Robles. He was a fascist spy, her handlers told her. He had to be executed. Josie said that Dos had come to Madrid to find out what happened to Pepe.

"Don't say anything to him," she was told. "Some of the Spanish were beginning to be worried about Dos Passos's zeal and, fearing that he might turn against their cause if he discovered the truth, hoped to keep him from finding out anything while he was in Spain."

And Ernest? It was all right to tell Ernest, her handlers told her. Ernest and Martha could be trusted. Let Ernest decide how to deal with Dos. In what amounted to an ironic twist of political fate, Ernest and Dos Passos were in the midst of a political role reversal. The apolitical Ernest, who wanted to write about nothing except hunting, fishing, and war as a disinterested observer, was now committed to the republican cause in Spain. Dos Passos, the dedicated leftist who slammed capitalism and bourgeois culture in his books, was now suspected by the republicans of veering to the right. If politics made strange bedfellows, Ernest and Dos were nonpareil living examples of it.

*   *   *

Dos went off on his own to see what he could find out about Pepe. The building Pepe lived in at 25 Fonseca was located in a grimy slum jammed with rundown stone houses. Dos climbed up the dirty stairs, slippery with a coating of grease. He found the right door and knocked. No one answered. Dos knocked again, this time as loudly as he could. He heard someone fumbling with the locks on the other side of the door. First one click and then another. The door had to be double- or triple-bolted. The door opened an inch, and Dos could see an eyeball peering out at him through the crack.

"Dos," the woman called out. "*Que maravilla!*"

"Margara?"

Pepe's wife opened the door wide enough for Dos to slip in, and then she bolted it again with the complicated array of locks. Dos studied her carefully. What happened to the pretty, carefree young woman he had known before the war? Margara was painfully thin, her skin drawn down around her cheekbones like a skull. Her reddish hair was soiled and unkempt. The apartment smelled dank, airless, musty, as though the windows had not been opened in a month. Margara sat down on a cot in the middle of the room and stared at the floor. She clamped her hands around her knees. Dos asked her if everything was all right.

"We can speak freely now," she said. "The children are at school." She asked Dos if he heard what happened to Pepe. Dos didn't have a clue. "What's wrong with Pepe?" he asked her. Margara told him the whole story, about the men who came in the dark of night and dragged Pepe off for questioning. All she knew was that they took him to a police station and asked him about the contents of his notebook. That's all she knew. So far they hadn't charged him with anything, at least nothing she had heard of.

"Charged him! With what?"

Pepe's brother was fighting on the side of the nationalists. He had been captured and was also a prisoner now. Dos knew that

Pepe and his brother had never gotten along. They didn't agree on anything, especially politics. Margara told Dos that she knew Pepe had been suspicious of the Russians, but he wouldn't tell her anything. It was too dangerous for her to know, he said.

"He turned off my questions, but I could see he was worried and harassed."

Dos was outraged. There had to be some mistake. If Pepe needed legal counsel, Dos would see that he was well represented. Dos knew lots of Spanish lawyers from his many trips to Spain. Margara told Dos that no one she contacted wanted to help. She knew some high-ranking officials in the republican government, but all they did was put her off, telling her they would see what they could do. But she never heard from them again. They all appeared to be skeptical about Pepe's loyalty to the cause.

"It's ridiculous," Dos said. "There must be some way of appealing to the law."

Margara just stared at him as one would observe a naïve child. "Law! You don't know the Spain of today!" Dos shook his head. This was a government that believed in democratic principles and justice for everybody, he was convinced. He would not rest until he had gotten some answers for himself. He told Margara he was leaving.

"I'll be back," he said, then vanished into the bowels of the dark stairwell.

*   *   *

Josie Herbst disliked Martha intensely from the time she first set eyes on her. For one thing, Martha was *not* Pauline, a woman whom Josie cared for a great deal, almost like a sister. What the hell was Ernest doing over here with this woman anyway? If that weren't bad enough, Martha said she was a journalist who was sympathetic to the republicans, but she *looked like* the enemy. In one of her dispatches, Josie described Martha "sailing in and out in beautiful Saks Fifth Avenue pants, with a green scarf wound round her head."

A few nights after Josie arrived, the Florida Hotel suffered a direct hit from a rebel shell that shook the walls and sent plaster cascading onto the heads of its inhabitants. Dozens of prostitutes came running out of the rooms of various correspondents onto the landing that overlooked the inner courtyard. As they passed, the dashing French writer and aviator, Antoine de Saint-Exupery, elegantly attired in a blue satin dressing gown, handed each of them a grapefruit from his private stash. Josie and Dos dashed out of their respective rooms, looking frightened in the midst of all the chaos. Then out came Ernest and Martha, smiling, somewhat acclimated to the routine violence by now.

Martha described the scene later: the scurrying prostitutes made her think of beetles emerging in the dark, "crying in high voices like birds." She also found Dos Passos amusing, clothed in his "pyjamas, uncombed, with his coat on."

More often than not, Martha referred to Ernest as "Scrooby" now, a shortened version of "Screwball." Ernest preferred to think of it as a nickname for his penis, and he called her "Daughter" or "Mooky," or sometimes just "M." The others laughed at their curious intimacies but admired their calmness in the face of so much danger. "Hemingway had the calming effect of a buffalo straying shaggily over the tundra, knowing its water holes and its pastures," said a military advisor to the republicans. "Because of this he invigorated our company." And they agreed with Ernest when he told them Martha was the bravest woman he had ever met.

They could not say the same of movie actor Errol Flynn, who descended on Madrid with a retinue of flunkies and cameras to record his every action in the warzone. Martha, herself, was uniquely unimpressed by the screen idol. "At lunch there was no more room at the table," she wrote, "due to the influx of shits now that all is quiet. Herbst and two Seldes and a nice handsome dumb [bastard] named Errol Flynn who looks like white fire on the screen but is only very, very average off."

That description was kind compared with comments made about the famous actor by other journalists in Madrid. George Seldes was overwhelmed at first by Flynn and his wife, French actress Lili Damita. Seldes thought they were "two of the most beautiful people I've ever seen." Flynn impressed him with his claim that he had "a million dollars which I've raised among the friends of republican Spain in Hollywood. We're going to build a hospital and buy ambulances for the republicans." But shortly afterward, Seldes discovered that Flynn's million dollars was a myth, a way for Flynn to get himself in front of the cameras while he pontificated about the loyalist cause.

"He was a goddamned liar!" Seldes exploded. "I've met three sons-of-bitches in my life. One was Mussolini, the second was D'Annunzio who betrayed Duse [a reference to Italian poet and fascist Gabriele D'Annunzio and his betrayal of Italian actress Eleanora Duse], and the third is Errol Flynn for his betrayal of the Spanish Republic to make publicity for himself for a Hollywood movie."

Ernest took Flynn out to the frontlines outside of Madrid and sized him up immediately as a "triple phony" as he watched Flynn quiver in his boots at the first rattle of machinegun fire. After having his picture taken for publicity photos, Flynn asked Ernest, "Do you know the address of a good, clean whorehouse?" Ernest just looked at Flynn as he vanished from the battlefront and headed back to safety. He left Madrid in a flash and flew to the relative calm of

130

Barcelona. The cameras were waiting for him there as well, and Flynn preened before them showing off some scratches on his face coated with mercurochrome, claiming he had been shot in the frontline trenches. The *New York Daily News* took the bait and ran the story with a headline saying, "Errol Flynn Killed at the Spanish Front"—which a later edition amended to "wounded" at the front. Flynn biographer Charles Higham claimed, with considerable documentation to back him up, that Flynn was actually in Spain as a spy for the Nazis.

Chapter Nineteen

Martha had yet to write an article for *Collier's*, limiting herself so far to taking notes and keeping a diary. Ernest told her she was ready to submit her first dispatch, but Martha insisted that she knew nothing about war or military matters, only about the lives of ordinary people in the streets—daily life.

"Not everyone's daily life," Ernest told her. The look in his eyes was all the encouragement she needed.

She went to work immediately, writing about the courage of civilians who live ordinary lives in the midst of paralyzing fear, with the lives of those they know and love being destroyed every day. Her prose was spare and a little less Hemingwayesque. She was beginning to find her own stride, her own voice, as she wrote: "An old woman, with a shawl around her shoulders, holding a terrified thin boy by the hand, runs out into the square. You know what she is thinking: she is thinking she must get the child home, you are always safer in your own place, with the things you know. Somehow you do not believe you can get killed when you are sitting in your own parlor, you never think that. She is in the middle of the square when the next one comes."

She sent the piece to *Collier's*, which published it a few months later. Encouraged by that early success, she wrote another article for the magazine, which accepted it and put her name on the masthead. Then the *New Yorker* accepted two additional articles in short order. Martha was on a roll. No longer was she a mere student being tutored by her favorite author—and now her lover. She was Martha Gellhorn, published novelist and war correspondent in her own right. Between articles she wrote in her diary.

"I like writing. In the end it is the only thing which does not bore or dismay me, or fill me with doubt. It is the only thing I know absolutely and irrevocably to be good in itself, no matter what the result."

And no one was prouder of her than Ernest, the master himself.

Ernest and Martha were both well aware of the atrocities committed on the republican side of the conflict as well as by the nationalists. Ernest would soon begin to work on a play set in the Florida Hotel, *The Fifth Column*, which depicted the torture of a rebel spy captured by the republicans. In his later novel about the Spanish Civil War, *For Whom the Bell Tolls*, Ernest's main character, Robert Jordan, laments the atrocities committed by *both* sides. George Seldes was euphoric in his praise of Ernest and his courage, describing him with glowing accolades.

"As for Hemingway's reportage from Spain, it was not only truthful, it was a brave thing to do at a time when Spain was being red-baited to death. As for physical courage, I tell you his daily or almost daily visits to the wrecked building in no man's land he used as an observation post were an exhibition of courage. From there he could see both the republicans as well as the Franco trenches opposite. But Hem and Herbert Matthews climbed out into no man's land almost every day and lay on their stomachs on the floor near a smashed second-floor window to watch the fighting. And Franco shelled everything, including this hideout."

Martha had also grown concerned about some of the communists she ran into in Madrid and on the front. She admitted in a letter to Eleanor Roosevelt that she found some of the communists supporting the republicans to be "sinister folk and very, very canny." But she chose to report the rebel atrocities in detail while ignoring those committed by the side she supported. The major flaw in Martha's reporting throughout her life was her tendency to leave out what she knew to be true—"all that objectivity shit"—in order to uphold a greater good as she saw it.

But Ernest was less than forthright with Dos when it came to the Robles affair. Dos was still hunting for his friend Pepe in an attempt to find out for himself what kind of trouble he was in. Josie Herbst had told Ernest about Robles' summary execution by his own government, but Ernest withheld the information from Dos for some reason—perhaps out of envy over Dos's cover story in *Time*. Ernest had been ignoring Dos, as everyone seemed to be doing since Dos arrived in Spain. So Dos decided to seek out his old buddy in the hope that Ernest could shed some light on the subject. Sidney Franklin ushered Dos into room 108 at the Florida Hotel, Ernest's well-stocked lair. Ernest was lying on the bed with a glass of wine in his hand.

"How much grub did you bring?" Ernest asked gruffly, taking Dos by surprise. No hello, no how do you do, just a blunt question.

Dos admitted that he had overlooked stocking up on food because he had other things on his mind.

"Then how do you expect to eat?" Ernest asked. "Martha! He hasn't brought a goddamned thing!"

Martha stepped into the room from the one adjoining it, the one with most of their provisions. She was royally decked out in a silver fox coat that she had picked up at the local market. Martha had disliked Dos from the moment they met. She disdained him almost as much as she did Josie Herbst—disdained all of Ernest's friends from the past, particularly the ones who had been friendly with Pauline.

"We might have known," she said.

Ernest softened a notch and poured Dos some wine from his bottle. Martha sat down in the chair and stared mirthlessly at Dos. "To the happy pair," Dos toasted them, not bothering to hide the sarcasm. At that point, Dos brought up the subject of Pepe Robles. Ernest rose from the bed and walked over to face Dos—to intimidate him, as it were, with his towering presence.

"What are you worrying about, Dos?" he asked. "Your professor friend's disappearance? Think nothing of it. People disappear every day."

Dos started to protest, but Ernest cut him off with a brutal attack. "Don't put your damned mouth into this Robles business! The Fifth Column is everywhere! Suppose your friend took a powder and joined the other side?"

"That could not be!" Dos shot back. "I've known the man for years. He's absolutely straight. Nobody forced him to give up a perfectly good job to come over to help his country."

Martha joined in with a cutting blow of her own. "People have different ideas about how to help their country. Your inquiries have already caused us embarrassment."

"You've got a typical American liberal attitude," said Ernest—Ernest the newborn revolutionary, the realist who reveled in the opportunity to teach his former friend a thing or two about war and politics. Dos bristled and glared at both of them. Two birds of a feather, he thought. There was nothing more to say to either of them. Dos had come to the end of the line. The atrocities committed by both sides in this war were equally repugnant. Dos's eyes were open now. He couldn't believe how far Ernest had swung to the left, even as he himself had grown more neutral. What the republicans did to Pepe was the last straw for him, the deal-breaker. He stared at Ernest who just glowered back at him.

"That was the end of it for us," Dos wrote afterward.

* * *

In the late spring of 1937, the communists under orders from Stalin moved to cement their control over the republican government by purging the non-communist elements from its ranks. They momentarily abandoned hostilities against Franco's nationalists and directed them instead on the anarchists and separatists within the republican government, conducting witch hunts for heretics. What a religious ring that had to it! The communists had replaced God and Church with their own version of what the State should be—omnipotent, omniscient, drunk with absolute power. The communists spared no efforts in their search for traitors to Marxist orthodoxy. George Orwell described in detail the kangaroo trials, the summary executions, the torture, and the bloodletting in *Homage to Catalonia*.

Ernest and Martha decided to return to the United States by way of Paris as the worst of this internecine violence was just getting started. They stopped at Shakespeare and Company, the bookstore owned by Sylvia Beach who had been such a staunch supporter of Ernest during his early years when he was still unknown and striving to get published. Ernest and poet Stephen Spender had agreed to give readings from their respective works on May 12 before an overflow crowd as a favor to Sylvia. Ernest disliked public speaking. His throat tended to constrict and give his words a nasal quality, but he had always loved Sylvia and remained loyal to her for her support when he needed it most. Ernest got up to read from his novel in progress, *To Have and Have Not*, the story set during the Great Depression in Key West featuring thinly disguised portraits of Sloppy Joe Russell and other colorful locals. He was visibly nervous in the beginning, delivering his lines in a monotone.

But then the excitement of his own words began to inspire him, and he grew more relaxed.

"His voice had lost the monotonous pitch, his mouth and half-moon mustache twitched even more," the *Herald Tribune* reported the next day. "He began to put expression into the clean, terse phrases…The picture of him which must have been taken some twelve years ago, when he was twenty-seven and very handsome, could be seen on the wall behind."

Ernest's old idol, James Joyce, was there to hear him read. Joyce was now an old and frail-looking fifty-five. His eyeglasses were thicker than ever. He would be dead a mere four years later.

Ernest took the boat-train to the coast, where he boarded the *Normandie* for the trip back to the United States. Martha would follow shortly afterward on a different liner and wait for him in New York while Ernest traveled south. Ernest had to face Pauline when he got back to Key West, and he wanted to face her alone. It was not going to be easy. In his own mind at least, his marriage was over. He wired Pauline that he would be arriving in New York on May 18 and would head straightaway down to Key West. Pauline wired back that it would be so good to see him again. She adopted a chatty tone, telling him about household matters, about the children, about how much she missed him while he was away. But Ernest could read the desperation between the lines.

This homecoming was not going to be easy.

Chapter Twenty

Ernest looked different to Pauline than he did a few months earlier. He had put on some weight and appeared a bit bloated from too much alcohol. Pauline could always tell when Ernest had been drinking too much—or more than usual. And he was not the kind, devoted husband she hoped to see on his return. He was gruff, strangely discontent, his darker moods more pronounced. Ernest did not like what Pauline had done to the property in his absence. For one thing, she had a brick wall built around the perimeter to give them more privacy from the crowds of tourists visiting Key West in growing numbers. Ernest disliked the tourists straining their necks on the sidewalk out front, but he didn't like the feeling of being fenced in. But worst of all, Pauline had installed a large salt-water swimming pool in the yard. She knew how much Ernest loved to swim, and she thought the swimming pool would be an inducement for him to stay home now and finish his novel. But when Ernest found out Pauline had spent twenty thousand dollars on it—two and a half times the cost of the house—he exploded. He flipped a penny at her and said,

"You've spent all my other money. You might as well take my last cent too."

Pauline saved the penny and had it cemented into the yard beside the pool, where it remains in full view today.

On May 5, 1937, Sloppy Joe Russell moved his bar to a building he bought on Duval Street for twenty-five hundred dollars when his landlord raised the rent one dollar a week at 428 Greene Street. The new place was one of the first stops Ernest made after his return. Josie Russell was in fine form, and so was Skinner dominating his perch behind the bar. Ernest went into the men's room to relieve himself, and when he came out he asked Josie what he had done with the old urinal.

"It's in the back," Josie said, "with other stuff I can't use anymore. Why?"

"Can I have it?"

Josie looked at him as though he were crazy. "Take it if you want. I was gonna toss it out."

"I've pissed enough money down that thing," Ernest said. "I feel like I own it now."

Pauline was speechless when Ernest brought it home. When Ernest was off on another one of his adventures, Pauline had it scrubbed out thoroughly, turned over backside down, and filled with plants and flowers in an attempt to hide its original purpose. That, too, remains in the backyard today near the site of the old pool.

Early in the morning of May 26, Ernest departed in the *Pilar* on a fishing trip to Bimini with a couple of friends on board. Pauline flew over from Miami with their sons, Patrick and Gregory, for a few glorious days of hauling in fish and basking in the sun. While Ernest was in Bimini avoiding the subject of their disintegrating marriage in his conversations with Pauline, Martha was having lunch with Eleanor Roosevelt in Washington, D.C., on May 28. During their lunch, Martha asked if President and Mrs. Roosevelt would be interested in seeing *The Spanish Earth* when Ernest and Joris Ivens completed the film. If so, they would all be happy to come to Washington to show it to them.

"Martha Gellhorn seems to have come back with a deep conviction that the Spanish people are a glorious people and something is happening in Spain which may mean much to the rest of the world," Mrs. Roosevelt wrote in her syndicated column.

Joris worked on the film in New York and Ernest divided his time between his novel and the text for the film. The narration was supposed to be delivered by an up-and-coming actor named Orson Welles, who would become famous a year later with his radio broadcast of H.G. Wells's *The War of the Worlds*, and a few years after that with his starring role in *Citizen Kane*. But after listening to Orson's voice-over, Ernest was dissatisfied and agreed to narrate it himself.

"Orson Wells was supposed to do it," Ernest told movie director John Huston a few years later.

"Orson, eh," said Huston. "And why didn't he do it?"

"Well, John," Ernest answered, clearing his throat. "Every time Orson said the world *infantry* it sounded like a cocksucker swallowing."

Ernest left Pauline and the boys in their rented house on Bimini and flew up to New York on June 4 to speak before the American Writers Conference in Carnegie Hall. He arrived just in time to see an excerpt from the film that Joris prepared for the occasion in front of a packed house. When it was over, Ernest stepped to the podium and thrilled to the thunderous applause of thirty-five hundred of his fellow writers. He appeared composed as he delivered his carefully crafted attack on the fascist menace threatening to embrace the world.

"Fascism is a lie told by bullies," he said. "It is condemned to literary sterility. When it is past, it will have no history except the bloody history of murder that is well known...But there is now and there will be from now on for a long time war for any writer to go to who wants to study it. It looks as though we are in for many years of undeclared wars."

His prescient remarks resonated well with most of the audience. But reporter Dawn Powell had a bit of fun with the proceedings in her write-up, saying that "about ten-thirty all the foreign correspondents marched on each one with his private blonde led by Ernest and Miss Gellhorn, who had been thru hell in Spain and came shivering on in a silver fox chin-up." As for Ernest's speech, Powell wrote that "Ernest gave a good speech" saying "that war was pretty nice and a lot better than sitting around in a hot hall and writers ought to all go to war and get killed and if they didn't they were a big sissy. Then he went over to the Stork Club, followed by a pack of foxes."

Spanish journalist Prudencia de Pareda was a bit kinder, writing, "Yes, there was some awkwardness, both vocal and physical—but he faced and beat them both. The audience had come for Ernest; he was there for them. He lapped up the warm acceptance."

Ernest met with Max Perkins to discuss his novel, and then returned to Pauline and the boys in Bimini to work some more on the book, which he promised to deliver in July. He told his wife that he intended to go back to Spain in the fall—again without her. Then he left her fretting in the sun and flew back to New York—to Joris, to Max, and most of all to Martha—on June 20, in time to get the film ready for a private showing before the president and Eleanor. The White House screening was set for July 8. Ernest, Martha, and Joris flew to Washington from Newark, New Jersey. On the way down, Martha warned them that the quality of the food and drink served up by the Roosevelts had deteriorated considerably over the years. It was now indescribably bad. The men laughed it off, believing she had to be exaggerating. Ernest was amply warned, but he was nevertheless in shock when he experienced the Roosevelts' hospitality first-hand.

"We had a rainwater soup followed by rubber squab, a nice wilted salad and a cake some admirer had sent in, an enthusiastic but unskilled admirer," Ernest wrote afterward. Mrs. Roosevelt was "enormously tall, very charming, and almost stone deaf. She hears practically nothing that is said to her but is so charming that most people do not notice it." President Roosevelt was "very Harvard charming and sexless and womanly, seems like a great Woman Secretary of Labor." The three visitors sweltered through the showing in the airless White House, without so much as a ceiling fan to circulate the humid summer heat. Ernest was shocked to finally see what he and Joris had produced on the screen before such an exalted audience.

"Afterwards when it is all over," he wrote, "you have a picture. You see it on the screen; you hear the noises and the music; and your own voice, that you've never heard before, comes back to you saying things you'd scribbled in the dark in the projection room or on pieces of paper in a hot hotel bedroom. But what you see in motion on the screen is not what you remember."

* * *

Ernest delivered the manuscript of *To Have and Have Not* to Max Perkins in time for an October 15, 1937, pub date. The novel that Ernest delivered was not his finest work, not really a cohesive novel so much as three novellas with a common theme strung together in single book. It was Ernest's most political book, set against the backdrop of the Great Depression in Key West and the attempted revolution in Cuba. It had a cast of characters based on people he knew who were involved in gun-running, smuggling, and murder. It is an exciting story, somewhat experimental in style with its hard-bitten prose, later adapted into a movie starring Humphrey Bogart and Lauren Bacall.

And then Ernest was off to Spain again on August 14, sailing across on the *Champlain* and Martha following this time on the *Normandie*. On board with Martha were acid-penned writer Dorothy Parker and equally acerbic playwright Lillian Hellman. Parker wrote about Martha working out every day in the ship's gym, where "all of Ernest's ladies began their basic training for the life partnership." Martha and Lillian disliked each other intensely from the start; perhaps the uniquely homely, slightly older woman was put off by Martha's good looks. In any event, Lillian sized her up and later criticized her "well-tailored" appearance, which made her look as though she were going off to cover the war for *Vogue*. For her part, Martha took a liking to Dorothy but found Lillian to be a "sullen" hag "with her thin upper lip, and the lids flat over her eyes and the insulting darkened teeth and the expression of polite spite." She had no right to inflict her misery on others, said Martha, "simply because one man left her."

Martha joined Ernest at the Hotel Foyot in Paris on August 23. Ernest was not in the best of moods when she arrived. He was poring through the page proofs for the British edition of his novel, but the more pressing concern was his doctor's advice following a recent physical examination. The doctor told him he was suffering from some damage to his liver as a result of his heavy drinking. He needed to cut his alcohol intake by half at least, said the doctor, and give up the heavy, spicy sauces he favored. The doctor also prescribed a sleeping pill to cure Ernest's chronic insomnia. Telling Ernest to cut back on alcohol and give up the food he liked was tantamount to telling him to stop breathing. He was an alcoholic and a sensualist. Booze and well-seasoned food were more than just fuel to him; they were the very elixir of life, along with sex and other earthly pleasures. He had recently turned thirty-eight, still a fairly young man, but many years of hard living were starting to take a nasty toll on his body.

Soon they would be heading south to Spain again—a country brimming over with the best of what life had to offer, even in the midst of the country's hellacious struggle for survival.

Chapter Twenty-one

On September 6 they crossed the border, first stopping off in Valencia. The news was not good for the republican cause, whose troops were in retreat throughout Spain, fighting a defensive battle against Franco's nationalists. The nationalists were in control of the northern provinces, including Basque country. Rebel planes and submarines attacked virtually everything that sailed in the Mediterranean delivering supplies to the republicans. The Vatican had recognized Burgos as the seat of the new nationalist government. Many of Ernest's and Martha's republican friends had been slaughtered in the fighting.

"I thought I knew everything about the war," Martha said to Ernest. "But what I didn't know is that your friends got killed."

Perhaps the major problem for the republicans was the withdrawal of military support by Stalin in the face of ongoing nationalist attacks. Stalin was rethinking his strategy, and while he had not yet signed the nonaggression pact with Hitler and would not do so for two more years, his crusade to purge the Russian military of dissidents at home required a greater concentration of energy there. He recalled his best field tacticians from Spain to deal with his internal strife and left the republican ranks in shambles after cleansing them of non-Marxist elements. The republicans attempted an offensive to take control of Madrid and succeeded briefly in splitting the rebel army in Brunete. But their depleted reserves suffered horrendous losses and fell short of the goal.

"You could pass a high pile of rubbish," Martha wrote, "and smell suddenly the sharp rotting smell of the dead. Further on would be the half-decayed carcass of a mule, with flies thick on it. And then a sewing machine, by itself, blown out into the street."

Ernest and Martha surveyed the wreckage through field glasses and observed Franco's soldiers wandering through deserted buildings, while off in the distance beyond them republican soldiers washed in a stream. The nationalists counterattacked and overran Santander. Shortly afterward, Franco commanded the entire Atlantic Coast and the middle of Spain—roughly two-thirds of the country. His next goal was to drive a corridor to the Mediterranean coast and split the nation in half.

"Now we learned to know the wounded, the various ways of broken flesh," wrote John Sommerfield, a volunteer in the republican army, "the limbs sliced off clean and left whole on the ground, or blown into a red pulp stuck with white fragments of bone and still hanging by throbbing veins to living bodies…we learned the faces of men dying and not knowing it, greenish, livid, with impersonal, gaping mouths."

Ernest grew annoyed with Martha when she said she wanted to return home to earn some money speaking about the war in Spain. He accused her of money-grubbing when the republicans were suffering mounting losses; Ernest had enough money for both of them. But in reality he was becoming irritated with her inchoate independence now that she had learned what she needed to know about her craft from him. She was like a star student striving to break free of her mentor. While Ernest had encouraged her writing ambitions and did all he could do to bring her along, he was also concerned that the day would come when she would no longer need him as much. His first two wives had been compliant and lacked career ambitions of their own. Martha was a different species altogether. For one thing she was nine years younger than he was, while Hadley was eight years older and Pauline four years older. Martha was also more glamorous and self-assertive. She had a strong will that was starting to clash more frequently with his.

146

Ernest retaliated by depicting Martha in a less-than-complimentary light in the play he was writing. Now that the novel was done, Ernest turned his attention back to *The Fifth Column*. The original storyline for the play required no female lead, but Ernest wrote one in anyway, portraying himself as a counterspy in Spain named Philip Rawlings and Martha as his attractive blonde lover, Dorothy Bridges. Philip is an amusing fellow whose main fault is that he drinks too much. In one scene, which Ernest eventually expunged, Philip complains about Dorothy putting him off his stroke by pressuring him to marry her when he would rather return home to his wife. Ernest described Dorothy/Martha in Philip's words, saying "Granted she's lazy and spoiled, and rather stupid, and enormously on the make. Still she's very beautiful, very friendly, and very charming and rather innocent—and quite brave."

Lazy! Spoiled! Stupid! On the make! These were hardly words designed to turn up the heat on their love affair, despite the inclusion of "beautiful," "charming," and "brave" among Dorothy's personal traits. At the end of the play, Philip leaves Dorothy, telling her "You're useless really. You're uneducated, you're useless, you're a fool and you're lazy." But Ernest did give Dorothy some of the best lines in the play. "Oh don't be kind," Dorothy answers Philip. "You're frightful when you're kind. Only kind people should be kind." Ernest, undoubtedly, was suffering from guilt pangs over his treatment of Pauline. Years earlier he had blamed Pauline for breaking up his marriage to Hadley, and now he was finding reasons to blame Martha for his all-but-doomed second marriage. Someone had to be the scapegoat, as long as it wasn't Ernest.

Martha decided to stay on in Madrid with Ernest a bit longer instead of sailing back across the Atlantic immediately. Once again their rooms, numbers 113 and 114 this time around, were amply stocked with—well not exactly with the spoils of war, but with the best that war-torn Spain had to offer. The bed, the chairs, every square inch of floor space in one room was weighed down with tins of corned beef, cheese, coffee, soup, chocolate bars, and of course alcoholic beverages of every variety. No one knew for sure exactly where Ernest laid claim to these provisions, which led to more speculation that perhaps he *was* doing triple duty as a war correspondent, combatant, and a spy. With the galley proofs of *To Have and Have Not* corrected and the novel due out in a month, Ernest barricaded himself in the Hotel Florida to work on his play, while Dorothy—er, Martha—pecked away beside him on her own typewriter, generating articles about the war for her publisher in New York.

*   *   *

Now it was Ernest's turn to grace the cover of *Time*. The October 18, 1937, issue of the magazine featured a stylized painting of him in profile, fishing in the Gulf Stream. He was depicted as a man of action who was also a man of letters—the man of the moment—in a pose familiar to his wide readership. Now he had evened the score with Dos. The cover story was timed to coincide with the publication of *To Have and Have Not*, and on that score Ernest was less than pleased with many of the reviews. *Time*'s review was glowing, calling Harry Morgan, his main character, Ernest's "most thoroughly consistent, deeply understandable character." With the novel, said the reviewer, Ernest reestablished his position in the top rank of American writers. The left-wing press loved the novel, with *New Masses* hailing the author's "increasing awareness of the economic system and the social order it dominates."

But the literary *fictionistas* were less impressed. "Please quit saving Spain and start saving Ernest Hemingway," implored fellow novelist Sinclair Lewis. *The Nation* dismissed the work as a mere "transition to the kind of book that Ernest will write in the future."

148

But the naysayers could not restrain the sale of the novel, which quickly climbed to thirty-eight thousand copies in the midst of the grinding depression. People needed diversion to take their minds off their penurious condition, and Ernest was one of their favorite sources of entertainment. So what if his latest book was not his best; it was a damned good story that captured the spirit of the era.

In mid-December the snow began to fall heavily across northern Spain. Martha wanted to return home in time for Christmas, so she traveled to Barcelona while Ernest lingered a bit longer to observe the action from a hill in Teruel. He met up with her in Barcelona at the Hotel Majestic, where they had dinner together before Martha boarded the train to Paris. Back in the States, news of their affair was now appearing in gossip columns throughout the nation. Pauline read about it in Key West and grew frantic. Of course she had known all along that Ernest was off on another fling, but she believed he would get over it in short order and put it behind him, as he had done with that business with Jane Mason. But the gossip now was that he and Martha were more than just lovers; they were serious partners who might have been married by now were it not for Ernest's existing marriage to Pauline. Pauline could take it no longer. She flew to New York and crossed the Atlantic on December 20 aboard the *Europa*, while Martha was sailing the other way on the *Normandie*. Their ships were in view of each other in mid-passage. Pauline checked into the Hotel Elysee-Park on the right bank in the midst of a howling snowstorm, in time to greet Ernest when he arrived from Barcelona.

Pauline was in a red hot fury when Ernest set eyes on her. "Don't you see that Martha is a childish, egotistical, self-centered phony?" she demanded of him. She is "almost without talent." Pauline told Ernest she would jump off the balcony outside their hotel room—ala Jane Mason—if he didn't come to his senses. And look at you, she said. You're bloated and suffering with liver problems because of your drinking. Ernest couldn't deny her accusations. He felt like hell and didn't argue with her assessment of

Martha. Hadn't he said as much about her through the mouth of Philip Rawlings in his play? But he couldn't be without her. He wrote to Max Perkins that he was in a "gigantic jam." Yes, life does get complicated when you venture onto the thin ice of infidelity.

They remained together in Paris for twelve days to wait out the weather, while Martha spent Christmas with Edna and her siblings in St. Louis. On January 12, 1938, Ernest and Pauline sailed westward across the turbulent Atlantic on the *Gripsholm*, with one storm after another roiling the ocean and pounding their vessel. Their destination was Nassau in the Bahamas, a conscious decision they made to avoid reporters in New York who were clamoring to know about their ruptured marriage. From Nassau they flew to Miami. Pauline caught a puddle-jumper down to Key West, and Ernest boarded the *Pilar* and headed to No Name Key. Pauline met him there with their car and drove him the remaining distance to their home.

During the past thirteen months, Ernest had spent less than three weeks in their house on Whitehead Street. The new year had just begun, and it was off to a less-than-auspicious start.

Chapter Twenty-two

Ernest put the best face that he could on his precarious situation. As the Key West *Citizen* reported following an interview with him, "Expressing concern at the local criticism of his latest novel, *To Have and Have Not*, Mr. Hemingway regretted that this is so and said, 'I am delighted to be back in Key West. It is my home and where my family is. My best friends are here. No one has more admiration for the town, and appreciation for its people, their friendliness, the fine life and wonderful fishing here than I have.'"

At the same time, Martha was coming into her own as a celebrated lecturer and expert on the civil war in Spain. "With a short black dress setting off her taffy-colored hair hanging childishly about her face in a long bob, Miss Gellhorn looked sixteen but spoke in a luscious, deep, free-flowing voice with words of maturity and an emphasis of authority," wrote a reporter in *Oak Leaves*, a newspaper in Oak Park, Illinois—Ernest's hometown no less. Martha's hometown newspaper, the *Post-Dispatch*, was equally ebullient, talking about her "voice, the culture, the art of pose, the poise, gesture, diction which succeed upon the stage at its best."

She drew a crowd of three thousand people at the University of Minnesota— students, professors, and concerned members of the public who were anxious for news about the course of the war in Spain. Her fame was growing, thanks to her war dispatches and now her widely reported speeches. The *New York Times* called Martha one of the few popular female lecturers of 1938. She warned of a widening war that would inevitably involve the United States more deeply in European affairs, but her attempts to get the Roosevelt

151

administration to abandon its neutral position in favor of the republicans went unheeded. Her friend Eleanor Roosevelt, though sympathetic, was being attacked by the Catholic Church and felt pressured to adopt a low profile out of fear of hurting her husband, who was adamant about keeping his distance from the conflict. When Martha became ill after delivering twenty-two lectures in a single month, Eleanor Roosevelt advised her to take a vacation and "stop thinking for a little while."

But Martha was incapable of closing her mind to the violence in Spain. "The only way I can pay back for what fate and society have handed me," she wrote back to the president's wife, "is to try, in minor totally useless ways, to make an angry sound against injustice…The young men will die. The best ones will die first, and the old powerful men will survive to mishandle the peace…I have gone angry to the bone."

Martha and Ernest were both itching to get back to Spain. In their absence, Franco's forces had sent the republicans into full retreat. On the night of March 16, with a full moon illuminating the cold dark sky over Barcelona, German bombers mounted a devastating attack on the city, eighteen raids in all over forty-eight hours, raining bombs down on the most populated neighborhoods, killing thousands of residents and maiming many more who were trapped beneath falling ceilings, roof beams, tumbling bricks and mortar. When the bombers had completed their deadly mission and flown off into the distance, the blood literally ran like flowing streams along the gutters. Reporters wrote of witnessing horrifying sights "which Dante could not have imagined." The hospitals overflowed with the sick and dying, those with broken bodies, and the streets outside were filled with screaming men, women, and children. Those who had survived the attacks roamed through the gutted city mindlessly, most of them delirious with hunger. There was no food to be found anywhere.

The two lovers could no longer stand to be away from each other. Twelve pounds lighter after her arduous speaking tour, Martha traveled to Florida, to Miami where Ernest flew up to meet her. She wanted to be with the man who comforted her when she needed it and strengthened her resolve to keep on going when her spirits were flagging. Their match was not perfect. An element of competition had seeped into their relationship. But they were both determined to see it through. There was tension there. But there was love there as well. Their affection for each other had grown deeper, and never were they more aware of that than when they were apart. Pauline was incensed, and hurt to the core. She had worked hard since his return to get her husband back. And now his lover was back—almost literally in her own backyard. Martha had come to take him away again. And Ernest was champing at the bit to go away with her.

*   *   *

Ernest and Martha sailed across to Europe on the *Queen Mary* on March 19, 1938. Back in Paris once more, Ernest once again functioned as more than a war correspondent. He operated on a quasi-official level as well, contacting the American ambassador to France, Claude Bowers, to arrange an evacuation plan for Americans in the event of a total collapse of the republican government. Paramount on the agenda, he told Bowers, was dispatching ships to Spanish ports to evacuate American citizens who were sure to be executed by Franco's troops if they were captured. Bowers agreed and forwarded Ernest's recommendations to Washington.

"I heard from reliable sources that Hemingway acted as a liaison between the Spaniards and the British navy in the last days in terms of evacuating people," said Milton Wolff. "So he did have influence, though he was certainly not on the general staff."

Ernest helped raised money for the crippled and wounded streaming across the border into Marseilles to escape the hellhole that was Spain. Then he and Gellhorn boarded the night train to Perpignan with fellow journalists Vincent Sheean and Jim Lardner, the son of humorist Ring Lardner whom Ernest admired. In Perpignan near the Spanish border, they all observed the ragtag hordes of war refugees staggering along the roads, crouching in ditches, begging everyone they met for scraps of food to alleviate their hunger. Most had abandoned their villages before they were overrun by the enemy.

"There were those who came with only a bundle," Martha wrote, "pink or yellow or blue or dirty grey, and all strange shapes, clutched under their arms or balanced on their heads, some walking fast and others warily."

Ernest, Martha, and the others crossed the border into Spain, where they watched nationalist bombers dropping their loads and strafing everything that moved with machineguns mounted on the fuselage. They reached Barcelona, now leveled and strewn with debris in the aftermath of the bombing attacks. It was all very much like the "last days of Pompei," Martha observed. Martha wanted to stay there and send more details of the devastation to her editor at *Collier's*, but he wired her back immediately that he was not interested in the Barcelona story. "Stale by the time we publish," he said. Instead, he instructed her to go back into France, and then to Czechoslovakia and England to report on how the war was affecting the rest of Europe.

Martha had observed Ernest at his finest during the past few weeks. Years later, after their love had turned to spite and bitterness, she was able to fairly assess his courage and coolness in the midst of danger. "There was plenty wrong with Hemingway," she wrote, "but nothing wrong with his honest commitment to the Republic of Spain and nothing wrong with his admiration and care for men in the Brigades and in the Spanish divisions and nothing wrong with his respect for the Spanish people. He proved it by his actions."

Others agreed. Ernest remained in Spain after Martha left for France, and continued his efforts to help those around him, including other journalists. "Because Ernest was always a good man in a tight spot," wrote Denis Brian, "fellow correspondents were glad to have him along, especially those with him in a boat on the dangerous Ebro River. The boat was out of control and heading for a wrecked bridge when Hemingway grabbed an oar and used his great strength and skill to row them to the river bank."

Martha rented a car in Perpignan and drove slowly north toward Paris, stopping along the way to interview locals about the war. She took her time, gathering material for her next article, and when she arrived in Paris on May 26, Ernest was already there waiting for her. They discussed the war, of course, but Ernest had other things on his mind as well, most important among them Pauline's increasingly urgent telegrams from home. He had to return to the States and deal with his marital situation once and for all. Martha was anxious about his departure. How many men had professed undying love for "the other woman," only to return to their wives when faced with the stark reality of their predicament? That, after all, was the path of least resistance with fewer complications for all concerned.

She was trying to be "reasonable," Martha wrote to her mother. "I believe he loves me, and he believes he loves me, but I do not believe much in the way one's personal destiny works out."

Martha completed her assignment in Europe for *Collier's* after Ernest left on the *Normandie* for New York. Pauline was waiting for him at the Key West airport on May 31 when his plane touched ground on the flight from Miami. She was livid, unsmiling, trembling with rage. She herself had just returned from New York after spending some time with her sister Virginia in Connecticut. Virginia had always liked Ernest; in fact, at one point she had developed a crush on him herself but backed away when his relationship with Pauline took a serious turn. But now she couldn't stand him because of the way he treated her sister. Don't let him off the hook too easily, she advised Pauline. Make sure he agrees to a substantial financial settlement if you get a divorce.

Ernest, too, was miserable as he confronted his wife at the airport. Summer had already arrived in Key West, and the blistering sun beat down hard from the pale-blue canopy of sky. Pauline had brought their sons Patrick and Gregory along with her, perhaps as an appeal to his paternal instincts and his obligations as a father. Ernest's homecoming did not get off to an auspicious start. With their handyman and general factotum behind the steering wheel, their Ford convertible with a dented fender approached the intersection of Simonton and United Streets. Suddenly, a WPA worker driving a busted-out jalopy lost control of his car, rolled over, and skidded sideways into Ernest's Ford. Ernest jumped out immediately, ready for combat. He stood toe to toe with the other driver, both men cursing each other out. A local cop appeared before either antagonist could throw a punch and arrested the two of them.

"I will not pay damages!" Ernest yelled. "I'll counter-suit any suit he brings up! I was struck!"

With no injuries to anyone, only further damage to the already battered cars, the presiding magistrate washed his hands of the matter, Pontius Pilate-style, and dismissed the case. The matter ended there. Ernest and the other party cooled down, and both of them laughed it off. The next day Ernest made a joke of the incident and told a reporter, with some exaggeration, "It's much more dangerous to be in Key West and have an old jalopy without brakes crash into you than it is to be under fire from airplane bombs, artillery fire, and machineguns as I was twenty-four hours a day."

The accident was a temporary diversion from his problems at home. Ernest had left the war in Spain behind, but the battle of Key West was just beginning.

Chapter Twenty-three

Josie Russell was the only friend in Key West Ernest could count on. Some of the regulars at Sloppy Joe's had cooled to him now, many unhappy with his portrayal of them and people they knew in *To Have and Have Not.* Everyone else who knew Ernest and Pauline, including Charlie and Lorine Thompson, sympathized with Pauline in the escalating war on Whitehead Street. Ernest retreated to his office across the catwalk in the other building on the property for longer and longer stretches. He and Pauline argued constantly about everything except the main issue between them: Martha Gellhorn and her continuing presence in his life. In distancing himself from Pauline, Ernest was pushing away more than his wife and the mother of two of his boys. Pauline, who had been a writer for *Vogue* in Paris before she met Ernest, had also been his primary editor during the past ten years—a period in which Ernest had written most of his major books. She had functioned first and foremost as his bullshit detector, telling him what to tone down and what to leave out when he exaggerated too transparently. Ernest always ran his work before Pauline first before he shipped it off to Max Perkins in New York.

"I don't think any of the books written about Ernest have given Pauline the credit for the part she played in his life," said Lorine Thompson years later. "You see, most of his best books were written while he was living in Key West. I feel that Pauline kept Ernest's nose a little bit to the grindstone…I think she did everything to keep Ernest at work, to make conditions favorable for him to work. Pauline's Uncle Gus, Gus Pfeiffer—there's no getting around it—with the money he gave Pauline made it possible for Ernest to spend a great deal more time writing than working on other things, and to take his time doing it."

Ernest began to feel more and more like an outcast in his own town, and like a stranger in his house. He drank even more heavily, some days pounding down a dozen or more drinks a day. He spent his days and nights with Pauline and the boys, but he ached for the latest woman in his life and couldn't wait to be with her again. He didn't want to admit it yet, but he was growing tired of Key West. His innate paranoia led him to believe that the situation had reversed: the town had turned on him rather than he on the town. With the Overseas Highway now completed, linking the Keys to the mainland, new hordes of tourists poured into Key West, many of them trying to get a glimpse of the famous writer behind the brick wall that barricaded Ernest from life outside. He had to get away, and the easiest way to do that was to take the *Pilar* down to Cuba, leave his frustration and his worries behind and escape into his greatest passion outside of writing, fishing for marlin.

He and Josie Russell departed for a brief outing in the Gulf Stream near Havana, but Ernest's heart was not completely in it. When he returned to Key West, he was more agitated than ever, more erratic than before. Pauline and some of their guests thought he was bordering on insanity. When he couldn't immediately lay his hands on the key to his writing lair, he flew into a rage, grabbed one of his sidearms and blasted the lock off, shattering the doorjamb into splinters.

"He was like a crazy man waving the pistol around," said Lorine Thompson. "I didn't know what he was going to do."

Pauline sent the children away with the Thompsons to stay with them for the night. Pauline left Ernest home and went by herself to a costume party she had planned at the Havana-Madrid Club. At home alone with his family and friends gone, Ernest downed several whiskeys and stormed down to the club. Pauline watched him stagger in and cringed when he let a drunken guest prod him into a fight, asking Ernest why he thought he was so tough. Ernest unleashed a powerful right, clipped the man on the point of

159

his chin and left him lying unconscious on the floor. Pauline retreated in tears, humiliated to the bone by her husband's behavior.

All this may have been a reflection of Ernest's worsening alcoholism and, perhaps, of the sickness gnawing away at his soul. He was deeply in love, no longer with Pauline but with Martha who had returned to her own family nest in St. Louis. They wrote to each other every day, professing their love in letters that became progressively passionate. Ernest was living a lie at home and it was eating him alive. He and Martha wanted to be together, yet Ernest had yet to take the next logical step and sever the umbilical cord that linked him to Pauline. He and his wife were separated in every way but actual fact. They went through the pretense of celebrating their birthdays together in July when Ernest turned thirty-nine and Pauline forty-three. Then they packed their car full of gear—rifles, shotguns, pistols, stacks of ammunition in addition to their clothes and other paraphernalia—for a hunting trip out west at the L-Bar-T ranch in Wyoming, near the northeast entrance to Yellowstone National Park.

As they passed through Florida, Gregory accidently scratched Ernest's eye, which required stopping off at a hospital to have it tended to. By the time they arrived at the ranch, Ernest was wearing an eye patch and dark glasses to cover the salve leaking out of his aching eye. His mood had grown stormier than ever, matching the deluge they had driven into. The skies opened up and kept them cabin-bound for a solid week under low dark clouds and pounding rain without letup. Ernest, Pauline, and the boys were confined within four close walls with scarcely an opportunity to ramble through the woods to relieve the tension. Escape came in the form of a telegram from NANA, asking Ernest to return to Spain to report on the war, which now looked all but hopeless for the republicans. Martha had already gone over by herself on assignment from *Collier's*.

Their plans for a family vacation now ruined beyond repair, Ernest left for New York alone, and Pauline made arrangements to rent an apartment on East 50th Street for her and the boys. She could no longer bear to spend her days in the small-town atmosphere of Key West without Ernest, with rumors multiplying daily about the battles taking place on Whitehead Street. She told Ernest that she would wait there until he got back from Europe. She maintained some glimmer of optimism that her marriage could still be saved, that Ernest would outgrow this infatuation with Martha—as he did other infatuations in the past—and come home to her. On August 31, the *Normandie* sailed out of New York Harbor with Ernest on board, carrying him across the Atlantic on his fourth and final visit to the war in Spain.

* * *

Franco and his forces occupied almost all of the country, and the republican government existed now in name only. The international brigades had abandoned the battlefield, leaving the republican remnants to suffer the wrath of the nationalists by themselves. Every day the battered legions crossed on foot across the border into France, bloodied, hungry, tired beyond description, clothed in rags, their eyes dulled by hopelessness and defeat. Ernest traveled back and forth between Paris and the Spanish border, describing the aftermath of the fighting for NANA and working on short stories as a warm-up for the big novel he planned to write about Spain—the one that would turn out to be the greatest and most ambitious novel he would ever write, by most accounts. Martha traveled throughout Europe, covering the preparations for all-out war that appeared increasingly inevitable each day.

In New York, Scribner's published Ernest's play along with a selection of his short stories in a single volume; *The Fifth Column and the First Forty-nine Stories* was launched on October 14, 1938. Max Perkins had been less than enthusiastic about the play but agreed to publish a limited edition in deference to his celebrated author. The reviewers were equally disappointed by Ernest's latest effort, ignoring the stories while pummeling the play. The *New York Times* found it monotonous. *The Nation* said it was "almost as bad" as *To Have and Have Not*, which was "by far the worst book" Ernest had ever written. *Time* found the play "ragged and confused." Influential critic Malcolm Cowley called the character Dorothy Bridges a "Junior Leaguer" and said that "if Philip hadn't left her for the Spanish people, he might have traded her for a flask of Chanel No. 5 and still have had the best of it." Ernest responded in typical fashion, blaming Max Perkins and Scribner's for not coming to his defense with a series of well-placed—and expensive—ads to counter the critics.

The lovers crossed back over the Atlantic on November 24, with plans for Ernest to spend Christmas with Pauline and the boys in Key West and for Martha to be with her mother and her own family in St. Louis for the holidays. Martha had become even more anxious during the past few months. Ernest had not yet made the final break from his wife, even though he told Martha it was just a question of time before he did. Martha could almost see him vacillating from day to day, professing his deep love for her and telling her he wanted to marry her, while simultaneously believing he could keep his double life going indefinitely. If he didn't end it with Pauline soon, she would have to break up with him. It was a miserable Christmas for both of them. The fights resumed on Whitehead Street, and Martha languished in the bosom of her family, questioning whether she and Ernest had a future together. Ernest flew up to New York as soon as the new year began to work on the stage production of his play, and Martha traveled there on January 14, 1939, to join him. But before she so much as had a chance to say "Hello, darling, how are you?" she picked up the

Daily Mirror on the morning of January 15 and read the following article:

"Hemingway was accosted in the Stork Club by a man who insisted on rubbing his hand over the writer's face while muttering, 'Tough, eh?' Quintin Reynolds, magazine writer, advised Hemingway to 'give him a poke, but don't hit him too hard.' The author of *Death in the Afternoon* arose and clipped the unwelcome visitor on the chin. When he was lifted off the floor he gave his name as Edward Chapman, a lawyer. Hemingway previously proved his claim to a hairy chest in a scrap with Max Eastman in the fall of 1937." Eastman had attacked Ernest in one of his articles, and the two men grappled with each other afterward in Max Perkins's office.

Two days later, syndicated columnist Walter Winchell put a different slant on the story in the same newspaper. According to Winchell, the lawyer "fell from his chair from too much wooflewater." Ernest never laid a hand on him, reported Winchell. "It just didn't happen." No matter though. The public believed what it wanted to believe. Ernest's reputation as a man of letters *and* a battling man of action was further inflated.

Martha told Ernest that his indecision about their relationship had become unendurable for her, and he assured her that he would end things as soon as he got back to Key West. But even then he procrastinated. His plane left New York in a heavy snowstorm on January 24, and when he got back to Key West he and Pauline got ready for a visit from Ernest's mother, who had yet to set eyes on her youngest grandson, Gregory. Ernest had been alienated from his mother for years, unreasonably blaming her for his father's suicide, and he detested her so much that he rented a room for her in the Casa Marina Hotel rather than have her stay at his house. Grace Hemingway arrived on February 7 for an awkward week-long reunion and departed for home on February 14.

While Grace was there on the island—with them, but not quite *among* them—Martha was vacationing with her own mother a hundred miles away as the crow flies, due north in Naples, Florida. Pauline would have been hysterical if she knew about that, so Ernest figured it was better not to inform her. One day after Grace left town, Ernest sauntered over to the P&O ferry bound for Havana. As far as Pauline was concerned, Ernest was just going off on another fishing excursion. In Ernest's mind, this trip was going to be more permanent. He and Martha had made plans for her to join him in Cuba. Without telling Pauline in so many words, Ernest had left the house in Key West for good.

PART FOUR

HEMINGWAY AND GELLHORN

Chapter Twenty-four

When he reached Havana Ernest rented rooms in two different hotels: one on the fourth floor of the Ambos Mundos, his favorite trysting place years earlier with Jane Mason, where he holed up to start his new book, and the second room in the Sevilla-Biltmore with a stock of provisions—a large ham, sausages, bread—where he slept. As he explained to Max Perkins a couple of months later, the only way he could get any privacy was to "tell everybody you live in one hotel and live in another. When they locate you, move to the country."

Ernest spent the next five weeks there, cutting back on his drinking, writing furiously every day, exercising regularly, and trimming his weight back under two hundred pounds. Martha claimed that she joined him in Havana as early as February 18, while others said she didn't get there until April. But it appears unlikely that both of them would have put up with such a lengthy separation. Each couldn't wait to put their affair on a more permanent footing. More than likely, the earlier date is the correct one. In the mornings, they ambled together over to the Ambos Mundos to pick up their mail and then went about their business. Ernest quickly lost himself in his story about the Spanish Civil War. The book developed its own momentum. It fairly exploded out of him as he channeled it onto the reams of blank paper stacked in front of his typewriter. The novel flowed like a rushing river. Ernest hadn't written with this kind of passion in years. He knew it was going to be good—far better than good, the best he had ever written. He worked surely and rapidly, a man possessed.

When the first flush of energy finally spent itself, Ernest took the ferry back to Key West by himself with several chapters in hand.

He wired Max Perkins that the book was "flowing along beautifully." Pretty soon Max would be getting the monumental novel that he knew Ernest could write, the one Max had so patiently been waiting for him to deliver. On April 5 Ernest boarded the one possession he cared about above all others in the world, the *Pilar*. When he motored back to Havana in his boat, Ernest's life with Pauline had effectively come to a close.

While Ernest was away, Martha made a futile attempt to tidy up the slovenly room stacked with cured hams and sausages, alcohol, guns, and fishing gear that served as their homestead. The chaos and mess that grew like a fungus across the room was bad enough in Madrid during wartime conditions, but in peacetime Havana it was unacceptable as a domestic living arrangement.

"I am really not abnormally clean," Martha said later. "I'm simply as clean as any normal person. But Ernest was extremely dirty, one of the most unfastidious men I've ever known."

She was taking over the house-hunting, she told Ernest when he got back to Havana. Ernest had no problem with that as long as she left him alone to work on his book. Martha checked the local listings and found a one-story Spanish-style farmhouse set on fifteen acres on top of a hill overlooking San Francisco de Paula, fifteen miles outside of Havana. It was called the Finca Vigia, or Lookout Farm.

The place was a train wreck when Martha set eyes on it, but the rent was cheap at one hundred U.S. dollars a month. The swimming pool was filled with green sludge, and out-of-control weeds had taken over the tennis court. Inside, the house was hideously furnished and in dire need of repair. The house was built in 1886 and looked as though it had been abandoned decades earlier. But Martha envisioned the possibilities. Colorful flowers and plants flourished throughout the property in the tropical heat and humidity. The central living room was spacious and there were enough rooms for both of them to have separate spaces to write in. Most important, local labor was cheap. Using money she saved from her *Collier's* assignments, Martha hired painters, carpenters, electricians, and a couple of gardeners to get the place in shape. She ordered furniture to replace the nondescript items in the house.

It took the workmen a little more than a month to complete the restoration. Ernest and Martha moved into the Finca Vigia together on May 17, with Ernest barely breaking stride as he poured out several thousand words a week on his book. Martha began an autobiographical novel of her own, about a young journalist covering the spillover effects of the Spanish conflict in Eastern Europe. This marked the first time Ernest had set up housekeeping with a younger woman, the first time he would be living with someone without a trust fund to sustain him when the money dried up. Royalties from his earlier books had begun to flag, but a movie offer for *To Have and Have Not*—despite the poor reviews— reopened the money floodgates again.

Back in Key West, Pauline decided she could no longer live there without Ernest. News of their crumbling marriage was the talk of the town. Her friends commiserated with her, but she hated running into others on the Island of Bones who greeted her with pity in their eyes. The cruel irony of her situation was not lost on Pauline; once she had been the Other Woman in his life, and now she was the wife being replaced by someone new. She packed the boys up and made plans to rent an apartment in New York, and from there to travel to Europe to put her old life behind her if she could. It would be the first time since her marriage twelve years earlier that she would go there without her husband.

*　*　*

The two lovers established a mutually agreeable routine. Ernest rose at first light and began to write almost immediately. Martha adapted to his schedule since he preferred to work in their bedroom instead of his study. The bedroom was a large, comfortable room with white walls, yellow tiles on the floor, and windows facing south toward Havana that let in streaming rays of light and fresh, perfumed air when the breeze was right. Martha marveled at his self-imposed discipline. She wrote to a friend that he disappeared into a shell "exactly as if he were dead or visiting on the moon. He handles himself like a man who is ready to do the world's championship boxing match. He has been I may say about as much use as a stuffed squirrel, but he is turning out a beautiful story. And nothing else on earth besides matters to him…I learn a lot as I go on."

Martha's book was not going nearly as well. She felt that her writing was flat, lacking color and passion. The words were dead on the page, filling her with dread about her own talent as a novelist. "The empty pages ahead frighten me as much as the typed pages behind," she said. Only her "dogged determination and pride" kept her going, forcing her to churn out at least a thousand words a day like a soldier grinding out mile after mile on foot because he had to. She was aching to tell the story of the armies of refugees traipsing like zombies across the European landscape, but only passion and conviction could capture their true plight. She envied Ernest's work, which was "magic, clear as water and carrying like the music of a flute."

They kept to their routines until two or two-thirty in the afternoon, when both of them closed up shop for the day. It was an exhausting schedule; it had been years since Ernest worked so well for such a long stretch, and he was exhilarated by his output. Martha was frustrated, but she plugged on because she was a writer with a story to tell and a need to get it down. After lunch they played tennis together on the refurbished court, swam laps in the sanitized pool, or went out on the *Pilar* to fish for marlin. They both loved to swim;

Ernest had once jumped into the shark-filled Gulf Stream with a knife between his teeth to free a line on the *Pilar*.

Then they went for drinks at the Floridita and walked along the Prado, the wide boulevard where small black birds called negritos swarmed in the evenings and people sat on benches under the towering oak trees. Ernest was normally a gregarious man, a gracious host who welcomed crowds of visitors attracted to his magnetic personality. But he kept to a solitary agenda during these early months in Cuba with Martha, afraid to talk about his book in progress for fear of ruining it, and unwilling to let guests divert him from his daily flow of work. He knew he had to keep at it without letup until his reservoir of energy ran low and needed to be replenished.

By August it was time to take a break from their punishing routine. They took the *Pilar* back to Key West, where Ernest loaded up the new Buick he had bought after his accident there with rifles, shotguns, and enough gear for an extended stay at the Nordquist Ranch in Wyoming. He missed his sons and made arrangements for them to join him when he arrived. Ernest had maintained friendly relations with his first wife Hadley who had since remarried and was enjoying a fishing vacation with her husband in nearby Cody.

"Life is quite complicated," Ernest had written to Hadley before he left Cuba. "Important thing for me to do is not get discouraged and take the easy way out like your and my noted ancestors. Because very bad example to children." The easy way out that he mentioned was suicide, thoughts of which had plagued him even at this early stage of his life; indeed, they were rooted in his psychological makeup and had grown worse after his father shot himself years earlier. As manically exuberant as Ernest was about the progress on his latest novel, the depressive down slope was equally debilitating.

He had taken along with him the first seventy-six thousand words of the novel he would call *For Whom the Bell Tolls*, which he planned to work on in Wyoming. Martha had a rough first draft of her own novel, which she planned to call *A Stricken Field*, a title she got from a book about a fourteenth-century battle that Ernest had been reading. They drove north toward St. Louis, where he dropped Martha off to spend some time with her mother, and then he continued on the rest of the drive to Wyoming. If Ernest thought life was complicated, as he had written to Hadley, it would turn into an entanglement beyond all imagining when he got to the ranch. Ernest had picked up his firstborn son Jack, or "Bumby" as he was nicknamed, in Cody after a brief visit with Hadley and her husband, and Patrick and Gregory were flying in from New York after their European vacation with their mother. What Ernest didn't know beforehand was that Pauline was planning to accompany them in a last-ditch effort to save the remnants of her tattered marriage.

Chapter Twenty-five

Ernest was in shock as he hugged his boys who ran into his open arms at the airport. Pauline followed behind them, smiling broadly as though nothing was amiss between them. She wanted to make the family reunion complete, she told him. Ernest was mute as he stared at her. He had taken the coward's way out and never told her in so many words that their marriage was over, but surely she must have understood that by now. Yet here she was, smiling at him sweetly, greeting him as though the past two years with Martha were just a passing interlude in their lives. To make matters worse, she had caught a cold in New York and was running a fever, which required some tender love and care from him to get her through it.

At the ranch, Ernest found himself ministering to her, bringing her meals and making her rock and rye cocktails to relieve her misery. Ernest could not let the farce continue any longer. "It's over," he told her. He was going to marry Martha. Pauline stared at him blankly, unwilling or unable to absorb the impact of his statement. Then she crumbled as the reality of the situation set in. As their son Patrick said later, "the knock-out punch" that his father delivered unleashed a torrent of tears that gushed out of his mother without letup. She began to cry, and no amount of consoling could appease her. She cried uncontrollably. The tears kept coming, the sobs wracked her body. Her agony seemed endless. Patrick and Gregory flew to her side, but nothing they could say or do stanched the flow. It went on interminably, until finally there was nothing left inside, no more tears, no more pleading, nothing but hollow emptiness. *Now* she knew her marriage was over. There was no hope of saving it.

Their vacation plans ruined, Ernest made arrangements for Pauline and the boys to be driven back to New York. Then he called Martha and told her what had happened. He asked her to fly to Billings, Montana, where he would pick her up. A change of venue was in order. They would be going to Sun Valley instead, outside of Ketchum, Idaho. The location was a sportsman's dream, set on an expansive rolling plain with trout streams surrounded by the Sawtooth Mountains. The land abounded with antelope, elk, deer, and smaller game including quail, partridges, and ducks. It had recently been developed by Union Pacific Railroad president Averill Harriman into a resort, complete with a hotel, chalets, restaurants, swimming pool, tennis courts, and nearby ski runs. In a promotional campaign to attract wealthier members of the public, Harriman invited movie stars and literary celebrities to stay there free of charge until the resort's commercial prospects took hold. Ernest was the ideal guest, a literary rock star who was an avid outdoorsman.

Ernest and Martha arrived late at night in his black Buick stuffed with rifles, fishing rods, and stacks of books and luggage. They checked into suite 206 at the hotel, a spacious corner accommodation with stone fireplaces in both rooms and mesmerizing views of the mountains along the horizon. They planned to stay for about six weeks, working on their books in the morning and unwinding in the afternoon, playing tennis, fishing, hiking into the foothills, and hunting for game. Ernest taught all his women how to fish and hunt, sports they were well advised to take up enthusiastically if they wanted to see much of him when he finished working. Martha became a decent shot despite her core inclinations. Tillie Arnold, the wife of the resort's official photographer, took an immediate liking to Martha and described her as a "barrel of fun and sharp as a tack."

In October, the snow began to fall in the higher elevations, signaling that winter would soon be arriving. Martha received a telegram from *Collier's* asking her to go over to Finland to cover the threat of a Russian invasion. It was an assignment that Martha felt she could not turn down. She was first and foremost a journalist, a war correspondent, and she needed to pursue her craft despite any misgivings from Ernest. Ernest was miffed that she would be going off on her own, but he used humor to put the best slant on it.

"What old Indian likes to lose his squaw with a hard winter coming on?" he asked her.

"Keep an eye on this big clown," Martha told Tillie at a going-away party Ernest threw for her in the lodge. "See that he's shaved and cleaned up when you go out on the town." Ernest had a penchant for wearing the same clothes several days running and letting his beard get scruffy around his ever-present mustache.

On November 10 Martha set sail out of New York on a Dutch freighter, the *Westenland*, with forty-five other passengers. The ship was bound for Belgium carrying wheat and had to pass through heavily mined water in the English Channel. Martha could see the mines bobbing in the waves as she looked out from the deck, and she caught sight of bloated bodies from the wreckage of another Dutch ship that had been blown up the day before. She was not without trepidations of her own about this assignment. She wrote to her mother, lamenting this "dull assignment in the frozen north." To Ernest she wrote that, after reporting about what was going on, her major goal was to "come home quick."

No sooner was Martha off to cover the war than Ernest turned their suite into a replica of his room in Havana before Martha found their house. He loved to play poker, shoot crap, and drink with anyone he could round up when his women were not around, and he invited guests to his quarters, which he jokingly called "Hemingstein's Mixed Vicing and Dicing Establishment." But inwardly he was miserable. He told his newfound cronies that he was "stinko lonely" without Martha, and he wrote to Martha's mother that he was having a "very lonely time" with her daughter gone. Ernest was particularly fond of Edna, who was a sixty-year-

175

old version of her daughter, and she found his warmth and humor endearing. They bonded right from the start, an important issue for Martha who was devoted to Edna.

Martha made her way to Helsinki from Belgium after a stopover in Stockholm. Her hotel room was lined with blackout paper to hide the lights inside from Russian bombers. The day she arrived, at three in the afternoon, Russian planes zoomed in low over Helsinki through a heavy fog and destroyed a residential neighborhood with bombs that emitted poisonous gas. After they left, Martha walked through the broken streets to observe the "shapeless and headless" bodies strewn among the wreckage.

"It is going to be terrible," she wrote to Ernest. "The people are marvelous, with a kind of frozen fortitude. They do not cry out and they do not run; they watch with loathing but without fear this nasty hidden business which they did nothing to bring on themselves." She told him she loved him dearly and couldn't wait to get back to the warmth of Cuba, to be there with him as his book progressed. "This book is what we have to base our lives on," she wrote. "The book is what lasts after us and makes all this war intelligible. And as I love you I love your work and as you are me your work is mine. Let's never never leave each other again." When he got her letter, Ernest wrote to Max Perkins that Martha was as courageous as they come.

"She got out to that front when not a single correspondent had been there."

Martha filed story after story about the Russian aggression and the brave Finnish civilians, some of them small boys and women, who volunteered unflinchingly to protect their homeland against their militaristic neighbors. She endured the cold, dread Nordic darkness as long as she could, and when an American military attaché asked her if she would like to hitch a ride back to the States, she answered simply, "Christ yes." She sent a telegram to

Ernest wishing him "Happy New Year and all of it together beloved," and let him know when she would be back on native soil.

*　　*　　*

She arrived in Cuba on January 19, 1940, happy to be back at the Finca Vigia despite the unusually cold Cuban winter. Ernest was overjoyed to have her with him again, and he howled out loud when she presented him with a mock contract stating that she promised "never to brutalize my present and future husband in any way whatsoever" and recognized "that a very fine and sensitive writer cannot be left alone for two months and sixteen days." She signed her document, somewhat prematurely, "Martha Gellhorn Hemingway."

Ernest normally wore his hair long, but when Martha saw him after their separation his hair hung in long strands over his ears and down the back of his neck. He wasn't going to cut it, he said, until his book was finished. Ernest looked as disheveled as ever, and he had started to gain back some of the weight he had shed nine months earlier. The title was now set for the novel; from John Donne's poem "No Man is an Island," Ernest was captivated by the line "never send to know for whom the bell tolls; it tolls for thee." Max Perkins was ecstatic about the five hundred pages Ernest had already shown him. "All knocked out," he cabled Ernest. The novel so far was "absolutely magnificent and new," and the title was "beautiful."

The cold snap broke in March, and Ernest asked his three sons to join them in Cuba to go fishing on the *Pilar*. This was the first time the boys saw their father living with a woman who was not their mother. Martha fell in love with them as soon as they landed in

177

Havana. Bumby was the oldest at sixteen and had a "body like something the Greeks wished for," she said. Patrick was an avid reader at eleven, and Gregory—Gigi, Ernest called him—liked to shoot craps with his father. They were all "as funny as their papa," Martha wrote to a friend, and she was delighted to be "an instant mother of three." The boys fell in love with Martha as well and nicknamed her "The Marty." They were intrigued by her spicy language, and Bumby said she was the first "attractive lady I ever heard use the 'f' word."

Martha's novel was published first, in March 1940. Alas, the only positive review came from Eleanor Roosevelt who called *A Stricken Field* "a masterpiece." The reviews that mattered were almost uniformly negative. One said the book read more like reporting than creative fiction. The *Saturday Review* wished that the main character, who was a fictionalized version of Martha, was "less noble and more real." The most scathing review was not so much a review at all but, rather, a personal attack on Martha and Ernest and their so-called "indulgent" lifestyle in Cuba while the rest of the world was going to hell. Ernest was boiling mad after he read the diatribe and would undoubtedly have called on the author in person if he had been in New York. Martha was more upset about Ernest's reaction than her own. He was "writing smoothly, with ease and magic and like an angel," Martha wrote. He was producing the "finest novel any of us will read in this decade," and it was a "stinking crime" and "barbarous" to try to derail him from his work.

But Ernest could not be derailed. He continued to work slavishly on the novel after the boys left, and he made good on his promise not to cut his hair, which began to resemble the foliage on their property. It was not long before his total self-absorption in his novel began to grate on Martha, whose own work was not moving along nearly as smoothly. She was despondent about the reception her novel had received and could have used a bit more attention to her battered ego. But Ernest pretended to have a hide as thick as an elephant, although he was as prickly as they come when the barbs were directed at him. He told her to get over it and get busy with her "five finger exercises"—his term for working on a new book.

Martha loved life in Cuba, but not to the exclusion of life beyond the island. It was fine for Ernest to barricade himself in their bedroom most of the day, lost in the world of his imagination, but Martha needed to be out there writing about the events shaping the world at large. She didn't want to admit it, but her strength was in reporting about what was going on rather than in writing fiction—even fiction based on facts. She bought a radio to listen to news of the war in Europe, but Ernest banned it from the house, saying he didn't wanted to be distracted from the story he was writing. He apologized for being "thoughtless, egotistic, mean-spirited and unhelpful," but then he continued as before with his work.

Martha spent most of her day putting words without passion down on paper, while Ernest focused his passion on his latest novel to the exclusion of everything else, even *her* until he was done for the day. Then they went out to play—fishing, tennis, drinking in the Floridita with some Basque pelota players Ernest had befriended, everything in short that struck a chord with *him*. When she began to complain a little about feeling confined, Ernest told her she was "like a racehorse with two speeds: running away and asleep."

That was not the message Martha wanted to hear. Notwithstanding the mock contract she had drawn up after her return from Finland, Martha left the island alone in June on a trip to New York to visit some friends.

Chapter Twenty-six

In July *For Whom the Bell Tolls* was almost finished. Max Perkins was anxious—more than anxious; he was on the verge of a nervous breakdown—to get his hands on the final manuscript in time for a fall publication just three months away. He had ordered an initial first printing of seventy-five thousand copies—which was already sold out in pre-publication sales to bookstores—and he needed to get final copy to the printer as soon as possible to stay on schedule. Ernest went up alone to New York and checked into the Barclay Hotel to complete the final pages, which he fed in small batches to a courier who raced them over to Scribner's. Max checked the pages for grammatical errors as they came in and sent them to the printer, with instructions to set them in galleys as quickly as possible. Ernest told Max that he felt like "a blind sardine in a processing factory."

On July 31, 1940, the *New York Times* ran a story saying that "Ernest Hemingway up from Cuba where he has been rounding out his new novel *For Whom the Bell Tolls* has been in New York the last few days. The new novel, which Scribner's will bring out in October, is a love story with the Spanish Civil War for a setting."

Eleven days later, another *New York Times* reporter named Robert Van Gelder visited Ernest in his quarters at the Barclay. New York City was suffering through a classic summer heat wave, and the temperature inside the hotel room matched the sweltering conditions outside. Ernest had surrounded himself with a coterie of drinking and gaming companions to keep him company after he finished writing for the day. They included a New York lawyer, a Spanish Civil War veteran, and an anonymous claque of camp-followers, all of them sitting around an ice bucket filled with a fifth of scotch and a bottle of soda water.

"Hemingway looked elephant big, enormously healthy," Van Gelder wrote in his August 11 article. "His talk is unevenly paced, a quick spate and then a slow search for a word. His chair keeps hitching across the floor toward the other chairs, and then as he reaches a point, a conclusion, he shoves the chair back to the edge of the group again."

Elephant big! Ernest gave the appearance of being bigger than he actually was. His height topped out a shade above six feet, but he had a large frame capable of carrying two hundred pounds without too much effort. With an extra twenty pounds on it, he looked immense, as large as a man two or three inches taller. Latter-day examples would include heavyweight fighters Rocky Marciano and Mike Tyson. Neither man stood taller than five feet ten or eleven, but their well-proportioned physiques layered with solid muscle gave off the aura of men who are not to be messed with.

Ernest sweated profusely in the company of his friends, his wire-rimmed glasses cutting into the bridge of his nose. His eyes were watery, blurred from focusing on typescript all day long, day in and day out. When the writing was done and the galleys were being prepared by the printer, Ernest boarded the train to Miami, and from there he got on the Pam Am Clipper to Havana. Martha and Edna were waiting for him when his plane set down. Ernest greeted Edna as effusively as he embraced Martha. Edna loved Ernest, but she observed him with a more objective eye than her daughter did. Enjoy the moment, she told Martha. "But do not marry this man. He will break your heart like he did his other wives." Yes, Edna loved Ernest. But she was wise enough to size him up as something other than son-in-law material.

*　　*　　*

Shortly after the galley proofs of *For Whom the Bell Tolls* arrived in Cuba for Ernest's final approval, Martha dropped her bombshell on him. She loved him dearly, but she didn't think it was a good idea for them to get married, she said. They both valued their freedom and independence too much. Ernest was devastated, unable to sleep through the night. At four in the morning he got out of bed and wrote her a long letter, saying she had given him "a good sound busted heart."

"He knew that for the last eighteen months he had been no gift to live with," Martha wrote later. But he put a guilt trip on her, reminding her how he had helped her get launched with her own writing. If she didn't want to marry him, she should just tell him flat out so he could take the *Pilar* back to Key West and maybe take the easy way out—Ernest's not-so-subtle hint that he was suicidal from time to time. "Mr. Scrooby," his pet name for his penis, had started to think of itself as "us," Ernest wrote.

There was no question that Martha loved the man she had idolized from the time she began to read his books, but she resented being sucked into his vortex to a point where she felt suffocated by his overwhelming presence. Yes, she loved him, and yes her career wouldn't have progressed to the degree it had were it not for his support. But Ernest was a man who needed to be in control of everyone who passed in and out of his gravity field. Martha was as fiercely individualistic as he was. She had resisted being subsumed by all of her other lovers.

"I didn't sign on to be a footnote in someone else's life," she said later.

182

Ernest's final ploy was to dedicate his novel to her at the last minute, before it was in print. "This Book is for Martha Gellhorn," his inscription read. It was the ultimate act of seduction. Martha relented. She was his "Mookie," his "Chickie," and he was her "Bongie." "Mr. Scrooby" belonged to "us." Martha caved in. Of course she would marry him, she said. To herself she thought, somehow or other she would make the marriage work.

For Whom the Bell Tolls was published to rapturous reviews on October 21, 1940. It was the Big Book the literary elite had been waiting for Ernest to write for the past ten years, and the one that would resonate with the reading public like no other book of the decade. "It's one of the greatest things written about the war," wrote George Seldes.

The *New York Times* thought it was "the best book Ernest Hemingway has written, the fullest, the deepest, the truest."

It "sets a new standard for Hemingway in characterization, dialogue, suspense, and compassion," said *The Nation.*

The novel reached "a deeper level than any sounded in the author's other books," intoned *The New Yorker.*

The *Saturday Review of Literature* believed *For Whom the Bell Tolls* was "one of the finest and richest novels of the last decade."

Even Edmund Wilson, who had been critical of some of Ernest's earlier output, wrote "Hemingway the artist is with us again; and it is like having an old friend back."

Only the far left-wing press found reason to complain about the novel and slammed Ernest for suggesting that republican atrocities were as repugnant as those committed by Franco and his nationalists. But the public agreed with the mainstream press. The novel flew out of bookstores like migrating birds. The Book of the Month Club ordered two hundred thousand copies. Within the first few months of publication, nearly half a million copies had been sold, and Paramount Pictures offered $110,000 for the film rights. There was no longer any doubt about who owned the title of the Heavyweight Champion of American Writers; Ernest had won it in a knockout. His novel was "selling like frozen Daiquiris in hell," he wrote to Hadley, to whom he had given all the royalties from his novel *The Sun Also Rises* when he left her for Pauline.

Finally liberated from the daily grind of intense, self-imposed labor, Ernest and Martha returned to Sun Valley with Ernest's boys. This time they were joined by an ever-expanding celebrity crowd, anxious to cash in on the free food and lodging provided by Harriman. Ernest's divorce from Pauline was granted on grounds of desertion two weeks after his novel came out. One month after publication, on November 21, on their way to Idaho, forty-one-year-old Ernest and thirty-two-year-old Martha got married before a justice of the peace in the dining room of the Union Pacific Railroad in Cheyenne, Wyoming. One reporter referred to the marriage as a "pairing of flint and steel."

Exactly one month after that, December 21, Ernest's old friend from their youthful days in Paris, F. Scott Fitzgerald, drank himself into an early grave. Pathetically, once Ernest's most notable competitor, Fitzgerald wrote in a letter to Ernest that his latest book was "better than anybody else writing could do…I envy you like hell." On Scott's bookshelf was a copy of *For Whom the Bell Tolls*, signed by Ernest with the inscription, "To Scott with affection and esteem, Ernest." The circle was complete, measured in tight intervals through the fall and early winter of 1940—publication, divorce, remarriage, death, and a new life for the glamorous, honeymooning couple.

Sun Valley was alive with superstars when the newlyweds arrived. Tall, lean, handsome movie star Gary Cooper was there with his wife Veronica, affectionately known as "Rocky." Cooper was a bona fide Montana cowboy who had made it big with several high-profile movies, including the 1932 adaptation of Ernest's novel, *A Farewell to Arms*. He was slated to portray Ernest's main character, Robert Jordan, in the film version of *For Whom the Bell Tolls*. Also present among the celebrity set was writer Dorothy Parker, who had endeared herself to Hemingway with some glowing reviews of his books, and her bisexual husband Alan Campbell; Dorothy stated publicly that her husband was "as queer as a billy goat."

Ernest and Martha fell into a pleasurable routine, playing tennis with Dorothy and Alan, hunting with Gary and Rocky, hiking into the mountains, and of course wining and dining without restraint in the evening and far into the night. Ernest loved to organize daily outings along the creeks that carved their way through the mountainous terrain. Before long everyone was calling him "the General," a title he relished. His boys took to the region like birds to the air. Bumby fished "as if the whole fate of mankind depended on it," Martha wrote, and the three of them were "rare boys" who were being raised "with genius" by their father who ignored "all of the rules."

Martha was at first taken with the striking Gary Copper, with his thin, muscular build and glittering eyes, and she told Ernest that he should make an effort to dress more neatly like he did. Gary dressed casually in western gear, a style Ernest loved, but the movie star changed his clothes every day and didn't walk around with food stains on them. Ernest ignored her. Martha quickly became bored with Gary's conversation, though, and lamented in a letter to Max Perkins that "the famous folk were…a pain in the ass." All they talked about was "box office returns," and she was getting "angrier and angrier about such idiocies."

Flush now with royalties from his latest novel and a lucrative offer for the movie rights, Ernest bought the Finca Vigia for $12,500 on December 28, just after he and Martha returned to Cuba for the holidays. While they were there basking in the Cuban sun, with Ernest settling in for an extended period of relaxation after finishing his book, Martha dropped another bombshell on him. She wanted to go to China to cover the Japanese invasion of the country for *Collier's*.

Chapter Twenty-seven

China was about the last place on earth Ernest wanted to go. He had just published what promised to be his most successful book, and a few months at home enjoying the accolades of his peers and the enthusiasm of the reading public seemed more than reasonable to him. But Martha was insistent. *Collier's* wanted to send her to the China front to report on what was going on, and she came close to begging her husband to go with her. If Ernest wanted to see much of his wife during the next few months, he had little choice but to acquiesce. But the tipping point for him, the challenge that promised to make the trip more exciting than a mere adventure as Martha's traveling companion, was the opportunity for Ernest to go there as a spy for the Roosevelt administration.

Before they left the U.S., Martha and Ernest went to New York to visit their editors. Ostensibly, Ernest would be going to China as a war correspondent for *PM* magazine, and he told *New York Post* columnist Earl Wilson that he planned to travel light with "binoculars, two pairs of boots (one high, one low), a leather jacket, a sheep-lined vest, an old tweed shooting coat with leather patches on the elbow, a few shirts, and socks." After suffering through an exhausting round of inoculations, he and Martha made an important stop in Washington, D.C., where they were briefed by Treasury Secretary Henry Morgenthau and his right-hand man, Harry Dexter White.

The situation in China was complicated. The country was divided into three parts at the time. The Japanese occupied the coastline and the northeast quadrant—about two-thirds of the country; the Kuomintang or nationalists under Chiang Kai-shek controlled the southwest interior away from the sea; and the communists held sway in the northwest. Chiang presented himself as the only democratic alternative to either a Japanese or communist takeover of the entire country, and in doing so he had earned the tacit support of the Roosevelt administration. No one knew too much about China's internal affairs; much of the information people *thought* they knew was supplied by Henry Luce, the publisher of *Time* who was known as "Father Time." He was the son of a missionary, married to his second wife Clare Booth Luce, and he had a soft spot for Chiang Kai-shek while remaining blind to Chiang's dictatorial ambitions.

But Roosevelt wanted to know more about the "real" China, the conditions in the villages and on the farms, and Morgenthau asked Ernest if he was willing to be his country's eyes and ears there. It seemed odd that such a directive would come from the treasury secretary rather than from the state department, but Morgenthau was more than a financial strategist. He was Roosevelt's banker who had lined up much of the financing for the New Deal, and he understood the power money wielded in global politics. His main foreign policy goals were checking Japan's imperialist designs in Asia and defeating fascism. He was also worried about Soviet expansion beyond its borders. Through Morgenthau's influence, the administration had been funneling money into Chiang's coffers to bolster his position, but the secretary was incensed by Chiang's financial demands and wanted to know where all the money was ending up—in support of Chiang's war effort or in his personal bank account. When he asked the famous author if he was willing to assume the role of spy, it was like asking a growing boy if he wanted to play King of the Hill. Ernest was taken by all things clandestine and military; had he not been a writer, the rank of General would have suited him fine. His friends in Idaho had nicknamed him well.

Before they left the country, Ernest and Martha flew to California with a stopover in Hollywood to discuss the movie version of *For Whom the Bell Tolls* with Gary Cooper and Ingrid

Berman, who would be playing the female lead. They listened to famed movie mogul Cecil B. DeMille give his views on the film industry at a banquet, and then they traveled north to San Francisco where they boarded the *Matsonia* en route to Honolulu. It was a decrepit old vessel, creaking noisily with every roll of the ocean in extremely high seas. The two of them spent much of their time drinking in their cabin while they rocked and rolled across the Pacific. Martha was motivated to make the journey, spurred on by a need to keep her journalism career moving ahead, but Ernest was in a foul mood when they docked in Hawaii. The claque of reporters who awaited their arrival annoyed the hell out of him, and the garlands of flowers draped around his neck by local dignitaries and hula dancers were the final straw threatening to break the camel's— or the elephant's—back.

Ernest was snarling, "grinning like a wolf with bared fangs," Martha noted mischievously as the photographers snapped their photos. "The next son of a bitch that touches me, I am going to cool him," he whispered to Martha.

They were forced to endure an afternoon with Ernest's aunt, who insisted on giving them unwanted advice during a tedious lunch. And they had to put up with a banquet thrown in their honor by the "King and Queen" of the island, complete with a torch-lit pageant at which Ernest and Martha both got piss-eyed drunk in an effort to get through the festivities with their sanity intact. Finally, mercifully it seemed, they were able to escape on a Pan Am flying boat bound for Guam.

"Those big Pan Am flying boats were marvelous," Martha wrote later. "We flew all day in roomy comfort, eating and drinking like pigs, visiting the captain, listening to our fellow travelers, dozing, reading, and in the late afternoon the plane landed on the water at an island. The passengers had time for a swim, a shower, a dinner, and slept in beds."

Ernest hadn't wanted to go on the trip in the first place, but Guam seemed like a welcome reprieve after the forced jocularity of Hawaii.

*   *   *

Hong Kong was a different city in 1941 than it is today. It was a ramshackle tumble of wooden buildings; narrow streets crammed with rickshaws, bicycles, and people; no skyscrapers; a single bank; and a handful of larger homes higher up on the base of Victoria Peak where the rich folks lived. Martha was horrified by "the sheer numbers, the density of bodies. There was no space to breathe. Why do they have to spit so much?" she wondered. "You can't put your foot down without stepping on a big slimy gob. And everything stinks of sweat and good old night soil." The night soil was a euphemism for the buckets of human shit that were emptied out every night and spread around for fertilizer. Ernest, however, was delighted. This was life in the raw, a grand human experience such as he had experienced in his early days covering wars in remote regions of the globe.

Ernest had a natural gift for picking up foreign languages. He was proficient if not fluent in Spanish, French, and Italian, and now he attuned his ear to the local patois—an amalgam of Pidgin English, Chinese, and other exotic strains. Martha saw a side to him that she hadn't discovered before. He made himself at home in whatever element he found himself. She was stunned that he was actually carrying on basic conversations in this alien tongue within days of their arrival. His great gift was observing speech and behavior patterns, absorbing them into his persona, and then writing about them truthfully, beautifully, and creatively. Martha was appalled by the human suffering she encountered; Ernest examined it with a clinical detachment.

They checked into the Hong Kong Hotel on Pedder Street, one of the only presentable hotels downtown, an ancient structure with paddle fans on the ceiling, an antique toilet, and a spacious lounge in the lobby that looked as though it had been ripped from the pages of a Somerset Maugham novel. Ernest set up his headquarters there, commandeering a padded leather chair where he began to hold court the day they arrived. Martha once again observed her husband in wonderment, marveling at his talent for sucking into his orbit an unsavory crowd of locals and other mysterious types.

"In the twinkling of an eye," Martha wrote, her husband had "collected a mixed, jovial entourage."

He sat there in the middle of the claque, drinking, telling jokes, and listening to the improbable stories of Chinese businessmen, racketeers, taxi drivers, cops and other civil servants, and a rough-looking character from Chicago named Morris "Two-Gun" Cohen, who claimed to be working as a hit man for a Hong Kong mobster and looked the part. Martha dismissed his routine at first as another example of Ernest "loafing" while she ached to be out in the countryside, observing peasant life on the farms. What she realized soon enough was that Ernest wasn't loafing at all; he was working—learning about life in China from the mouths of people who knew it more intimately than anyone else.

Martha sat in on some of these marathon talking and drinking sessions for as long as she could stand them, but she was odd-woman-out in an all-male club and she felt uncomfortable in the group. In any event, it was clearly not her style. She told Ernest that she wanted to travel into the interior to observe conditions there firsthand. But Ernest had no inclination to abandon the camaraderie of his rogue's gallery of chums. He laughed and said to the group,

"Martha is going off to take the pulse of the nation." The men laughed out loud with Ernest. Martha left in a snit and made arrangements to go off on her own. When Ernest started to light firecrackers in their small hotel room, she knew it was time to leave.

The chief—the *only*—means of air transportation in primitive, wartime China was via the China National Aviation Company. CNAC consisted of two DC3s and three DC2s, rickety old aircraft with metal seats thinly draped with canvas and a toilet behind a green curtain that required no flush mechanism; there was a hole in the floor that allowed human fertilizer (night soil) to drop willy-nilly onto the ground—or onto whomever was standing in the wrong place on the ground. Ernest later said that China was a vast "shit-filled country."

CNAC's schedule was haphazard at best. The planes took off when there were enough people and cargo to transport, and whenever one of the airline's few qualified pilots was available. Martha was lucky. She booked a ride on one of the DC2s that took off at four-thirty in the morning with seven Chinese passengers and her. The pilots preferred to fly in pitch darkness and foul weather to avoid Japanese antiaircraft guns that were positioned to blast CNAC planes out of the sky. Martha sat white-knuckled in her hard, uncomfortable seat as the American pilot named Roy rose sharply to avoid the Peak, which was all but invisible against the ebony sky. Indeed, the only illumination came from shell bursts around the plane as it flew over Japanese lines.

They landed safely five-and-a-half hours later in Chungking, later spelled Chongqing, the largest city in southwest China valuable for its strategic position as a large Yangtze River port. The airstrip they landed on was located on a narrow island beneath more towering cliffs, and it was notorious for being submerged under as much as sixty feet of water at least two months a year. At other times, the water level rose and fell unpredictably, sometimes flooding the airstrip without warning. The other passengers departed quickly and disappeared into the city, a gray stretch of rubble at the top of the cliff. Martha and the American pilot ate a meager breakfast of rice and tea. She regarded the young man with curiosity, but she learned that it was better not to ask what adventurous Americans and Brits were doing in this horrific warzone when they could be enjoying the comforts of home. Then they took off again, the two of them and a new load of Chinese passengers. The plane passed over a few grim villages and isolated farms, flying just high enough to clear mountain tops before dipping low into valleys while Roy checked out conditions on the ground.

"I go where I'm looking," he explained perfunctorily to Martha. She gathered that the route he took was a random adventure in itself; he was obviously looking out for Japanese artillery encampments along the way and was prepared to fly around them if he had to. A few hours later Roy spotted the next stop on their itinerary, Kunming, through a thick haze that all but obliterated the ground.

"Yep," he said without further elaboration. Deftly, he dove down sharply through the yellow smog that had been thrown up by Japanese bombs earlier in the day, and touched down on a runway marked with white oil drums and pockmarked with bomb craters. Kunming was a provisional headquarters for the nationalists, with an underground network of tunnels lined with offices and barracks in the event that Chungking fell to the Japanese.

Martha was freezing cold and miserable by this time. She felt as though she had been flying for eternity through an icy wasteland with a roughneck for a pilot, who literally held her life in his fingertips at the controls. But she still had not reached her final destination. Again Roy lifted Martha and yet a new troop of passengers up from the ground as he expertly rose above mountains and dived into valleys, ever on the lookout for enemy encampments. Frozen to the bone, Martha finally landed in Lashio, Burma— today's Myanmar—sixteen hours and fifteen hundred miles after she had left Hong Kong. It was the adventure of a lifetime just reaching her destination. For Roy it was all in a day's work. He and his fellow pilots made the run regularly every week.

Lashio was important because of its location at the end of the Burma Road, which was nothing less than an engineering miracle. Everything passed over this mountainous route—oil, weapons, food, other supplies needed to sustain the Chinese war effort. The road snaked through the Himalayas at staggering heights and carved its way through rock at steep inclines that slowed traffic to no more than twenty miles an hour. Snow and ice covered the solid rock surface most of the long Chinese winter. Huge boulders littered the road, loosened from the high mountain walls by both gravity and regular bombing raids by Japanese aircraft. Yet, no sooner had the enemy planes abandoned the skies after their bombing sorties than teams of Chinese construction crews scurried across the rock surface to repair the wreckage. It was a dance repeated over and over almost daily.

The Chinese had virtually no defenses to ward off the Japanese attacks except for their indefatigable patience and long history of survival. Two hundred thousand Chinese laborers had built the serpentine road covering more than seven hundred miles across China to its terminus in Burma, and they were not about to let a few Japanese bombs undermine their superhuman effort. The Burma Road was critical to China's struggle against Japan, and it was a transportation link to the outside world that was a major source of interest to Ernest's contacts in Washington.

Chapter Twenty-eight

Martha's rest stop in Lashio consisted of a wooden shack with iron cots and a hot shower—heaven itself after her grueling journey. But Lashio would not be home for long. At one-thirty in the afternoon, after they got word that a couple of dozen Japanese planes had completed their bombing run over Kunming, Roy and Martha took off again for the provisional capital. Kunming "was a big walled city," Martha wrote, "entered by a great carved painted gate. The houses were made of timber or mud brick, with curving eaves. The Japanese claimed to have destroyed it but, as they destroyed, the Chinese residents repaired. Endurance was the Chinese secret weapon. The Japanese should have understood that, and everybody else had better remember it."

A few days later Martha was back in Hong Kong after "flying in what looked like béchamel sauce for hours." She found Ernest where she had left him, holding court in the lobby of their hotel and drinking with his motley cast of buddies. While Martha had been away, he had written to Edna to reassure her that her daughter was all right, "treating the men like brothers and the women like dogs." Martha resented that description when she heard about it later, but by then Ernest's embellishments of the facts were the least of the problems that had erupted between them. Martha complained to Ernest and his entourage about the plight of the masses drowsing away in opium dens, cavorting in brothels, breaking their backs in labor fit only for beasts, children forced to do slave labor in dimly lit factories, all of them half starved to death with sometimes only a small ration of rice and tea to sustain them through the day. But she blamed the people themselves as well as the masters who abused them, and Ernest responded by telling his friends that "Martha loves humanity but can't stand people." The men laughed along with Ernest, but his pithy accuracy in summing up her political bent bothered her more than his humor at her expense.

"The trouble with you, Martha," Ernest told her, "is that you think everybody is exactly like you. What you can't stand, they can't stand. What's hell for you has to be hell for them. How do you know what they feel about their lives? If it was as bad as you think, they'd kill themselves instead of having more kids and setting off firecrackers."

To mollify his wife, Ernest moved her into a newer hotel in the countryside near Repulse Bay away from all the poverty. The hotel was surrounded by flowering English gardens and decorated inside with chintz. Waiters served pink gins to the guests inside the compound that was insulated from the constant spitting and stench of sweat and night soil that offended Martha's sensibilities. Ernest once again surrounded himself with a new group of drinking companions, but Martha was less dismissive after she realized the true nature of his so-called "socializing." While she had been away, Ernest had expanded his circle beyond the likes of Two Gun Cohen and the assortment of Chinese racketeers and businessmen. He had also cultivated the friendship of U.S. Rubber Company executive Carl Blum; New Zealand industrialist Rewi Alley; head of British intelligence Major Charles Boxer; historian Emily Hahn; aviation expert W. Langhorne Bond; Argentine diplomat Ramon Lavalle; U.S. Consul General Addison Southard; and other China hands who had valuable information to share about military and political conditions in China.

Southard, in particular, was astonished at how quickly Ernest grasped what it took others years to learn for themselves. After picking all their brains, Ernest formulated a comprehensive view of the military dynamics at work throughout the country. Ernest reported in his dispatches to Washington that it was "seemingly inevitable" that the Japanese would invade Southeast Asia some time in 1941. They would not attack in summer or early autumn, he predicted, since that was typhoon season. He dismissed other months as unlikely and stated that December was the only month that made military sense to him. His forecast was spot on. It landed on Morgenthau's desk and, by extension, on the desk of Harry Dexter White. Ernest had no way of knowing at the time—nor did Southard or anyone else in government for that matter—that White was a Soviet spy who would later be accused of espionage.

*   *   *

Now that he had extracted all the intelligence his friends had to offer during their marathon bull sessions, Ernest was as anxious as Martha to head into the interior and observe firsthand what was happening on the ground. Two-Gun Cohen proved to be more than the buffoon that Martha had originally taken him for. Through his contacts, he had arranged for them to meet Mrs. Sun Yat-Sen, the widow of the early leader of the Chinese republican movement. She was one of the three powerful and glamorous Soong sisters and was willing to introduce Ernest and Martha to her sister May-Ling Soong and her husband, none other than the Generalissimo himself, Chiang Kai-Shek. The third sister was married to millionaire premier H.H. Kung. Through a combination of beauty, marriages to powerful men, plus their own sizable inheritances, the three sisters wielded significant power behind the scenes.

This was what Ernest had been hoping to accomplish from the start: a chance to size up Chiang for himself and report his impressions back to Washington. Martha's main goal was to write about the squalor she found as accurately as possible. In an article for *Collier's* entitled "Time Bomb in Hong Kong," Martha described the gut-wrenching, widespread poverty and the wide gap that existed between the small rich elite and the great mass of peasants. She resented Chiang and his wife before she met them and was prepared not to be taken in by their reputed charm and hospitality.

Ernest and Martha loaded up on supplies of flea and lice powder, boiled water, mosquito nets, and enough whiskey to carry them through the next phase of their journey—or so Ernest thought. On the night of March 24, 1941, they stood on the tarmac amid gale force winds waiting for a flight out of Hong Kong. The wind delayed their departure until eleven in the morning, when they lifted off the ground through a seemingly impenetrable fogbank. They flew over Japanese lines and landed on a small landing strip in Namyung during a torrential downpour, where they were greeted by two Chinese escorts named Mr. Ma and Mr. Ho.

"Mr. Ma was all round; round specs, round nose, round cheeks, round, permanently smiling," wrote Martha, who instantly disliked the man and distrusted what she perceived to be his phony amiability.

For the next twelve days, Ernest, Martha, and their escorts traveled south down the North River by boat, then mounted horses and rode to the front where they witnessed heavy fighting between Chinese and Japanese troops. In essence they were camping out in horrendous conditions, with nothing more than tattered mosquito nets to keep the bug-swarms at bay, and a bowl of dirty water when they could find it to brush their teeth and wash up. Martha was driven close to the verge of insanity by the omnipresent filth.

"You're a nutcase if you even think of washing yourself or brushing your teeth out here," Ernest told her. "You need to control your mania for keeping clean."

Martha ignored his advice and plunged her face into the fetid water, all the while complaining nonstop about the experience. "Cheer up," Ernest said, laughing. "Who wanted to come to China?"

It was the first of many times he would ask her that question; it became his constant refrain every time she lamented their circumstances. After the third or fourth time it began to grate on her. Ernest was less amused, however, by the Chinese generals they met during their journey who developed an inordinate fondness for the whiskey he carried with him into the warzone. It tasted a hell of a lot better than the sour rice wine and battery acid whiskey they were used to consuming, and they downed it by the tumbler-full in their many toasts to one another and their American allies. Ernest observed his rapidly dwindling supply, which threw him into a greater panic than the threat of being blown up by Japanese artillery.

Under Mr. Ma's and Mr. Ho's guidance, Ernest and Martha spent a memorable night in Tintack, "the disease center of South China," as Martha described it. She repeatedly asked Mr. Ma if the town was safe after listening to countless residents hacking and spitting up phlegm throughout the night.

"Oh yes. Is more safe. Maybe," he answered. In the morning Martha and Ernest saw the black flag flying over the town, a sign that they had landed in the midst of a cholera epidemic. After a breakfast of rice and tea, their party set off on the next leg of their adventure into the heartland. Their hosts provided them with a pair of pathetic miniature ponies, which shivered from the biting cold worse than their riders did. Ernest's horse was so small that the author's feet dragged along the ground. When they came to a stream, Ernest took pity on the bedraggled beast, wrapped his arm around the animal's belly, and carried him across to the other bank.

"Put that horse down," Martha yelled at him.

"I will not," Ernest said.

"You're insulting the Chinese. Put it down!"

"My first loyalty is to this horse," Ernest answered.

"You must drop that horse! *Please*."

"Okay," Ernest finally relented. "Poor old horse. Walk by yourself if you can."

When the whiskey supply ran dry, Mr. Ma commiserated with Ernest's predicament and commandeered a large jug of Chinese wine. Ernest drank thirstily from the vessel and passed it over to Martha. She took a swig and asked him, "What's in here?"

"It's called spring wine. Considered very high class. The Chinese drink it as an aphrodisiac."

Martha observed elongated objects at the bottom of the jug. "What's in here?" she demanded.

"Are you sure you want to know?"

"Yes."

"Well, snakes. But *dead*. Martha, if you throw up, I swear I'll hold it against you."

Finally they arrived in Chunking, where they were escorted to a house up on the cliff populated with bedbugs and a coterie of lizard-eyed thugs, henchmen and bodyguards of Generalissimo and Madame Chiang. The well-armed hoodlums lounged around on the sofa and chairs, glaring insolently at the American guests while they waited for orders from the great leader himself. Ernest took in the sordid surroundings and laughed so hard he had to sit down to support himself. Martha glowered at him, unable to find anything amusing in the situation. When Ernest stopped howling, he stood up and said to her, "Well, I guess I'll go out and see what the boys in the corner saloon are drinking. What'll you do?"

"Stare at the wall," she said.

At this point Martha realized that she had ignored her husband's advice about bathing to her own peril. She gazed in horror at the skin peeling away between her fingers in a yellowish ooze laced with blood. She had fallen victim to a condition Westerners referred to as "China Rot." She was exhausted, sick, distressed, and also suffering from dysentery. Ernest, on the other hand, seemed impervious to the filth as he drank with the locals and returned to the house, sprinkled lice powder around and chased bedbugs, wishing he had a pistol at his disposal to make quick work of the fleeing vermin.

"I'm going mad," Martha told him.

"Honest to God, Martha, you brought this on yourself. I told you not to wash."

"I just want to die."

"Who wanted to come to China?"

Chapter Twenty-nine

April 14 was the day Ernest and Martha had been looking forward to for the past few weeks; it was the day they were invited to have lunch with Chiang and his wife in their well-guarded home. The two writers had expected to be wined and dined in a palace, and they were surprised by the modest middle-class tackiness of the Chiangs' house when they arrived. Most likely the Chiangs had made a conscious decision to downplay their wealth to keep up the appearances of their "democratic" leanings. It's unlikely that their tastes ran to nondescript furniture and doilies, judging by Madame Chiang's appreciation of expensive clothes and jewelry.

Madame Chiang rushed in to greet them first, ahead of her servants. She was all smiles and practiced charm, with her lovely figure set off with a short-sleeved, body-hugging, ankle-length dress, diamond earrings, and just the right amount of perfume and lipstick. The women studied each other closely. A colleague had once described Martha as someone with a knack for romping through a warzone in "well-tailored slacks," and Madame Chiang was quick to observe her attempt at elegance in such dire conditions. On her part, Martha had resolved not to be seduced by Madame Chiang's polished veneer, and she focused instead on her ruthless love of power and her reputation for manipulating her public image.

Moments later Chiang Kai-Shek appeared by his wife's side, smiling, bowing slightly, extending his hand in greeting. Both Ernest and Martha were surprised by how slight the man was. For such a powerful leader, a military tactician and virtual dictator in his sphere of China, he presented anything but an imposing figure. He was neatly dressed in a tight military tunic and Sam Browne belt. His head was shaved and he wore a clipped British-style mustache that made him look like a caricature of the man Ernest and Martha expected to meet. Behind his back, his aides referred to him as "Peanut." Yet his smile was an immobile slash across his face. It appeared as though the man was made of frozen steel. The smile revealed his toothless mouth, which shocked the visitors. Later they learned that for him to greet anyone without his false teeth was considered the highest compliment, the privilege of letting others see him as he actually was. Ernest and Martha absorbed every detail of this slow-motion drama playing out in front of their eyes.

The two couples sat down to lunch, served by a small platoon of fawning servants who deposited one course after another in front of the guests. Chiang spoke first about the communist menace threatening his country, a plight he seemed more alarmed about than the prospect of a Japanese takeover. The communists were master propagandists and manipulators of public opinion, Chiang said. Ernest listened intently, offering little. He was a skilled collector of intelligence who knew how to listen and how to respond to get the information he wanted. Martha, on the other hand, grew increasingly restless. She would meet Chou En-Lai within days of their lunch with the Chiangs and come away impressed by him and his vision for China. Chou was second in command of the communists behind Mao Tse-Tung.

Chou was the only decent man she met in China, Martha wrote. "If he had said, 'take my hand and I will lead you to the pleasure dome of Xanadu,' I would have…asked for a minute to pick up my toothbrush and been ready to leave."

Martha was not interested in being blindsided by Chiang and his wife, whose manipulation of journalists often made the communists look like amateurs. Chiang claimed to be concerned about the communist threat, but he was not beyond lunching with the Soviet ambassador in an effort to stalemate the communists in his own country. Both Ernest and Martha understood that the rivalry in China between Chiang and Mao was more of a power play than an ideological spat. Martha's temper got the best of her, and she directed her ire at Madame Chiang.

"Why do you not take care of your lepers rather than make them beg in the street?" Martha asked her. Martha underestimated exactly whom she was dealing with. The loveliest Soong sister of all was as ferocious as she was beautiful. Madame Chiang's eyes flashed, beaming hatred at her presumptuous interlocutor.

The Chinese were humane and civilized, unlike Westerners, Madame Chiang snarled. "China had a great culture when your ancestors were living in trees and painting themselves blue."

Her remark took Martha by surprise, but Ernest suppressed a laugh as he stared back and forth at the two women. In a flash, Madame Chiang took a different tack entirely and was smiling again. She had one of her servants bring her a straw hat and a jade brooch set in silver, which she presented to Martha as gifts, as though nothing had transpired between them. The Generalissimo continued with his evisceration of Mao and his band of communists and the threat they posed to Western civilization, apparently unfazed by his wife's behavior. When lunch came to an end, the Chiangs sent Ernest and Martha on their way in a blizzard of smiles and good cheer. As they left, Ernest's laughter erupted out of him like a volcano that could no longer be contained.

"I guess that'll teach you to take on the Empress of China," he bellowed.

*　　*　　*

Astonishingly, Martha wrote an article for *Collier's* describing their lunch date with the Chiangs in the most adoring terms possible. We know how she really felt about them because she wrote in a memoir many years later that "these two stony rulers could care nothing for the miserable hordes of their people and in turn their people had no reason to love them." Separately, she wrote to a former boyfriend, "Madame Chiang, that great woman and savior of China. Well, balls."

But in her piece for the magazine, she said Madame Chiang was "as beautifully constructed as the newest and brightest movie star." She was "entrancing" and an "executive of great talent" who worked eighteen hours a day. "No coolie has a longer day." Putting her article in perspective, most American publications considered it unpatriotic to attack a U.S. ally during wartime, particularly one so closely linked to the Roosevelt administration. *Collier's* could well have instructed Martha to tone down her remarks if she expected to see them in print. The celebrated historian Barbara Tuchman explained the situation in one of her books.

"As America's ally, China could not be admitted to be anything other than a democratic power. It was impossible to acknowledge that Chiang Kai-Shek's government was what the historian Whitney Griswold, future president of Yale, named it in 1938, 'a Fascist dictatorship,' though a slovenly and ineffectual one. Correspondents, even when outside the country and free of censorship, refrained from reporting the worst of the Kuomintang on the theory that to do so would be to help the Japanese, and besides it would ensure that the correspondent could not return. It became an established tradition that no journalist 'wishing well to China,' as one of them wrote, could visit Chungking without going into ecstasies over the beauties of Madame, the heroic determination of the Generalissimo, the prowess of the Chinese armies and the general nobility of all hands."

Martha merely fit into the mold formed by the rest of her colleagues, while Ernest wrote little about the political orientation of the Chiangs and reserved his observations for the scrutiny of his contacts in Washington.

*   *   *

Martha's experience with China Rot grew more and more perplexing, to the point where she was forced to don thick white gloves over a foul-smelling unguent that was supposed to cure the malady. "I was about as alluring as a leper," she admitted. Ernest kept his distance the best he could. But the tipping point for both of them occurred during a flight to Rangoon when Ernest's few remaining drops of gin, which he had been nursing to last out the journey, flew out of his paper cup when turbulence rocked the plane over the Burma Road. Ernest cursed viciously while their fellow passengers wailed and screamed, terrified that the aircraft would be rent in half. Martha experienced spasms of guilt as the airplane shook violently. "I regretted bitterly having nagged him into this horror journey," Martha wrote, "and would never forgive myself for causing his death, cut off in his prime, his work unfinished, his children fatherless; my heart was breaking with sorrow."

They landed safely with Ernest in as black a mood as Martha had ever seen him while she was "racked by guilt." The heat was unbearable when they exited the plane. As Martha described it, "you felt you could cut the heat and hold it like chunks of wet blotting paper." They checked into a stifling hotel with nothing but a lethargic ceiling fan to move the air in slow motion across their bodies. Ernest resembled a beached whale as he stripped off his clothes and lay down on the marble floor, the coolest surface in the room. Martha laid beside him, naked herself except for the heavy, malodorous gloves. She was moved to tears over what she had put her husband through during the past few months and turned toward him, touched his shoulder, and whispered in his ear, "Thank you."

Ernest jumped. He stared at her and howled, "Take your filthy dirty hands off me!"

Martha was crushed. She had tried to comfort the man she loved, a man who had appeared to be all but indestructible under the worst conditions imaginable, and this is what it all had come down to. They stared at each other in silence, and then they simultaneously rolled onto their sides screaming with laughter as the sweat cascaded off their bodies and pooled onto the marble floor. They had lost their dignity piecemeal during their sojourn in China, but they had not lost their sense of humor.

Chapter Thirty

Back home in the United States at the end of May, safely removed from the horrible stench and relentless filth of China, Ernest and Martha stopped first at the White House where they were debriefed by their intelligence contacts. Ernest filled them in on China's lack of resources to mount a sustained counterattack against the Japanese, Russia's involvement in China's internal affairs, the escalating rivalry between Chiang and Mao, and his own assessment of battle conditions throughout the country. Ernest believed that America would be drawn into the war when the Japanese attacked the Philippines or Malaysia in an attempt to gain "control of the world's supply of rubber." Chiang Kai-Shek was hardly a reliable ally, but the U.S. had little choice but to continue to back him in the hope of tying the Japanese up in a protracted land war in China. That strategy would be less costly if it succeeded, Ernest said, than building more battleships to engage the Japanese directly. Ernest also advocated partitioning China between the communists and nationalists to forestall a civil war.

Then Ernest and Martha were off to Cuba, stopping first in Key West to pick up his sons Patrick and Gregory, Josie Russell, and the *Pilar*. The plan was for the two men to make a night passage across the Gulf Stream on Ernest's boat and for Martha and the boys to fly down from Miami on the Pan Am Clipper. Josie was in effect the older brother Ernest always wanted, a bosom buddy, a two-fisted drinking companion, and the type of salty fisherman and bootlegger Ernest relished. Ernest, Josie, Martha, and the boys fished and enjoyed their long days in the sun. The men arranged to take a break and go to New York for the Joe Louis—Billy Conn heavyweight championship bout at Madison Square Garden. Alas, Josie never made it. The story in the August 8 *Key West Citizen* understated the sad details:

"Joe Russell died at 3 o'clock yesterday afternoon in a Havana hospital. Ernest Hemingway...telephoned Joe Russell, Jr. here last night to tell him of his father's death. The elder Russell had gone into the hospital for a minor operation and was said to be recovering only a few hours before death came, apparently from a stroke."

Ernest's longtime friend had been seemingly indestructible. Josie was only fifty-one, and his death hit Ernest like a mortar blast on the battlefield. The man of letters was left without adequate words to describe his grief. "Mr. Josie died," was all he could say about it as he made arrangements to ship Josie's body back to Key West.

In the days that followed, Ernest lost himself in the towering stacks of unanswered mail that had accumulated during the past few months. He was increasingly concerned about his younger brother Leicester who was drifting—literally drifting—with a British friend in a leaky boat searching for U-boats in the Caribbean. Ernest would soon embark on that mission himself, but with better equipment courtesy of the U.S. government. Ernest realized that his brother was heedlessly risking his own neck in an attempt to do something useful with his life, and he secured a job for Leicester in the Office of Naval Intelligence in Washington.

Ernest was adrift as well after his months in China, and he was anxious to get on with a new writing project. The most frustrating time for any writer—and the most *dangerous* time for one who liked to drink—was the period between books. A writer with no book to write is no fun to be around. Ernest was an autobiographical writer whose fiction and nonfiction came directly from his own life, and he had already used up his best experiences of the past two decades. China was fertile ground for any writer searching for a subject for his next book, but for some reason it failed to come together for him.

Ernest's discontent put further pressure on his sometimes strained relationship with Martha whose own work was flowing more smoothly now. His mood soured further when the Pulitzer Prize Committee announced that it would not be granting a fiction award for 1940. Ernest and much of the literary world believed that the award would be granted to *For Whom the Bell Tolls*. Ernest's thinly disguised disappointment was transparent.

"If I'd won that prize," he said, "I'd think I was slipping. I've been writing for twenty years and never have won a prize. I've gotten along all right."

Martha, on the other hand, had developed her own momentum. She had finished a book of short stories and taken her title from, of all places, a letter written to her by Pauline. "The heart of another is a dark forest," Pauline had stated in her letter, and Martha simply lifted the first part of that sentence for her book title, *The Heart of Another*. When Ernest saw it, he told Martha that Pauline had gotten the quote from Dostoyevsky or Turgenev, but the actual source was Willa Cather. Thanks to Ernest, Martha's new opus was published by his long-time publisher, Scribner's. He generously told Max Perkins that her latest effort was her most adult book so far, and he mocked her former publisher, Duell, Sloane and Pearce, by saying they should be known as "Dull, Slum and Pus." Ernest took Martha's photo for the dust jacket, which Martha said made her look "Isadora Duncanish," with a mane of "wild hair and an expression of combined bewilderment and sunstroke."

Beneath it all, however, Martha was growing bored with life in Cuba. She wanted to get back to Europe and cover the war for *Collier's*. Ernest seemed content to spend his days fishing from the *Pilar*, and Martha put on her game face, accompanying him on his long days trolling for marlin in the Gulf Stream off Cuba. Ernest wrote Max Perkins that "it was good to have both a loving wife and a sporting companion," but Martha was finding it harder to disguise her restlessness. "I find in myself a total inability to retain interest," she wrote to her former lover Allen Grover. "Right now it all sorta stinks." She was delighted when Ernest left ahead of her on their fall outing in Sun Valley. About his absence, she told the poet Hortense Flexner, one of her confidantes, "by Christ, how I enjoy it!"

But in her exasperation, she recognized more than she cared to see about her husband in herself. "I wish to be hell on wheels, or dead," she wrote to Hortense. She believed that she and Ernest were a little bit afraid of each other. They each knew that "the other is the most violent person either one knows, and knowing something about violence we are always mutually alarmed at the potentialities of the other."

Their relationship was beginning to sound more like one of Ernest's boxing matches than like a marriage made in heaven.

* * *

Martha had also become bored with the endless rounds of drinking, hunting, fishing, and hiking with the celebrity crowd in Sun Valley. She found the place to be "holy hell," filled with streams of vapid conversations with mindless actors. Harriman's resort was "the west in an ornamental sanitary package." Referring to F. Scott Fitzgerald in a letter to Max Perkins, Martha wrote that "Hollywood *ruined* Scott, unless he was terribly dead before." Ernest loved being the center of attention and he lapped up the incessant compliments like a cat at a bowl of milk. Film director Robert Capa immortalized Ernest's every move with his camera, and film agent Leland Hayward and his wife, actress Margaret

Sullavan, fawned over him like star-struck movie fans themselves. Martha felt more and more like an outsider in their midst.

Her book was published in October and received the mixed reviews that Martha had grown accustomed to by now. It would have been bad enough if the critics judged her work on its own merits. But hardly any of them failed to comment that her stories were heavily influenced by her husband. He apparently had cast a "Svengali spell" over her work, according to the *New Republic*, which often deteriorated from merely "aping" Ernest into the swamp of outright "mush." Martha was incensed by that assessment more than any other. She was in serious danger of becoming a footnote in Ernest's life—a fear she expressed at the beginning of their relationship. She was being subsumed by his outsized fame. It did not help that Ernest wanted Martha to publish her new book under the name Martha Hemingway, further clouding her identity. She resisted him on this, although she did agree to copyright the book as Martha Gellhorn Hemingway. Ernest told her to ignore the critics; she was not writing for them. Just do your work and to hell with them. He wrote to Charles Scribner that "Martha is fine and very beautiful and happy."

But Martha was not fine and she was not happy. She was miserable in fact. Her only solace was Ernest's sons, whom she had come to love as though they were her own. She longed to be back on her own again, reporting on the war in Europe, working as a journalist, which she felt was her true calling. Ernest's sloppiness was also getting to her. She wished he would bathe and change his clothes more often. He exuded an odor of whiskey and manly sweat that she found increasingly off-putting. If her life with Ernest continued as it was much longer, she was going to scream or have a nervous breakdown. Martha needed to get away at least for a little while.

The Japanese attacked when Ernest said they would, in December 1941. But it was not an attack on Southeast Asia that

212

drew the U.S. into the war. Rather, it was a sneak bombing raid on the American military base in Pearl Harbor on December 7. "We'll probably get [the war] for a Christmas present," Ernest said before the attack. "Or maybe wake up New Year's morning with an unshakable hangover."

As the U.S. prepared for war, Martha was more anxious to get over to the European theater as a war correspondent. But again she ran into the familiar problem of *Collier's'* and other major publications' reluctance to hire women in that capacity. The U.S. military itself did not want women covering the action, which meant she would have trouble gaining access to the battlezones. Martha could go as a freelancer, if she wished, and file dispatches with no guarantee of publication. She would have to cover her own expenses. Whether or not her work saw the light of day depended on the quality of the reportage turned in by the men on the scene—her main competition. Martha would have to compete with the best staff reporters from *Time* and the major newspapers to get her work in print. She would have to beat the best of the best at their own game.

Salvation of sorts came in the form of an offer from her editor at *Collier's* to report on the presence of German U-boats in the Gulf Stream. Enemy submarines were attacking oil tankers in the area with impunity. The world's largest oil refinery was located on Aruba, and early in the morning of February 16, 1942, U-boats sent seven tankers to the bottom of the sea and bombarded the refinery without suffering so much as a scratch on their hulls. The situation had grown critical; without a steady flow of oil from the refinery, the American and allied war effort would be crippled. Nineteen vessels went down in flames in February, nineteen more were blasted to smithereens in March, eleven more in April, and a staggering total of thirty-eight were obliterated in May alone. Twice as many oil tankers had been sunk in the Caribbean as were destroyed in the North Atlantic passage to Europe. Nearly three hundred ships would be lost by the end of the year. Drastic steps needed to be taken to remedy the situation.

The drastic remedy came in what amounted to a letter of marque and reprisal, allowing private boats to attack, destroy, and capture enemy ships at sea. Anyone owning a seaworthy vessel approved by the government could, in effect, function as a privateer in the war effort against the Axis powers. An Associated Press release on June 27 spelled out the details:

"In a move to put a great fleet of small boats into the war against submarines off the Atlantic and Gulf coasts, the navy called today for all owners of seagoing craft to volunteer the services of themselves and their vessels…Boats found to be qualified will be equipped with radio, armament and suitable anti-submarine devices as rapidly as possible."

There were only three routes available for U-boats to enter the waters off Cuba, all of them narrow and treacherous. One was through the Straits of Florida, another through the Old Bahama Channel off the northeast coast of Cuba, and the third through the Yucatan Channel off Cuba's southwest coast. Ernest was more than game to take up the challenge. The "general" was happy to expand his areas of military expertise to include the rank of "admiral." Martha, too, was eager to report on U-boat activity in the Gulf Stream while her husband engaged in a useful war effort instead of returning to his indolent existence on the island. If she couldn't report on the ground war in Europe, she could at least write about the Axis threat not far from home.

Martha got up to speed reading everything she could find on naval warfare, submarine tactics and strategy, weaponry, and the location of small islands in the region. She was ecstatic. "I am in a state of bliss," she wrote to Bill Davis, a friend of Ernest. "I love the life of the wandering journalist very much." In her journal she entered, "If you have no part in the world, no matter how diseased the world is, you are dead. It is not enough to earn your living, do no actual harm to anyone, tell no lies…It is okay. It is not dirty. But it is dead. I want to be part of what happens to everyone."

Chapter Thirty-one

Documents released for the first time in 2010 revealed that Ernest's experiences as a privateer in service to the U.S. government were more than a quixotic effort to stop the sinking of Allied ships by German U-boats—at least at first. Through his contacts in Washington, he was given a stipend of five hundred dollars a month to establish what amounted to a spy ring in Cuba. Ernest, in his magnetic fashion, quickly assembled a rogue's gallery of spies and combatants made up of dockworkers, gamblers, a Catholic priest, an Olympic athlete, and a few gunrunners—a makeshift entourage he dubbed the "Crook Factory" or "Crook Shop" on different occasions.

Ernest and his crew left on patrol every day in the *Pilar*, which was outfitted by the government with machineguns, grenades, satchel charges, and other equipment that was hardly a serious threat to the firepower of the U-boats. Nevertheless, Ernest's plan was to come upon a submarine just as it was surfacing, lob grenades into the open hatches, and shoot those who tried to escape when they were most vulnerable. The *Pilar* plied the waters around Cuba ostensibly as a fishing boat offering itself as bait for German submariners hoping to confiscate food and useful supplies. For hours each day in the open water, they picked up radio conversations in German, hoping to gain vital intelligence information to turn over to Washington. Martha, meanwhile, went off on her own assignment for *Collier's*, happy to leave the men to their own devices. Ernest knew U-boats were in the area from listening in on their radio traffic, and he heard about the damage they inflicted on oil tankers almost daily. But—perhaps luckily for him and his cohorts—they failed to engage any in combat. Before long he and his men got bored. Among the supplies they had stocked on the *Pilar* were innumerable bottles of whiskey, rum, and wine.

Before long, the sorties across the Gulf Stream turned into drunken bouts of drinking and dining on the spicy Cuban food served up by Ernest's chief cook and bottle washer, Gregorio Fuentes. When the men emptied their bottles, they tossed them overboard and used them for target practice.

Ernest's exploits in the Gulf Stream with his reckless ensemble grew to legendary proportions and reached the ears of FBI chief J. Edgar Hoover in Washington. Hoover was an odd mixture of puritanical martinet and closet sexual adventurer, who was not a fan of Ernest's over-the-top lifestyle to begin with. Hoover distrusted his motivation and his earlier sympathies for the republicans in Spain. He knew that Ernest had no love for the Bureau, referring to some of its agents as "members of the Gestapo." Reports of wild parties and the boozing sessions aboard the *Pilar* did not go down well with Hoover. Almost from the beginning, Hoover pleaded with the president without much success to shut down Ernest's operation. But the U.S. ambassador to Cuba, Spruille Braden, was an ally of the author and valued his intelligence reports as well as Ernest's capacity for alcohol.

"He could consume an astonishing amount of liquor—any kind of liquor—without appearing to feel it," Braden wrote. "I don't know how many cocktails we had before dinner; but Ernest didn't take cocktails, he took absinthe drip. During the dinner we had red and white wine, followed by champagne...Afterward I had highballs, but Ernest went back to his absinthe drip. And he remained cold sober."

Ernest continued to serve his country in a critical region, searching for U-boats, preparing to take them on in combat at great risk to himself, his boat, and the men aboard it, all the while downing prodigious quantities of alcohol during the patriotic adventures at sea.

When Martha returned from her own travels throughout the area on an assignment that took her to exotic places like St. Barthelemy and Virgin Gorda between St. Thomas and Antigua, she came back to a husband who was up to his usual childish antics, as far as she was concerned. Ernest struck her as a grownup boy using the war to drink and cavort with his coterie of misfits instead of seriously engaging in the effort to defeat the Nazis. Their fights grew nastier and more intense, and Martha could not wait to get away again on her work for the magazine. Ernest wrote her love letters while she was away, telling her of life at the Finca, giving her news about the boys, and supplying anecdotes about their growing legion of cats. But after Martha wrote to him, complaining about the confinement of Cuba, Ernest responded with a letter containing humor laced with acid.

"Boy can you hit," he wrote. "Do you know where the heart of another lives?" That was an obvious dig at her ripping off Pauline to get a title for one of her books. "Boy how my hero can hit cuando no hay enemigo and who you are giving it to loves you like a fucking dope."

It was not all bad between Ernest and Martha. She did love their home on the island; it was her discovery and creature after all. And she still loved the man she had idolized since she was a very young woman. There was enough volatility in their relationship to mesmerize a woman like Martha who craved excitement and adventure above all else. But there was competition as well. She could never hope to equal let alone surpass his reputation. She still felt like one of his students, a role the reviewers would never let her forget. And there was a lazy side to Ernest that she had never seen before. He had attempted no serious writing since his last book came out—a major drawback for a man given to hedonism and sensuality as he was. Martha couldn't wait to get back to him when she was away, and she couldn't get away fast enough after a couple of weeks of seeing him again.

* * *

On June 26, Ernest's sons descended on Cuba to celebrate Patrick's fourteenth birthday. Jack or Bumby, Ernest's firstborn with Hadley, was now eighteen, and the middle son, Gregory, was eleven. They all had schoolboy crushes on the thirty-three-year-old Martha who was more like an older playmate than a stepmother—Bumby's second stepmother after Pauline. The boys were in awe of this lovely blonde woman's vocabulary, which included the word *fuck* in every third sentence or so. And they also loved life at the Finca Vigia, the lush growth that threatened to overtake the property, and the collection of animal life that abounded inside and out. In addition to their father's cats, a tribe that seemed to multiply almost daily, the Finca was home to several dogs, ducks, roosters, and armies of tarantulas, centipedes, scorpions, and assorted ants and insects that feasted on wood, paper, linen, silk, and bread. Ernest placed cans of kerosene throughout the house in a never-ending war against the invaders, which added a pungency to the perfumed floral aromas drifting in through the windows.

Bumby was especially taken with "an enormously old ceiba tree…with its large, high-reaching roots extending from the bulbous trunk like sinuous flying buttresses of smooth, gray bark. Many orchid plants live on its trunk and among its broad branches," he wrote. Gregory was mesmerized by the green vegetation, the variegated flowers, and the view of Havana lit up at night from the hills above the city. Martha, too, enjoyed summer with the boys, swimming in the pool each day, playing tennis with Ernest and his sons in the afternoons, and drinking in the bars along the Havana waterfront at night. But beneath it all, she felt frustrated and restless.

"During that terrible year, 1942, I lived in the sun, safe and comfortable and hating it," she wrote. She told Eleanor Roosevelt that she was growing tired of her role as the *de facto* den mother and housekeeper who kept the house from falling down around everyone's head. Ernest didn't mind living among clutter and chaos, but it was driving Martha closer to the edge. Visitors arrived unannounced at all hours, welcomed by Ernest who craved the camaraderie of his fellow spies and roustabouts, the Basque jai alai players who drove up from Havana to drink Papa's liquor and party with the author, and assorted riffraff from God knew where that had gravitated into the magnetic pull of Ernest's orbit. Martha never stopped marveling at her husband's ability to gather around him legions of cronies wherever he went, but it was wearing out the little patience she had left. She no longer had any privacy or any sense of identity in this all-male world. She needed to get out among some kindred spirits.

"When she was away she longed for him," one biographer wrote. "When she was home she found it difficult to put up with his exasperating habits…When nothing changed she boiled up with frustration and knew only one way out, to get away for a while."

In October, Martha told Ernest that she needed a break. She left Cuba on a trip to New York City, where she checked in at the Lombardy Hotel and had dinner with friends. She wrote Ernest that she wished they could be together, "alone for a while," and he replied that he loved her "because your feet are so long and because they get cold and because I can take good care of you when you are sick also because you are the most beautiful woman I have ever known."

From New York, Martha headed down to Washington to visit Eleanor Roosevelt. Martha was chilled by the cold, damp autumn air after the heat of Cuba. She promptly came down with a cold and retreated to the Lincoln bedroom on the second floor of the White House—a bedroom that a later president would immortalize by charging guests exorbitant rates to sleep there. Another prominent visitor during Martha's stay, Alexander Woollcott, the fat acerbic critic and member of the Algonquin Round Table with Dorothy Parker and others, couldn't wait to get inside the Lincoln bedroom after Martha left. As Woollcott wrote to Rebecca West, the room was dear to him "because it had more recently been occupied by Martha Gellhorn." It was the closest he would ever get to actually fucking Ernest's wife.

While Martha was away, Ernest and his crew got the closest they ever would to engaging a German sub in combat. In November they spotted a large vessel towing a smaller boat spouting smoke as it headed eastward toward Cuba. The *Pilar* closed the distance between them, keeping the alien crafts under surveillance for the better part of an hour. As they neared the two ships, they could see that the smaller boat was a submarine being towed into port by a Spanish warship, the *Marques de Comillas*. Once the *Pilar* was observed, the Spanish ship veered away at top speed leaving Ernest's boat in its wake. Ernest reported the sighting to the American Naval Attaché in Havana, who noted that "the observers, two reliable Americans and four Cubans, state they were within five hundred yards of the boat in question when the incident occurred."

When Martha returned to Cuba, she incited Ernest's wrath by taking some of his tomcats into Havana to have them spayed while he was off on one of his submarine hunts. He would rather have shot them than have them neutered, he screamed at Martha. He hated "wimmies," he told her, "because it was a wommy who sent them off to have their balls cut off."

Life in Cuba was no more agreeable for Martha than it was before she left. She put up with it for a few weeks and then told Ernest that she was leaving for St. Louis to spend the holidays with her mother who was alone now that her children were scattered all over. Ernest remained in Cuba in the company of his man-swarm buddies and his sons, who came to visit periodically. No sooner were they apart than Ernest and Martha began to miss each other terribly again. She had always vacillated with her lovers over the years, desiring their company when they were apart and struggling to free herself of their embrace when they were together. It was no different with Ernest.

She wrote to him, calling him her "darling house-broken cobra (cobra because no one knew where it would strike next)...Take care of yourself beloved and the childies and the animalies...and I will be home quick as a winklet."

Unable to realize her dream of going to the war in Europe as a correspondent, Martha started to work on a new novel while she was in St. Louis. The words flowed freely, encouraging her to write to Max Perkins that it was "the first time that I have ever written all the time with pleasure...I had three weeks on it and they were almost like a beautiful drunk, they were so happy...I always used to see E so tired but so happy when he was writing, and I was usually just tired and doubting."

Encouraged by Ernest, Martha continued to work on her book in Cuba in a furious burst of creative energy. Ernest was delighted with her progress and became impatient with her periodic spells of self-doubt. He frowned when she told him "I wish we could stop it all now, the prestige, the possessions, the position, the knowledge, the victory. And by a miracle, return together under the arch at Milan, you so brash in your motorcycle sidecar and I badly dressed, fierce, loving." Just believe in what you're doing and get on with your work, he told her.

It was good between them while the writing was going well, but when her insecurity returned, their arguments grew more frequent and nasty. Why can't you bathe and wear clean clothes once in a while, she wanted to know. Why are you so obsessive about cleanliness, he asked her. There were no logical answers to those questions. Ernest's other wives and girlfriends had found his grooming, or lack of it, somewhat endearing. Martha, on the other hand, was a stickler for cleanliness and style as she had demonstrated even in the midst of war. They had different perspectives, exacerbated all the more by their mutual frustrations. They needed and were dependent on each other for different reasons. But the divide was widening between them. They pulled apart for a while, then drew closer again. But each new rift was broader than the last one. It appeared all but inevitable that the breach and the insults and the wounds would eventually become too severe for either of them to overcome.

Chapter Thirty-two

Despite Hoover's dislike of Ernest, the *Pilar* continued its sub patrols through the spring and summer of 1943. FBI minions in Cuba reported that "the American 38 foot motor boat PILAR, black hull and green deck, was operating eastward along the north coast of Cuba on a scientific mission and identifies itself on aircraft approach by an American flag during the day and flashing 'V' at night."

When Ernest was out to sea, the mail-boat arrived once a week with new chapters of Martha's novel for him to scrutinize. Ernest stayed up late at night in his cabin illuminated by an oil lamp, making corrections on her manuscript before shipping them back to Cuba with the next mail delivery. As much as Martha wanted to be free of Ernest and go off on her own, she still depended on him for the confidence she needed to fulfill her goals as a writer. A later generation of psychobabblers would have labeled their marriage a codependency, with each one enabling the other to cling to their relationship past the point where it was healthy and productive.

In early June, the U-boat activity in the channels leading into the Gulf intensified. The government authorized the *Pilar* to step up its own operations in the myriad keys near the Cuban coast—Cayo Frances, Cayo Chico, Cayo Magano Grande, and others. Ernest christened this latest phase of his sub-hunting duties "Operation Friendless," in honor of one of his favorite cats at the Finca. For the next few weeks he and his crew searched the waters and trekked across small islands dotting the Gulf looking for *fugitivos* and *enemigos*. Martha put her weeks alone at the Finca to good use, working away on her novel and finishing it with none of Ernest's drinking buddies around to distract her. After forty days of patrolling the sea without spotting any enemy subs, the men aboard the *Pilar* grew more and more belligerent. The supplies of beer, rum, and gin were running low and Ernest had all he could do to keep order on his boat. It was time to go home. Mr. Scrooby needed some attention from Martha. When he dreamed one night that he had made love to a Polar bear with Martha's face, he knew it was time to head back to shore.

Ernest needed a new engine for the *Pilar* after the punishing weeks at sea, and his men rushed off to the nearest bars to get roaring drunk and find other people to fight. It wasn't long before Martha's reverie was dashed by a new round of parties at the Finca now that Ernest was back. Ernesto has returned, the word spread immediately across Havana. Once again the hordes came visiting in droves as Papa Ernesto hosted a pig roast on his property, complete with enough beer, wine, rum, whiskey, and gin to float an armada of seaworthy vessels. The ostensible occasion was Ernest's forty-fourth birthday coming up in July, but in reality he would have found another reason—*any* reason—to celebrate with the best and worst citizens Havana had to offer. A drunken priest blessed the enormous pig roasting over the banked coals, and the jai alai players started to toss balls and other objects around at one another's heads. After one of them beaned another with a hard roll, Papa rose to his feet before a fight could break out and declared,

"On my birthday you can't throw rolls until dessert. *No hast'el postre!*"

Martha put up with all of it as long as she could. Finally, a reprieve came in the form of the break she had been looking for all her life. *Collier's* asked her if she would be willing to go to England, where the military rules were more relaxed, as a foreign correspondent. Martha could barely contain her excitement. Her novel was finished and now she could go away and pursue her craft with no entanglements—no entanglements except for Ernest and their life together in Cuba. When she told Ernest about her plans, he flew into a rage. Why did she want to run off to war? Why couldn't she stay put and develop her talent as a novelist? Why wasn't being his wife enough for her? Ernest's sons, who had come down for the summer, observed his third marriage disintegrating before their eyes, this time with no other woman involved. They also saw him visibly drunk for the first time.

"Papa would be just drunk out of his mind," Gregory recalled later, "but able to do it because [the chauffer] would drive the car home. He'd have all these drinks at the Floridita, just unbelievable drinking."

Martha asked Ernest to give up the sub patrols and go to England with her. All he had to do was put out the word that he was available, and he would have his choice of assignments from any magazine or newspaper he wanted. They all would be delighted to have his byline on their front pages. But Ernest dug his heels in. He loved his life in Cuba and had had enough of writing journalism after covering wars all over the globe. He wanted to get back to his fiction again, although he had been in a writing slump since *For Whom the Bell Tolls* came out three years earlier. Still, he had to get back in writing shape, cut back on the drinking a bit, and start a new novel. Ernest and Martha were both adamant about their plans. Martha was going to England regardless of what anyone said, and Ernest wasn't going to let his wife dictate his own course of action. Neither one would give in.

* * *

Martha left Cuba on September 20, 1943, and headed for New York where she had to jump through a few bureaucratic hoops to get her documentation in order. While she waited for her papers to clear, she saw the film version of *A Farewell to Arms* and a preview of *For Whom the Bell Tolls,* both movies starring Gary Cooper. Once again she tried to entice Ernest to join her and share the war experience with her.

"I am sad," she wrote Ernest. "Only there isn't anything final, is there? This is just a short trip and we are both coming back from our short trips to our lovely home. And then we'll write books and see the autumns together and walk around the corn fields waiting for the pheasants."

Ernest wanted to be out on the water again searching for U-boats, but he was devastated to learn that the government was pulling the plug on all the submarine patrols in the area. He spent his time mostly alone, with "thirteen cats, five dogs, fighting cocks, and pigeons" keeping him company, drinking heavily, and brooding about his errant wife. Martha wrote constantly, telling him that everyone in New York was asking about him and wondering why he didn't go over with her to write about the war.

"I have to live my way," she wrote, "or there would not be any me to love you with. You really wouldn't want me if I built a fine big stone wall around the Finca and sat inside." A week later her tone changed and she admitted that she found their life in Cuba "remote and somehow awful."

That's not what Ernest wanted to hear. He wanted his wife back with him in Cuba. But she would not return. His loneliness turned into anger. His mood grew darker and took a vengeful turn. In the past when anyone crossed him, Ernest did more than just get even; he went after them on a search and destroy mission. Now Martha had become his enemy. She had turned against him. He would find a way to make her pay for that.

PART FIVE

THE BELL TOLLS FOR THEM

Chapter Thirty-three

Martha looked in the bathroom mirror in the Berkshire Hotel and saw the first signs of aging on her face. She had a fleshy face, the kind that got jowly and led to chipmunk cheeks with the passage of time. She was shocked. Her father had been right—up to a point. She had talent. But she had been using her good looks as currency over the years, trading them for relationships with successful men who could help advance her career.

It had not been smooth sailing for Martha who bided her time in New York for longer than she anticipated, delayed by bureaucratic snafus. She corrected the page proofs of her novel, finally titled *Liana*, while she waited. She fumed when she saw a pre-publication notice of her novel, referring to the author only as "the wife of Ernest Hemingway." No matter how far she roamed, and how distinctive her own work would become, she couldn't slip out from under Ernest's all-embracing shadow. She fretted about every passing day when nothing seemed to be happening and worried about the face that stared back at her from the mirror. Her doubts returned and her self-confidence waned without Ernest by her side to bolster her ego.

"You belong to me," she wrote to him. "Some time the war will be over. We have a good wide life ahead of us. And I will try to be beautiful when I am old, and if I can't do that I will try to be good. I love you very much."

She made her first attempt at preserving her youthful good looks by embarking on a round of beauty treatments that included facials, vitamin injections, dental visits to fix her receding gums, hair appointments, and a rigorous exercise program. She shopped for the latest fashions since she wanted to look her best when she arrived in battle-scarred London. She had been the best-tailored correspondent in Spain during the Civil War, and she would present herself in the best light in London as well.

Martha's clearance to travel to wartime London came through in late October, and she boarded a Pan Am Clipper on a journey that took twelve days in all, with stops along the way in Bermuda and Portugal. Martha had not seen London in five years, and the city she arrived in looked far different than the metropolis she remembered. Many of the landmarks she was familiar with had been cratered from German bombardment, and the skyline was altered beyond recognition by jagged concrete structures where stolid stone buildings had once reigned supreme. Everyone was in uniform: nurses with dark cloaks and red linings, young soldiers with berets and the blue trimmings of their parachute regiments, American GIs in their distinctive camouflage battle gear. Martha was impressed by the stoic civilians who had endured months of relentless bomb raids; "Nothing becomes them like a catastrophe," she wrote later. "Slowness, understatement, complacency change into endurance, a refusal to panic, and pride, the begetter of self-discipline."

Martha moved into a flat in London's West End but started complaining immediately about the living conditions, particularly the layer of concrete dust that had assumed a constant presence in the air for as long as the bombing continued. Wartime conditions only intensified her fastidious nature, but she knew better than to write to Ernest about her queasiness, knowing that he would make fun of her and ask her the same question he had asked in China: who wanted to go there anyway? Instead she wrote to him about the reception she had received as his wife, flattering his ego by saying she profited "from the glory and power of his name." In an effort to smooth things with him, she wrote that she was "the very ordinary wife of an extraordinary man." She even proposed that he come over and write a series of articles about the war, knowing that they might overshadow her own efforts. But Ernest did not bite. He wrote to his son Patrick that his wife was a "selfish and ambitious" woman. To Max Perkins he confided that he hadn't "done a damn thing I wanted to do now for well over two years, except shoot live pigeons occasionally." Martha, he wrote, "does exactly what she wants to do willfully as any spoiled child. And always for the noblest motives."

Liana turned out to be Martha's most successful novel to date, quickly selling out its first printing of twenty-seven thousand copies and hitting the major bestseller lists. The reviewers referred to her by her own name, one saying that she had "come artistically of age." Ernest was less than pleased by a review that claimed she handled her characters with more restraint and subtlety than her husband did. She was his creature after all, and as much as he wanted her to succeed on her own merits, he also wanted to be acknowledged as the mentor who made her what she had become. Martha's newfound success made Ernest even more irritable than he already was, more anxious to take revenge than he was before she left.

*　　*　　*

Martha returned to Cuba after an absence of five months, only to find the Finca in a slovenly state with empty booze bottles strewn everywhere and her husband in a dark, menacing mood. Nothing she could say or do could mollify him. Ernest's behavior toward Martha bordered on madness. His own son Gregory said later that his father "changed into a different person" during this period, more paranoid and more abusive than he had ever seen him. It was as though Ernest's inner demons had been set loose, with the dark depressive side of his nature erupting unrestrained to the surface.

"Ernest began at once to rave at me," Martha said later. "He woke me when I was trying to sleep to bully, snarl, mock—my crime really was to have been at war when he had not, but that was not how he put it. I was supposedly insane, I only wanted excitement and danger, I had no responsibility to anyone. I was selfish beyond belief…I put it to him that I was going back, whether he came or not."

"I was a fool to come back from Europe, and I knew it," Martha wrote to Eleanor Roosevelt.

No sooner had Martha left Ernest stewing by himself in Cuba than he left for New York to exact his revenge. If he couldn't keep his wife at home in his bed with him, he would see to it that her means of escape was blocked at the next turn. Ernest could have had his pick of any publication in the country. They all would have been ecstatic to sign the most celebrated writer in the world as their war correspondent. But Ernest went directly to *Collier's* and offered his exclusive services to Martha's editor, in effect giving him the choice of keeping Martha on the payroll and passing up the literary coup of a lifetime, or making the wife a stringer and hiring her famous husband. The editor did what he had to do; the alternative would have been a one-way ticket to the unemployment line for him.

Martha was paralyzed by Ernest's knockout punch. Again she turned to Eleanor Roosevelt for solace. "The way it looks, I am going to lose out on the thing I most care about seeing or writing of in the world, and maybe in my whole life," she wrote to the First Lady.

Others thought Martha got no less than she deserved. Ernest's friend, the writer Winston Guest, regarded her as a "tough, mercenary bitch. She explained to me that she picked Ernest because of his ability as a writer and possible remuneration from books," he said.

Martha defended herself, saying it was all "rubbish. I loved him as long as I could and when I lost all respect for him as a man—not as a writer—I said so and withdrew and that was that."

Ernest and Martha had become two strong-willed combatants at this stage of their marriage. Neither was prepared to give an inch, both were determined to get their own way whatever the cost to the other. The writers who lived and gathered in New York in the days before Ernest left for the warfront remembered him as huge, tipping the scales somewhere around two-twenty, sporting a full pepper-and-salt beard. Despite his bloated size, he was full of energy and spitfire. He ran into the novelist John O'Hara in Costello's bar one night and bet him ten bucks that he could break O'Hara's supposedly unbreakable blackthorn walking stick in half. O'Hara, three sheets to the wind himself, took Ernest up on the challenge, then looked on horrified as Ernest draped a couple of napkins over his head, placed the club on top of the napkins, and snapped it in two pieces. Another writer, Dawn Powell, said she was "exhausted" by Ernest's immense gusto. He was "someone who gives out more in six hours than most people do in a lifetime. He leaves you groggy."

Ernest was indeed more energetic than he had been since his submarine patrols. He was all pumped up with adrenalin fueled by his quest for revenge against Martha who was shell-shocked, reeling unsteadily from Ernest's act of vengeance. But she looked more glamorous than ever after her series of beauty treatments, all dressed up in tailored new outfits to go back to war, but with no job now to take her there. Still, she would find a way to get over there again somehow. She would find a way to gain access to the battlefront and write about how war affected ordinary people where they lived. And she would get *Collier's* to publish her dispatches because they would be too good to ignore. If Ernest thought he had defeated her, he had better think again.

Collier's got more than a war correspondent when it put Ernest on the payroll; the magazine hired an intelligence agent as well, a writer with combat experience who would be granted access to the thick of the action. Ambassador Braden had been extremely impressed by Ernest's activities as a sub-hunter, and he gave Ernest a letter commending him for his "highly confidential intelligence activities," and for "performing certain other work, likewise of a confidential nature, involving personal risks and ever-present danger." Ernest also had contacts in the OSS, the wartime predecessor of the CIA that was formed to conduct intelligence operations behind enemy lines. Secret documents from the period indicate that the OSS refused to recognize Ernest as an official operative, but nonetheless acknowledged that he had "conspicuous abilities for this type of work," which the agency was willing to put to good use in a clandestine capacity. There was little question but that Ernest would be going to Europe not only as a writer, but also as an agent for the federal government traveling into the warzone without portfolio.

Chapter Thirty-four

Martha begged Ernest to let her travel with him aboard a seaplane bound for London, but he brushed her off saying that no women were allowed on the specially arranged flight. Martha found out later that the passengers on Ernest's plane included the actress Gertrude Lawrence, who was flying across the Atlantic with food supplies for friends in London. Martha turned once more to Allen Grover, who arranged passage for her on a Norwegian freighter carrying a load of dynamite, amphibious personnel carriers, and other military equipment. Martha was the only passenger aboard the uncomfortable ship, which had no amenities and contained a crew of boisterous sailors who spoke little or no English. Martha read nonstop to pass the time and ruminate on the state of her marriage.

"I find I cannot think of him in kindness but only with dread," she wrote in her diary on May 10, 1944. In a letter to Hortense Flexner, she confided, "He is a rare and wonderful type...He is a good man, which is vitally important. He is however bad for me, sadly enough, or maybe wrong for me is the word; and I am wrong for him...I feel terribly strange, like a shadow and full of dread...It is all sickening and I am sad to death, and afraid...I want my own name back, most violently, as if getting it back would give me some of myself...We are, basically, two tough people and we were born to survive."

The crossing was agonizingly slow, taking three weeks in all as the freighter plodded slowly through heavy fog and churning seas heavily populated with German wolf packs looking to send Allied cargo ships to the bottom of the ocean. Martha landed in Liverpool on May 31, only to learn that Ernest had arrived two weeks earlier and was recuperating in a London hospital following a serious automobile accident. A doctor named Peter Gorer had offered Ernest a ride back to his hotel one night from a party hosted by photojournalist Robert Capa. The good doctor was at least as drunk as Ernest was after a long night of drinking, and both men failed to see the steel water tank that loomed on the side of the darkened street at three o'clock in the morning. The crash propelled Ernest headlong into the windshield, splitting his forehead with a long gash that required fifty-seven stitches to close up. Ernest's already battered knees were also smashed again. The injury would leave him with a concussion, ringing ears for weeks afterward, and new scars to accompany others on his forehead, arms, and knees resulting from a series of earlier injuries.

Martha headed to the hospital as fast as she could and found her husband, his head covered by a huge wraparound bandage that looked like a turban, hosting a party for a new band of cronies. There was a well-stocked bar alongside his bed, with Ernest and the others imbibing freely. In the room with him were novelist Irwin Shaw, CBS correspondent Charles Collingwood, *Time* correspondent William Walton, Robert Capa, and a few others including a small, pretty, thirty-six-year-old journalist with short curly hair named Mary Welsh whose byline appeared in *Time*, *Life*, and other major publications.

*   *   *

Ernest had met Mary in a restaurant near the Dorchester Hotel shortly after his plane landed in England. She was sitting at a table with Irwin Shaw, who would gain fame in 1949 with his war novel, *The Young Lions*. Irwin pointed out the burly man sitting at another table across the room. "That's Ernest Hemingway," Irwin said. She looked over just as the rugged, good-looking man glanced across in her direction. Their eyes locked. Before she could turn away, he rose from his table and strode directly over to Irwin and Mary. Ernest barely looked at Irwin. Instead, his eyes drank in the compact woman with the tight sweater that perfectly complimented her trim figure. Irwin introduced them and Ernest sat down.

"It's been nice knowing you," Irwin said to Mary later.

"What do you mean?"

"You'll see."

Before Martha so much as set foot on English soil after her arduous journey across the Atlantic, Ernest told Mary within days of meeting her, "I don't know you, Mary, but I want to marry you. I want to marry you now, and I hope to marry you sometime. Sometime you may want to marry me."

Lucky Mary!

She was as taken with him as he was with her. After Martha arrived on the scene, Ernest made a date to take her out to dinner to discuss their faltering marriage. She waited patiently in her room, but Ernest never showed up. On his way to pick her up, Ernest ran into Mary and took her out to dinner instead. Ernest's thirst for revenge was not yet slaked. When Ernest and Martha did appear together, their friends remembered him reducing her to tears with the most castigating language they had ever heard a man direct at his wife in public.

Mary Welsh was no stranger to marriage and romantic relationships herself. Born in Minnesota in 1908, the same year Martha was born, she aspired to become a writer from the time she could read. Her first marriage was to a drama student from Ohio named Lawrence Cook when she was already thirty-two. She divorced him shortly afterward and moved to Chicago to take a job at the *Chicago Daily News*. She met another reporter there named Will Lang, with whom she had an affair while they worked together on various assignments. The next stop for Mary was London where she found a job on the *Daily Express*, which sent her to Paris to cover war preparations in the years leading up to World War II. When France fell in 1940, Mary went back to London to cover the war on British soil. At this time she accused a fellow journalist named Andy Rooney (yes, *that* Andy Rooney who was there reporting for *Stars and Stripes*) of plagiarizing her material—a charge that was eventually settled amicably. Mary then married another reporter in London, an Australian named Noel Monks, who was away on an assignment when the most famous writer on planet Earth appeared at her table while she was dining with Irwin. Mary was having affairs with Irwin and possibly one or two other journalists in London before Ernest swooped in to claim her.

Those looking for similarities between Mary and Martha had a laundry list to choose from: both were attractive, ambitious, talented writers from the Midwest a few months apart in age; both had a history of relationships with successful men; and both were unhappily married in the spring of 1944. One was pulling away from the most famous writer of his generation, while the other was being sucked into his orbit. It's a tossup as to who was getting the better deal here. Or maybe not.

*   *   *

D-Day was looming on the near horizon as the three protagonists jockeyed for position. On June 6, 1944, one hundred and sixty thousand allied troops would be landing on the Normandy coast, marking the beginning of the end for Nazi Germany. D-Day—Decision Day, Disembarkation Day, or Operation Overlord as it was alternatively called—had been in the planning stage for months and waited only for the proper weather and tide conditions to set it in motion. June 5 was a lousy weather day; June 6 promised to be somewhat better, but not ideal. The operation involved five separate landings in all by American, British, and Canadian troops under the command of American General Dwight D. Eisenhower.

Eisenhower planned to set the invasion in motion with five thousand ships carrying his men and hundreds of military vehicles across the English Channel. Eight hundred planes would be launched over France, dropping thirteen thousand paratroopers behind enemy lines while an additional three hundred bombers released their deadly charges on top of German troops defending the beaches. Despite his bandaged head and knees, Ernest planned to be among those going ashore with the combatants. Martha wanted to be there as well. The problems she faced were twofold: how was she was going to get there now that Ernest had thrown his roadblock in her path? And, if she did manage to secure a ringside seat for the invasion, would *Collier's* publish her dispatches with Ernest occupying the prime real estate on the magazine's pages?

Chapter Thirty-five

Martha would not be denied the story of the decade, if not her lifetime. Displaying remarkable grit and determination to achieve her goal, Martha waited patiently in London for the invasion to get under way. "9:46 or so," she entered in her diary. "In 5 seconds the command will be given to the world." She described the sound of bombers roaring overhead on their way toward the English Channel: "the sound of a giant factory in the sky." She made note of the weather as she looked up at them: "Weather raw and cold." And notwithstanding her disappointment at being stranded in London, she thought about her husband: "Worried for E," she wrote.

Without knowing exactly what she planned to do, Martha set out for the coast of England. Later that night she walked along the docks where she ran into a military policeman guarding a large white ship with enormous red crosses painted on its side. "I'm here to interview nurses for my magazine," she told him as she presented her press credentials. To her astonishment he waved her through. Once aboard the ship, Martha looked for the nearest bathroom and locked herself inside until she felt the ship inch its way out of port into the open sea. When she slipped out of the bathroom she located a stash of whiskey. "The weather gets rainier and colder every minute," she wrote. "Badly spooked…I was very scared, drank, got unscared." Martha stayed awake through the long, cold, blustery night, prowling alone through the dark corridors of the vessel. At the first light of dawn she saw " a seascape filled with ships…the greatest naval traffic jam in history…so enormous, so awesome, that it felt more like an act of nature than anything man made."

Then she was in the midst of battle. "Double & triple clap of gunfire," she wrote in her diary. "Unseen planes roar. Barrage balloons. Gun flashes. 1 close shell burst…Explosions jar the ship." Soon her ship was alive with teams of medical personnel, nurses and doctors just over from the States, merchant seamen in blue denim, all of them scurrying around purposefully as the war exploded all around them. Martha had her ringside seat as the hospital ship came to rest in the American sector on Omaha Beach. She saw the giant bulldozers scooping up mines on the beach just as the men ran ashore. She saw the artillery shells slamming into German positions on the cliffs beyond the sand. And she saw the bloated bodies floating by, some of them drowned when they left their landing craft too soon and sank under the waves beneath the weight of their own equipment, "swollen greyish sacks." She saw arms and legs of others blown to bits by German guns.

At night Martha went to work with the nurses and doctors who waded onto the beach through waist-high water behind the soldiers. She pushed her way ashore with them, carrying one end of a stretcher, picking up the wounded and dead one by one and carrying them back onto the hospital ship. They picked up German wounded, too, and directed them into POW cages, a "terrible seedy bunch," most of them young and scared, and some of them grizzled with the scars of combat. "Great speed & efficiency of loading," she wrote. "Blood soaked bandages. Everyone watching in silence." In the light of the red flares that went up over the beach, Martha looked out at a landscape from hell, a "junk yard, with the boxy black shapes of tanks, trucks, munition dumps."

And then it was over for her. The military police discovered that she was the only journalist aboard and arrested her for crossing into the warzone without authorization. They sent her back to London where Martha set to work immediately, writing two articles for *Collier's* about all the horrific things she had witnessed firsthand. Martha had her story, the story of a lifetime. She would not be denied.

*　　*　　*

With his head and swollen knees covered with bandages, Ernest took his place with scores of infantrymen aboard the *Empire Anvil* as it plowed across the English Channel with hundreds of other transport ships bound for the beaches of Normandy. Ernest studied his briefing map, with the names of beaches destined to take their places in history: Sword, Juno, Gold, Utah, and most infamous of all, Omaha Beach. Omaha was where so many men drowned before they reached land as a result of navigation problems. It was where the fighting was fiercest because the Germans concentrated the largest number of troops there to defend the French coast. The landing at Omaha and the raging battle that ensued would be immortalized years later in the opening scene of the movie *Saving Private Ryan*.

With his head throbbing and his knees threatening to buckle under him, Ernest clambered down the rope ladder onto a landing craft, where he was transferred to another ship with another rope ladder, and finally onto a smaller landing craft crowded with grim-faced infantrymen. At dawn he scanned Omaha Beach with his field glasses, observing every detail as the men struggled to reach land. "The green water turned white and came slamming in over the men, the guns and the cases of explosives," Ernest wrote in a dispatch for *Collier's*. "Ahead you could see the coast of France. The gray booms and derrick-forested bulks of the attack transports were behind now, and, all over the sea, boats were crawling forward toward France."

Men were puking with seasickness, others prayed for salvation with no hope of retreat if they failed to punch through enemy lines. Only the sea was behind them, waiting to swallow them up if they turned back from their deadly charge. A thousand Allied soldiers would lay dead in the pebbled sand before the long

244

day ended, many blown to pieces, others riveted with machinegun bullets, easy targets for the German gun emplacements. Ernest took it all in, observing "the first, second, third, fourth and fifth waves laying where they had fallen, looking like so many heavily laden bundles on that flat pebbly stretch between the sea and the first cover."

The Allied forces finally broke through and forced the Germans to retreat. The enemy continued to fight on as best they could for some time longer, but the backbone of their resistance had been broken. A few days later Ernest was back in London, sitting in his room in the Dorchester Hotel working on his articles for *Collier's*. On June 15, while he was in the officers' mess of the 98th Squadron in Dunsford, a German V-1 bomb scored a direct hit on the building, raining plaster and other debris down on the men inside. Ernest was uninjured as he secured a piece of bomb shrapnel for a souvenir. A few days later he was airborne with the 98th, flying among eight groups of six B-25 Mitchell bombers on an afternoon run to bomb V-1 launch sites in Drancourt, France. Ernest sat stoically as antiaircraft shells burst all around them. He looked down to watch his plane unload its bombs "sideways as if she were having eight long metal kittens in a hurry." On June 29 Ernest flew on another mission with RAF Group Captain Peter Barnes.

"Ernest seemed to love the fireworks bursting all around us," Barnes said afterward, "and he urged me to press on...I knew I was supposed to keep Ernest out of trouble. I pulled away in a confusion of search lights and intensive flak. As we winged over, there was a huge flash behind us, and the airplane danced around like a leaf in a whirlwind. Someone got the V-1, but not us. Ernest seemed to have loved every moment of it."

The men Ernest served with admired his grace and courage under fire, but many of them wondered out loud why someone as famous as he was would risk his life when he didn't have to. "Hell," Ernest said, laughing. "I had to go to war to see my wife."

"He was a delightful character, totally oblivious of the fame and acclaim that had been his," said John Carlisle, a correspondent with the *Detroit Free Press*. "He wrote and talked as a realist. He was blunt and forceful, but everything was edged with a touch of subtle humor…he was a real, genuine guy. He didn't talk about himself." Underneath it all, Ernest was a fatalist. He had always believed that it was time to go when your number came up, and no one knew when that was going to be. He had a lifelong fascination with death that ran like a cancerous vein throughout his genetic makeup.

*   *   *

During the first week in July Ernest shaved his beard off, leaving just his bushy black mustache intact. At the same time, the doctors removed the bandages from Ernest's head, revealing a pepper-and-salt stubble where the hair was growing back. The effect lent him the appearance of a scruffy barroom brawler, which was not too far off the mark from what he was. He next headed back to France, where he joined the 22nd Infantry Regiment under the command of Colonel Charles "Buck" Lanham, with whom Ernest would develop a tight friendship that would last throughout most of his life. Buck left Ernest pretty much on his own, valuing Ernest's triple-threat role as a journalist, a combatant, and a gatherer of intelligence.

Ernest took off from the coast of France in a Jeep with his driver, Private Archie "Red" Pelkey, behind the steering wheel. The back of the vehicle was loaded with rifles and hand grenades. Ernest had a .45 caliber pistol strapped to his side and his cherished Zeiss field glasses strung around his neck. The Germans had retreated inland, but there were still pockets of stiff resistance as close as ten miles from the coast. As Red began the drive eastward from the coast of Normandy, Ernest studied the road maps that he had lifted from a dead German infantryman. Along the way Ernest spotted an abandoned German motorcycle and sidecar, which still had the key in the ignition. Ernest got out of the Jeep and started up the motorcycle, with Red following behind him in the Jeep. When they came across a chateau, Ernest got out and retrieved a couple of hand grenades from the Jeep. Then he and Red each lobbed one through an open window. One by one a troop of German soldiers came marching out with their hands held high. A report in Reuters captured the moment in an amusing snippet: "The private, with Mr. Hemingway, tossed hand grenades into the house and six of Hitler's supermen piled out and surrendered to Hemingway."

Red guarded their half-starved prisoners, who had no inclination to escape, while Ernest stormed inside. Keeping his priorities straight, Ernest went immediately into the wine cellar and emerged minutes later, his arms laden with the precious spoils of war: bottles of the finest fruit of the grape that France had to offer. Among them were a 1915 Chateau Lafite, a 1929 Chateauneuf du Pape, and a 1915 Rudesheimer. That night Ernest shared his booty with a crew of appreciative journalists and soldiers who caught up with them at the chateau.

"I recall Hemingway with a captured set of Nazi binoculars around his neck and a captured Nazi map case slung over his shoulder," said John Carlisle. "He was in his mid-forties then but already had gray in his hair...Hemingway found the wine cellar and picked out the best wine. He was absolutely fearless, as though war didn't bother him one bit."

"He made me laugh more deeply than anyone else I'd known," recalled *Time* correspondent William Walton. "He had such a sense of the ridiculous, and when he got a reaction he'd play on that same theme and carry it further, which made for great conversations. And there was a big streak of the ham in him."

In early August, Buck Lanham rendezvoused with Ernest and invited him to a party his staff was throwing at the command post to celebrate Buck's twenty-fifth wedding anniversary. Ernest said he couldn't come without giving Buck an explanation of why not. During the festivities a Nazi shell landed on the post and killed a few of Buck's men and slightly injured the Colonel. He told Ernest about the attack the next day, and Ernest explained to him that "the reason I didn't go is because the place had the stink of death about it." It was a line he had lifted directly from the pages of *For Whom the Bell Tolls*, in which Ernest's main character based on himself smelled the stink of death in the bloody battlefields of Spain.

The incident spooked Buck more than he let on at the time. A second precognitive event involving Ernest occurred a month later as Buck was preparing his first attack in the Battle of Huertgen Forest, which would turn out to be one of the bloodiest and longest-running infantry battles the U.S. army had ever fought. He told Ernest that he was going to relieve an officer under his command because he didn't have confidence in his leadership abilities.

"You won't have to relieve him," Ernest said. "He's going to be killed."

Buck was truly rattled after that remark. Moments later, he returned to his command post where his executive officer told him that a German shell had penetrated a narrow space between the logs of a dugout and killed the man he wanted to replace.

"That shook me," Buck remembered. "Hemingway would hate me to call it a 'premonition' and I'm ambivalent about it. I'm open-minded about ESP. If you live long enough you see many things you can't account for. Hemingway hated such talk. I don't know what he really believed. He veered back and forth between believing in nothing and in being a half-assed Catholic."

"He was very superstitious," Walton agreed. "He always said, 'I'm going to play everything, prayer, rabbit's foot, touching wood three times. We need all the help we can get.'"

Buck was an atheist, as Ernest professed to be whenever he grew weary of pretending he was a Catholic. But Ernest was also a gambler, uncertain of the outcome and looking to play the odds. He was surely familiar with Blaise Pascal's wager that it was better to believe in God, since if He existed you gained everything, whereas if He did not exist and you believed you lost nothing except for a few temporal pleasures. If you did not believe and He existed you risked losing everything including your soul. In Ernest's case, he hedged his bets and enjoyed his temporal pleasures at the same time.

Chapter Thirty-six

Martha looked inside the cover of *Collier's* and took pride in seeing her name displayed on the masthead next to Ernest's as the magazine's "invasion correspondent." She wrote a letter to her mother saying she was as "happy as a goat" and Ernest was alive and well, without going into details about the worsening state of her marriage. Her only complaint was that women correspondents were "treated too much like violets." Martha was aching to get back to France, to the action, but she still lacked military clearance because of her unauthorized crossing to Normandy on the hospital ship. Once again she was forced to rely on her female charms, this time with well-placed officers whom she seduced into letting her ride with them and their regiments to the warfront. She was forthright enough to admit that a man in her position would have had "far fewer doors" opened for him. Then again, a man wouldn't have had to resort to subterfuge to get to the war in the first place.

Martha traveled south into Italy and hooked up with the 8th Army, which was marching north after having liberated Rome. She delighted in the "huge hodgepodge" of ethnic groups from such far-flung countries as New Zealand, South Africa, India, Basutoland, Poland, and Canada. Martha hitched a ride in their armored carriers as they plowed onward through Umbria, encountering scattered German resistance along the way. "Shells coming over," she wrote in her diary, "whistling over like great birds. All danger hidden (big mines looking like carpenters' tool chests) blue sea and sky...Happy regiment—main feature. Soldiers all so independent." The summer weather was perfect as she swam in the warm blue ocean with the men, hunted for ducks and geese, and foraged for wine, wine, and more wine in abandoned cellars across the Italian countryside. Her experiences provided great material for the articles she sent across the ocean to *Collier's*.

"There they all stood," she wrote about a church service in a small Italian village, "the officers and the men, friends and partners, each one with his long journey behind him and each one with the long uncertain journey ahead."

In August Martha was in Florence around the same time that Ernest was liberating armloads of wine from damp, dark cellars in France. War raged in the streets, from doorway to doorway, from street corner to street corner, as German forces fought desperately to hang on to every square foot of land they still occupied and ward off their all-but-inevitable defeat. She stayed in a house with an elderly American while "outgoing shells whistled over the house like insane freight cars." In her diary she noted, "Ponte Vecchio all damage…Man killed going out to buy vegetables. The people of Florence could weep for the destruction of their city. So drab & soiled in war. Uffizi Gallery w. hole showing ceiling damage."

She met the U.S. army major while surveying damage on the Ponte Vecchio one evening. He was only twenty-six, ten years younger than Martha, but he was "tall and beautiful and funny" as they made love in the deserted Hotel Excelsior amid the clamor of mortar and machinegun fire in the streets outside. Afterward, she joined a Canadian regiment bound eastward through Tuscany toward the Adriatic coast to attack a remaining German stronghold. It was a memorable battle as she described it in *Collier's*, "a jigsaw puzzle of fighting men, bewildered terrified civilians, noise, smells, jokes, pain, fear, unfinished conversations and high explosives." She was especially concerned about the young men who would be killed "now when the end of the war was at last in sight."

At the end of August, she was riding northward through France in a Jeep that rolled over an embankment, flinging her out and breaking one of her ribs. Now she was the one injured in a car wreck as she continued gamely northbound toward Paris. Once again she would find out that Ernest had gotten there first. And not just Ernest. He had installed a young journalist named Mary Welsh in room 86 at the Ritz Hotel, the room right next to his.

*　　*　　*

Ernest watched the German artillery shells bursting all around him on his march away from the coast toward Paris. Buck remembered Ernest "standing poised as always on the balls of his feet. Like a fighter. Like a great cat. Easy. Relaxed. Absorbed. Intent. Watchful. Missing nothing."

Ernest told Red Pelkey that their goal was to get to Paris as soon as possible without taking too many chances with German mortar shells that thundered through the air directly overhead. The advice was sound and serious. His words were not those of a man who was looking for a quick end to his life on earth, notwithstanding his recurring bouts with suicidal thoughts. Red did his best behind the wheel of the Jeep, but no one could see the shell whistling down on them before it rocked the ground just yards from Ernest's motorcycle and sidecar. The blast upended the vehicle and propelled Ernest into a drainage ditch alongside the road. One report claimed that the shell had missed Ernest by only three yards, while Robert Capa, who was riding close behind snapping vivid photos of the action, said it landed maybe ten yards away. Three or ten, it was too close for comfort. Ernest lay in the ditch for more than two hours with Red beside him, while German machinegun fire ripped into the embankment, driving dirt into their faces every time Ernest raised his head to see what was going on. Reinforcements arrived in time to send the Germans into retreat so the Allied forces could continue their slow, perilous push toward Paris.

Ernest and his troops took command of the Hotel de la Mere in the rocky, tidal island of Mont-St.-Michel near the Normandy coast. Nazi officers had occupied the premises before abandoning it just a few days before Ernest arrived. He turned his gruff charm on the hotel's proprietors, who were happy to have their establishment liberated from the autocratic Nazis. Ernest took charge immediately, securing abundant rooms for himself, the soldiers, and his fellow journalists.

"He chose the wine, decided on menus," said Charles Collingwood. "He had great force of personality and a gift for organization.

John Carlisle thought that Ernest was "one of the happiest men I ever knew" at this stage of his life. He was "a guy with a great zest for life who enjoyed every minute of it."

But William Randolph Hearst, Jr., resented Ernest's celebrity status. "He was only a reporter the same as us, but he thought he was the Second Coming and acted like it." Hearst was in the minority in his assessment of Ernest, and his comments may have been colored by the stain of sour grapes. There is no question that Ernest was more than "only a reporter" like the rest of his colleagues. He carried in his pocket a letter from OSS directing military units to "provide Mr. Ernest Hemingway with small arms, grenades, or other captured articles he desires." Ernest was also a French intelligence operative who "was fighting with the Resistance before the liberation of Chartres." According to OSS documents, Ernest fought "during the liberation battle, at the site of a mass grave while the fires were still burning and the last Germans surrendering." Ernest was popular with the Maquis, the rural guerrilla bands of the French Resistance.

By the middle of August, just before Martha arrived in Paris to discover that Ernest had made it there before she did, Ernest and the Allied forces had fought their way into Rambouillet less than thirty miles southwest of Paris. Ernest met up with Colonel David Bruce, the head of OSS in France, who found Ernest ensconced in two rooms on the second floor of the Hotel du Grand Veneur. Ernest was acting as the *de facto* general of the Allied campaign to take Paris by storm. He and his men were in total control of the site, which was still surrounded by an armada of German tanks looking to reoccupy the town at the first opportunity. Ernest's rooms were the nerve center of the operation, the headquarters of the Allied push into Paris. French officers reported to Ernest regularly with intelligence about German movements in the area.

"There, in his shirtsleeves, he gave audience to intelligence couriers, refugees from Paris, and deserters from the German army," said Colonel Bruce. "Army gear littered the floor, revolvers of every nationality were heaped carelessly on the bed. The bathtub was filled with hand grenades and the basin with brandy bottles, while under the bed was a cache of army ration whiskey."

"Hemingway was carrying a gun, a sidearm, and he shouldn't have been," sniffed William Randolph Hearst, Jr.

Andy Rooney was there as well. "Hemingway had taken over this little hotel in Rambouillet," he remembered. "It had about thirty or forty rooms. And he was working with the French Maquis and had stored hundreds of guns and other weapons in a lot of these rooms."

"He discovered a barroom in this little town," said John Carlisle. "The guys in there spoke French; we didn't know who the hell they were. Finally, he told us it was the Maquis. These guys would come in there and make their secret reports, and this is where Hemingway hung out until they went out again on missions. He spoke excellent French and the French people loved him. The Americans respected him, but lots of the French, I found, adored him."

"He had done a pretty good intelligence job," said Andy Rooney, "using maps to locate German gun positions. He had also organized French Resistance in this hotel and they were conducting their own little war…We started out for Paris on August 24…I was over by a farmhouse behind a stone wall, all alone, sort of nervous because all of the rest of the guys are in tanks and I've parked my Jeep. And I see this figure moving down behind the stone wall. I'm nervous because I think he may be a German. And it turns out to be Hemingway, alone. So the two of us crouched there behind the stone wall for more than an hour. He talked about where the German gun positions were and what he'd been doing. It was a strange experience for me, and I was impressed."

And then they reached Paris. "Hemingway was following close behind my Jeep," said Hans L. Trefousse, who interrogated German prisoners and reported on what they said in English and French. "We crossed the Seine and entered Paris at Porte de St. Cloud. As we entered Paris together the cheering crowds were overwhelming. Liberation Day was a tremendous experience. While the French cheered, I said to some of them, 'There's a very famous American writer right behind me, Ernest Hemingway.'"

Ernest lost no time in heading directly to the Ritz on the Place Vendome, a hotel he had grown familiar with during his many years in Paris. He entered the premises in the company of a woman—an eccentric Spanish beauty whose name was neither Martha nor Mary. Ernest had met Elena years earlier during one of his trips to Spain during the Spanish Civil War, and he had been conducting an off-again, on-again romance with her whenever he was in Europe. The hotel's owner treated Ernest and his entourage to several rounds of martinis and a celebratory dinner. Outside the hotel the streets resounded with the sounds of gunfire, as every Frenchman with a rifle or sidearm was firing it into the air.

"Papa was barefoot," said John Carlisle, "and wearing a pair of khaki pants, and walking up and down the room with a good-looking gal dressed in a khaki outfit. She had a German Luger stuck in her belt, a bandolier of bullets around her, and a Free Forces of the Interior badge on her arm. Papa said to me, 'Pour yourself a shot of cognac.' I had a hangover so I poured a big shot. He said, 'For God's sake don't drink it all.'"

After dinner, Ernest and Elena began to argue in Spanish, their voices growing more heated and louder with each exchange. "What the hell is going on?" Carlisle asked. Ernest stood directly in front of him, looked him squarely in the eye, and said, "A woman never knows when it's over."

It was certainly over when Mary arrived in Paris and headed to the Ritz at Ernest's invitation. He put her up in the room adjoining his own, exactly where Martha found them shortly afterward.

Chapter Thirty-seven

Martha made her presence known immediately, even as she went out of her way to avoid her husband and the snide remarks he directed to his comrades in arms and fellow journalists loud enough for her to hear them. She understood that he was irate and his ego was wounded. He was not a man accustomed to having women leave him, not even temporarily so they could go off and pursue their own interests apart from his control. At the same time she was not about to jettison her newly found identity for the sake of saving her marriage—assuming that saving it was possible after all the damage that had been done. Neither one would cave in to the other in their battle of wills. They had come to an impasse and the bell was tolling loudly.

Martha spent most of her time writing about the last phase of the war and shipped her articles to *Collier's*, which was eager to put her reflections into print alongside Ernest's dispatches. She experienced a brief moment of *schadenfreude* when she overheard Ernest telling his new paramour Mary that she was built "like a spider." In his more affectionate moods, Ernest called Mary his "little pickle" or his "small friend." He told her over and over that he wanted to marry her. Mary would learn soon enough, Martha reasoned, what it was like to be consumed by his overwhelming passions. Ernest saw it differently, of course. He wrote to Martha's mother about her daughter's "silly inhumanity," complaining that she "loves to leave people. It is the bad scene that she plays best." To his firstborn son Bumby, Ernest wrote that he would trade Martha for "two non beautiful wives I might occasionally have the pleasure of going to bed with."

Ernest left Paris in late August in a convoy with Red Pelkey at the wheel of his Jeep, en route to join Buck's 22nd Infantry regiment for the push into Germany. The well-armed convoy of two cars, two Jeeps, and a motorcycle wandered through minefields all the way, exchanging gunfire with the enemy but arriving in Belgium unscathed. Buck came across Ernest in a farmhouse in Buchet, eating nonchalantly and taking notes for an article for *Collier's* with German shells exploding all around them.

"Another shell came through the wall," Buck remembered. "I told him to put on his goddamned tin hat. He wouldn't so I took mine off. We argued about the whole thing but he went on eating. He reverted to his favorite theory that you were as safe in one place as another as far as artillery fire was concerned unless you were being shot at personally. I pointed out that was precisely what was being done."

When the Allies took Brussels on September 4, 1944, Martha took advantage of the opportunity to follow the path the troops had taken and report on the celebrations taking place throughout Belgium. She traveled from Brussels to Antwerp, where she delighted in seeing German prisoners locked up in cages at the zoo. Her only regret was that the Allies had removed the lions first rather than leave them in there to feast on the spoils of war. The prisoners were separated into four cages: one for officers, another for enlisted men, the third for Allied collaborators, and the fourth for women who had prostituted themselves to the Nazis. Next Martha went to Holland, driving through Arnhem and Nijmegen, observing the bomb-gutted towns that looked as though they had been "abandoned years ago following an earthquake or a flood."

After several weeks touring through the formerly Nazi-occupied land, Martha returned to Paris where she found Ernest once again holding court at the Ritz in the midst of an adoring circle of soldiers, reporters—and a movie star. German beauty Marlene Dietrich had taken up residence there as well, and Martha couldn't help but notice that she and Ernest acted like teenagers in the first thrall of puppy love. Ernest affectionately called her "my Kraut" as Mary smoldered beside them. Yes, it was now Mary's turn to endure Ernest's meteorological swings in moods and affections. Martha couldn't deal with them any longer, nor could he with hers.

Martha was surprised when Ernest invited her to join him and his group for dinner. The evening started off cordially enough, but as the night moved along, borne aloft on a gathering cloud of alcohol fumes, Ernest's mood grew ugly. Without warning, he began to berate her in front of the others until, one by one, they peeled away into the night. Finally, there was no one left at the table except for Ernest and Martha. She couldn't take it any longer, she told him. He could go off and marry whomever he wanted at the moment—the cute American journalist who looked like a spider, a gorgeous movie star, or a guerrilla fighter from the hills of Spain with a string of bullets around her neck. She didn't care. She wanted a divorce. Ernest continued his verbal assault and Martha yelled back, each itemizing the other's faults ad infinitum. Eventually he wore her down, reducing her to tears. She pushed her chair back and flew away from the table, leaving Ernest there to continue ranting in an empty dining room.

Later that night, Martha exposed her soul in a letter to Allen Grover, one of her most sympathetic confidants along with Eleanor Roosevelt. "Who shall I talk to and who will tell me why I am doing what I am doing? If God has any benevolence for me he will spare me further horrid errors of the heart, when one tries to make permanence. I wish only to be unmarried; it seems neater. I am so free that the atom cannot be freer, I am free like nothing quite bearable."

To her mother, Martha admitted that her marriage to Ernest was doomed. "I simply never want to hear his name mentioned again," she wrote. "The past is dead and has become ugly; I shall try to forget it all entirely, and blot it out as with amnesia."

Ernest turned increasingly to Mary, professing his love and asking her to marry him. But she was having misgivings of her own. She admitted that her marriage to Noel Monks was all but over, but she told Ernest that she was feeling crushed by his overwhelming ardor. Mary wrote him a letter saying that she sometimes had to get away from his "domination because you are so big and you absorb me so that I lose myself, wanting only the soft easy business of flattery and admiration and gaiety that matters not." Beneath it all was a gnawing feeling that his passion for her contained a sharp edge of revenge—revenge against the wife who caused him so much grief.

Ernest was more hurt than he wanted to admit by the collapse of his third marriage. "Funny how it should take one war to start a woman in your damn heart and another to finish her," he wrote to Max Perkins.

*   *   *

The war may have finished their marriage, but the war was not done with either Ernest or Martha. At the end of September, Ernest was jolted by the news that some members of the journalist community were filing charges against him for being an armed combatant, which was a violation of the role of journalists spelled out by the third Geneva Convention. Ernest was furious and blamed the "liars" and "phonies" of the press who were jealous of his celebrity status that gave him access denied to them. On October 3, the Supreme Headquarters Allied Expeditionary Force ordered Ernest to report to the Inspector General of the Third Army in Nancy to respond to the charges. Fortunately for Ernest, his friends in high places jumped to his defense. Officers on General George Patton's staff told Ernest to deny all the charges at the Inquiry, the first step before a Court Martial. European OSS chief David Bruce would be in attendance as a witness.

Sitting before his inquisitors, Ernest answered the questions as he had been instructed to. Did he carry weapons and engage in combat?

"I offered my services to him in any way in which I might be useful," Ernest said, nodding in Colonel Bruce's direction, "providing that my actions did not violate the Geneva Convention or that any of them should in any way prejudice my fellow war correspondents."

Questioned further about his specific actions, Ernest replied that he "served only in an advisory capacity to Colonel Bruce. I did not command troops nor give orders but only transmitted orders."

What about accounts from various witnesses that Ernest had stripped off his correspondent's insignia, served as a colonel in the French Resistance, and occupied a room filled with mines, grenades, and war maps?

Ernest admitted that he removed the insignia by taking off his jacket and appearing in shirtsleeves, but only because it was hot. As far as his rank of colonel was concerned, Ernest said "It was the same way that citizens of the state of Kentucky are sometimes addressed as colonel without it implying any military rank." The weapons in his hotel room were stored there by the Maquis who were under the orders of Allied commanders.

"Were there mines in your room?"

"There were no mines in my room. I would greatly prefer not to have mines in my room at any time." Ernest was growing playful, warming to the charade.

War maps?

"I always travel with maps because I like to know where I am and where I am going."

"Are you saying that you never fought with the men?"

"I didn't fight with the men," Ernest stated emphatically. Later, after the proceedings were over and he was exonerated of all charges, Ernest laughed and denied that he had lied about his activities. "Why would I fight with the men," he said with a smile, "since I never had anything against them?"

*   *   *

While Ernest was in Nancy being questioned by the military tribunal, Martha headed to the ancient town of Soissons in northern France, situated alongside the Aisne River. The 82nd Airborne Division had taken heavy casualties in ferocious combat with German holdouts in the region, and Martha wanted to report on the aftermath of the battle and assist in any way she could. The weather had grown worse with an early winter setting in. Snow drove in from the north in a blinding swirl, the plasma for blood transfusions froze solid overnight, troops froze to death in their foxholes, and sodden blankets they used to stay warm became hardened, useless boards in the frigid air. Martha found a room in an abandoned house with no heat or running water. She went out on night patrols with a group of sergeants and their men, taking notes, following the soldiers making their rounds in the woods outside the village. That's where the military police found her and asked to see her military pass and accreditation. Martha had nothing to show them.

The MPs escorted Martha to General James Gavin's tent, which served as the 82nd's regional headquarters. Martha expected at least a dressing-down from the general, but she was more terrified than anything else of being deported back to the States, effectively ending her career as a war correspondent without proper press credentials. General Gavin was a year older than Martha at thirty-seven, the youngest divisional commander in the U.S. army. He was tall, slim, physically fit, and strikingly handsome. Martha entered the tent and faced his stare directly. His eyes moved over the cheeky blonde reporter who somehow managed to look glamorous and attractive in the midst of a battlezone. Martha later said his eyes emitted an intensity that was almost a physical shock. She felt an electrical charge running through her. The animal magnetism between them was a palpable presence. Martha knew immediately that she would not be sent back home. Gavin asked her for address in Paris instead. He laughed and told her that she would make a good guerrilla fighter with her talent for living on the edge the way she did. Martha wrote down the name of the hotel where she was staying in Paris, and then left with the General's blessing. She knew she would be seeing him again. At least she hoped she would.

Chapter Thirty-eight

James Maurice "Jumping Jim" Gavin was the stuff legends are made of. Born in Brooklyn, New York, on March 22, 1907, with the name James Nally Ryan, he never knew who his real parents were. His mother may have been an Irish immigrant named Katherine Ryan, and his father was either James Nally or another Irishman named Thomas Ryan. So the name that appeared on his birth certificate was little more than an educated guess on the part of hospital officials. When Jim was about two years old, he was placed in the Convent of Mercy orphanage in Brooklyn, where he remained until he was adopted in 1909 by Martin and Mary Gavin, a coal mining family from Mount Carmel, Pennsylvania. The Gavins had a tough time putting food on the table and keeping a roof over their heads, so Jim had to go to work when he was only twelve to help support the family.

Faced with the prospect of becoming a coal miner like his adopted father, Jim decided to run away from home. On his seventeenth birthday on March 22, 1924, he took the night train to New York and sent a telegram to his parents saying everything was all right with him, to prevent them from reporting him missing to the police. He immediately went to see a U.S. Army recruiting officer, who told him that he needed parental approval to join the army since he was under eighteen. Knowing that his father wanted him back home in the coal mine with him, Jim told the recruiter he was an orphan. He enlisted on April 1, 1924, and was sent to Panama.

His rise through the ranks was nothing less than meteoric. He read books about military history in the base library and was promoted to Corporal within six months. Despite his lack of a formal education, he lied about his age and was admitted to West

Point. He was a natural athlete who boxed at the academy and made a bad marriage to a woman who bore a daughter they named Barbara after he graduated. Following a stint in Fort Benning, Georgia, he was posted to the Philippines, where he grew alarmed about his country's inability to counter Japan's plans for expansion throughout the region. Jim was promoted quickly to Captain and began training at the Airborne School in Fort Benning in July 1941. His next command was as Commanding Officer of C Company of the newly established 503rd Parachute Infantry Battalion. On October 16, 1941, he was promoted to Major and wrote a manual about airborne tactics, using information he had gleaned from the Russians and Germans about paratroopers and glider troops. His military career escalated dramatically as American entry into the war drew nearer. He made Colonel as the commanding officer of the 505th Parachute Infantry Regiment in August 1942, and built the unit from the ground up. He led the troops under his command on long marches and training sessions, and promoted the concept of being the "the first out of the airplane door and the last in the chow line."

In February 1943, the 82nd Airborne Division was selected for the Allied Invasion of Europe and played a major part in Mission Boston on D-Day. Jim's role in the invasion of Normandy was dramatized by Cornelius Ryan in his book *The Longest Day*. In the movie made later Jim was portrayed by Robert Ryan, and then again by Ryan O'Neal in *A Bridge Too Far*. It was startling how the name *Ryan* was so prominent in his life; perhaps Ryan was his real father after all. Promoted afterward to Lieutenant General, Jim earned the moniker "The Jumping General," or more informally "Jumping Jim," from his men because of his practice of parachuting out of aircraft with his combat troops.

By the time Martha set eyes on Jumping Jim in his tent, the tall, lanky, handsome General was already a legend in military circles.

*   *   *

Ernest breathed a sigh of relief after being exonerated of all charges leveled against him and then made plans to meet up with Buck—as an armed combatant—during one of the last campaigns of the war for them. Observers could not help but notice that Ernest and Buck made for an odd couple in every way imaginable. What drew the two men together so closely? They looked like Laurel and Hardy as they shambled beside each other, Ernest tall and large, Buck short and wiry. But beneath the surface they were more alike than could be immediately discerned. Buck was the field commander that Ernest would have been had he not been a writer; Ernest was the famous author that Buck, who wrote poetry, would like to have been. They respected and loved each other like brothers.

"We told each other about our childhoods, our parents, our dreams, our hopes, our education, our women, our friends, our enemies, our triumphs and our disasters," Buck wrote later. "It was one of those rare occasions when two human beings suddenly find themselves in complete rapport and their separate worlds meet and merge."

When Buck rallied his troops by yelling, "Let's go get these Krauts! Let's kill these chickenshits! Let's get up over this hill now and get the place taken!" Ernest was the first one over the hill with him.

As the war wound down, Ernest immediately started to think about life back home. He wanted to return to Cuba, and he wanted Mary to join him there. He wrote to her about that "old whore, Death" that he faced every day. He told her what their life together at the Finca would be like, both of them writing in the morning, fishing on his boat in the afternoon, entertaining guests, enjoying the sights, smells, and tastes of Havana at night. Mary was beginning to

266

succumb to his passions, tossing aside her reservations, embracing the idea of an idyllic existence in a tropical setting with the man she had come to love.

"I am your woman my dearest Only One for as long as you'll have me," she wrote back, "and I will try to make that forever."

Mary was hooked, and Ernest once again felt the glow of having a woman beside him who would share his bed, his home, his life with his sons, and not try to run off to war to write about things she didn't need to see. He also started to think seriously about starting a new book after so much time had elapsed since his last one. It would be about the war of course. "I will just take my small piece of a tiny part of it," he wrote to Mary, "and buttress it with the forgotten sometimes punchy knowledge and the new will work the mess so the old magic will work—and then we will have the book, a day at a time."

With thoughts of Cuba and Mary very much on his mind, Ernest almost did not make it back from the battlefield alive. On a damp, chilly day in the German woods, Ernest heard a familiar sound overhead, one he remembered clearly from his days in Spain. Ernest listened for a moment and recognized the familiar hum of the aircraft engine supplied by the Germans to Franco's forces years earlier. He yelled out, "Oh God! Jump!" His driver Red Pelkey, fellow correspondent Bill Walton, and Ernest leaped out of the Jeep just as the plane swooped low and stitched the vehicle with a deadly round of machinegun fire. The three of them lay in a ditch as the aircraft returned for an encore. It was a close encounter, with the old whore death failing to claim them by only a split second. Ernest knew it was time to go home, soon, before his luck, prayers, and the magic of his rabbit's foot ran out.

*   *   *

Jumping Jim tracked Martha down on his third visit to Paris. He had come calling every time his duties on the battlefield permitted, only to find that she was off to Italy, to Spain, to other parts of Europe digging up stories for *Collier's*. But the third time was the charm. He presented himself at the Hotel Lincoln and found her in this time. Their first meeting since their encounter on the battlefield did not go smoothly. Jumping Jim was used to having his way with women, many of whom wilted under his mesmerizing gaze. Martha was clearly taken with him as well, but she was not a pushover for any man. She was not about to be grabbed "like a package and pushed into bed," she said later. She turned him down, setting the dashing General back on his heels. They talked instead, getting to know and respect each other first. *Then* they went to bed "on a basis of high mutual esteem." When they weren't making love, they sat together in bed playing hand after hand of gin rummy and telling each other about their lives and interests.

Jumping Jim had many conquests under his belt by now— female as well as military conquests. But Martha was a different species entirely for him. He had been quick to forget the women he had slept with, but he would not forget Martha. Jumping Jim fell head over heels for her as he had never fallen before. In short order he was writing her long letters from the front dripping with passion, expressing his undying love for her. She was his "only rock in a great deal of quicksand. You are the purpose of my life. You have become my life itself. Darling, give. Write me a letter, goddamit, you are breaking my heart."

But Martha was not ready to give as much as Jim wanted in return—indeed, she never would be with any man who wanted to possess her. She loved him too, she told him, but the prospect of spending her life on an army base, even with a General, was nothing short of horrifying for her. The more she resisted, the more passionate his ardor grew. "Darling, I love you, I love you, I love you," he wrote. "It is a good love now. It is sturdy, dependable and solid, something that one can count on."

It was something for Jim to count on, perhaps, but not Martha. She enjoyed their lovemaking and their conversations, but already her attention was drifting to other men, men who were less intense, men who were funny and knew how to make her laugh as Ernest had. Even when Ernest was misbehaving and she wanted to throttle him, he had always come up with a line that made her double over with laughter. As Jumping Jim felt Martha cooling toward him, he tried another tack. He decided he would make her jealous. Marlene Dietrich was working her way through the American literary and military establishment as the war wound down. She loved being with Ernest, and she also cast her eyes on Jumping Jim. When Martha was not available to him one night, Jim spent the night with Marlene in her hotel.

Now Martha was faced with the prospect of her lover making love to her husband's favorite Kraut. It was all too incestuous for her, too ensnaring, too entangling, too damned complicated. She didn't need to be sucked back into Ernest's vortex by sexual osmosis, as it were. She was furious with Jumping Jim for thinking he could win her over with such a tawdry schoolboy trick.

Chapter Thirty-nine

The parallels between Martha and Mary became even more apparent after the war. Ernest returned to Cuba in March 1945 and made arrangements for Mary to join him there as soon as she returned from Europe. Martha's only misgiving about the living arrangement was her proprietary interest in the Finca Vigia. Ernest had bought the house with his own money, but she was the one who found the place and fixed it up. The idea of another woman sharing *her* tropical refuge with Ernest was irritating to say the least, but all things considered, Martha was happy to be off by herself pursuing her own interests.

When Mary arrived for a trial visit in early May, she encountered a scene that had become all too familiar to Martha and driven her to the precipice of madness when she was living there. Ernest was once again in party mode, and Mary was rattled to the bones by the endless rounds of feasting and drunken rowdiness that made the walls vibrate almost without letup. The Finca was alive not only with Ernest's literary guests from New York and elsewhere, but also with politicians, athletes, gamblers, and unsavory characters from every level of Cuban society. Mary was stunned that such a gifted man of letters would willingly turn his house into a den of boisterous, unrestrained, Saturnalian pleasures. She retreated to the bedroom and made an entry into her diary that could have been penned by Martha.

"Can only conclude I'd be an idiot to stay here and marry Papa. Our values, most of them, are antipodal. He puts a premium on bad manners, on violence, on killing (man, animals, birds, fish), on toughness, on death. I begin to realize how highly I value gentleness, conversation, non-violence. I'd better go while the going is possible and can be without too much bitterness."

But she didn't go when she might have. Ernest promised undying love and fidelity and vowed to change his ways, and Mary proceeded with her divorce from Noel Monks. Ernest drove her to the airport to catch a plane to Chicago for the hearing, and on the way he lost control of the car on a rain-slick road and crashed into a tree. Ernest suffered another split forehead and four broken ribs when he smashed into the steering wheel, and Mary's cheek was flayed open with blood streaming down her left cheek. It was all so familiar—broken bones, stitches on the forehead, blood, trauma, the very taste of death itself. How many times had Martha been party to it? Ernest returned to the Finca where he turned himself into the model lover, nursing Mary back to health, cutting back on his drinking and partying while his bones healed, and agreeing to Mary's needs for a more orderly life. Ernest's charm worked its magic, as it had so many times in the past. Mary melted, her doubts vanished. A month later she wrote to a friend that life with Ernest at the Finca was "so idyllic, so lush, so leisured, with everything so plentiful. I can sun in the altogether with only the Finca dogs, cats, servants, and children to disturb my privacy."

The truth was, Ernest needed to get back in writing shape for the task ahead. He had not written anything but journalism for five years now. He was anxious to begin work on another major opus, but he was also worried that he might not be able to equal the success of *For Whom the Bell Tolls* let alone surpass it. He knew it was his best book ever. It had taken so much out of him. It had drained him physically and emotionally. And yet he needed to cast his doubts aside and face the challenge. He was only forty-six years old, far too young to live on faded glory and coast as a professional celebrity for the rest of his life instead of acting like a serious novelist with his best work yet to come.

Mary's divorce became final in August, and she returned in October to a much renovated Finca, with new furniture to replace Martha's, new paint to cover the faded old paint, new rain gutters in place of the old sagging ones, and the whole place cleaned and shining inside and out. Ernest's legion of cats—even the wimmies whose wommy cut their balls off—were no longer allowed to roam freely through the house, driving Mary batty. In her absence Ernest had inundated her daily with letters, professing his undying love and steadfastness, promising to be the supportive husband she craved. The written word was his artform, of course, and his letters were more persuasive than his words were in person. Mary was hooked, like a marlin on the end of Ernest's line. When *Time* telegraphed her with an offer of a lucrative new assignment, she telegraphed back that she was "eager to continue current career of loafer fisherwoman housewife. So strike me off the rolls."

She had decided to make a go of life at the Finca with Ernest, despite her continuing tredpidations about being alone five out of seven mornings when he was working on his new book, about learning to fish and shoot "which bore the shit out of me," and about having so little company of her own that "I don't know why the hell I try to stay here." Ernest was on his best behavior while his courtship of Mary continued apace. He cut back on his drinking, stepped up his exercise routine to drop excess pounds, and "in bed he has certainly been better for me than any man I ever had," Mary entered into her diary on December 19, 1945.

Martha's divorce from Ernest became final just before Christmas, and they never set eyes on each other again. She never wanted to hear his name mentioned in her presence, she said, and she refused to grant interviews to anyone whose main goal was finding out what life with Ernest was like, rather than taking an interest in *her* literary efforts. And so it was that the paths of two great writers, two extraordinary and strong-willed human beings came together for a brief moment in eternity and then diverged and went their separate ways again.

Ernest and Mary married on March 13 of the following year, and it wasn't too long before the old Ernest returned with a vengeance. He rewarded Mary a couple of years later by falling in love with a "beautiful, jolly, nice, and ungloomy" Italian girl named Adriana Ivancich, who was young enough to be his daughter. Yes, Ernest finally had the daughter he always wanted, but in a more intimate way than even he had anticipated. As he had done in the past, Ernest invited her to Cuba to meet the wife. The pattern was unbroken, but Hadley, Pauline, or Martha no longer had to deal with it. It was Mary's turn now. Lucky Mary!

*   *   *

Martha drifted away from Jumping Jim and took up with Ernest's buddy, CBS correspondent Charles Collingwood, who was funny and witty and made her laugh. She had an affair with another old crony of Ernest, *Time* correspondent Bill Walton, who fell much harder for her than she did for him. It was curious that a woman who couldn't get away from her husband fast enough wound up having flings with such close friends of his. Then again, perhaps it was just her way of evening the score.

Martha embarked on the most productive phase of her life once she was free of her all-controlling husband. Her war novel, *The Undefeated*, was published in 1945. The books flew off her typewriter with great regularity. She spaced them out three to five years apart until her death, fiction and nonfiction, an impressive array of creative writing that bore her trademark stamps of wit, empathy, and cynicism—the cynicism growing stronger as she got older. She made the mistake of adopting the child she always thought she wanted, a boy from an Italian orphanage whom she called Sandy, but she grew impatient with being a fulltime mother and left him in the care of relatives in Englewood, New Jersey. Their relationship became bitter when she made it clear he disappointed her, and the breach grew wider with time. Martha got married again in 1954, to *Time* editor-in-chief Tom Matthews, and divorced him nine years later.

Ernest entered a period of slow and steady decline, creatively, mentally, and physically. His next novel out of the gate, his long-awaited war novel published ten years after the previous one, was arguably his worst book ever. *Across the River and into the Trees* told the story of an American army officer and his affair with, ahem, a beautiful, young Italian countess. Any similarities to people living or dead were strictly coincidental, as the saying goes. This would the last full-length novel Ernest would publish in his lifetime. It was not even the best of bad Hemingway; it read almost as though Ernest had decided to parody himself as he had done with Sherwood Anderson twenty-five years earlier. One noteworthy critic, novelist John O'Hara, saw it differently, however. He said the book established Ernest as "the most important author since Shakespeare." Perhaps John was concerned that Ernest would have been moved to break another walking stick over *his* head the next time they met if he wrote anything negative about the novel.

Ernest had been in line for the Nobel Prize for literature, awaiting only the arrival of another novel on the literary landscape that was the equal of *For Whom the Bell Tolls*. Alas, the new book was not it. It would take his magnificent long short story or novella, take your pick, to put Ernest back in the running. *The Old Man and the Sea* weighed in at only twenty-five thousand words and ran to a little more than one hundred pages. And receive the coveted prize he did, two years later in 1954. It was all downhill for Ernest after that. At fifty-five years of age he looked more like a man of seventy, with a full white beard and white thinning hair brushed forward in a Julius Caesar-style comb-over. He drank more. He gained weight. His health declined. He became more paranoid than ever when the mad demons in his bipolar nature took up permanent residence in his mind.

His posthumous works were a mixed bag; only the wonderful memoir/novel *A Moveable Feast* equaled the greatness of the best work published in his lifetime. The other manuscripts he left behind were unfinished and patched together with varying degrees of success by his literary executors. It's hard to believe he would have been happy with *Islands in the Stream* and *Garden of Eden*, whose main characters were loosely based on F. Scott Fitzgerald and his wife Zelda. The critics got it wrong when they said the characters were reflective of Ernest's own sexual identity crisis. Zelda was the one who envied her husband's literary talent and tried to undermine him, not Hadley, Pauline, Martha, or Mary.

Ernest and Martha would have agreed on one thing after he was gone. Ernest was definitely not the marrying kind. He was every inch a man's man. Men who met him wanted to be just like him. Women were attracted to his earthy virility too, and he to them. He loved women, but usually more than one at a time, which made him less than reliable as a lifelong mate and partner. The women who got away were better off for not having married him. Martha would have been happier if she never had. When his women married Ernest for whatever reason—love, admiration, career advancement—they got the bad with the good, the depressive with the manic, the suicidal fatalist with the unbridled optimist. And they got his need to love more than one woman simultaneously. That was the package deal, as all his wives discovered sooner or later.

*   *   *

Ernest and Martha left this world the same way, on their own terms and by their own hand. Ernest, whose mind had been completely ruined by a series of electric shock treatments designed to "cure" his bipolar disorder, rose early on the morning of July 2, 1961, in his house in Ketchum, Idaho. He padded quietly down the stairs to the basement. He unlocked his gun cabinet and removed his favorite double-barreled shotgun. He walked up the flight of stairs to the foyer, placed the end of the barrel in his mouth, and tripped the trigger with his toe. The blast thundered through the house, waking Mary. She knew immediately what had happened. The clock on her night table read seven-thirty. She bolted down the stairs and found what was left of her husband lying there in the foyer in a pool of blood. He was less than three weeks shy of his sixty-second birthday.

When Martha heard the news she said she did not blame Ernest for not wanting to "stay around for a long rotting finale." She didn't want to do that either. For her the end came later. On Saturday, February 14, 1998, at eighty-nine years of age, she found herself sick and groaning with unbearable pain in her flat in London. Ovarian cancer ravaged her body and she was nearly blind, no longer able to do anything that had given her pleasure all her life. She could no longer write, no longer travel, no longer read. Everything she loved was gone. "I think it takes some kind of desperate courage to commit suicide," she had once written to a friend. "After all, it is the totally unknown risk." Martha took the pills from the bottle next to her nightstand and swallowed them all. The light, such as it was, dimmed around her as the life drained from her body.

And so, "Never send to know for whom the bell tolls," the poet said.

It tolls for them, and it tolls for thee, and it tolls for me.

Terminado! Finito! Fini!

Acknowledgements

While the concept for this book and its interpretation of historical events is my own, it would not have been possible without the work of many fine writers who came before me. I would like to acknowledge the following major sources, listed in alphabetical order by author:

Bibliography

Baker, Carlos: *Hemingway* (Princeton University Press, 4th edition, 1972)

Bellavance-Johnson, Martha with Bellavance, Lee: *Ernest Hemingway in Key West* (The Computer Lab, 2000)

Bennett, Michael J.: *When Dreams Came True: The GI Bill and the Making of Modern America* (Brassey's, 1996)

Bolloten, Burnett: *The Spanish Civil War: Revolution and Counterrevolution* (University of North Carolina Press, 1991)

Brian, Denis: *The True Gen: an Intimate Portrait of Hemingway by Those Who Knew Him* (Dell, 1988)

Burns, James MacGregor: *Roosevelt: The Soldier of Freedom* (Harcourt Brace Jovanovich, 1970)

Dickson, Paul and Allen, Thomas B.: *The Bonus Army: an American Epic* (Walker, 2000)

Diliberto, Gioia: *Hadley* (Ticknor & Fields, 1992)

Dos Passos, John: *Manhattan Transfer: a Novel* (Mariner, 2003)

Gellhorn, Martha: *The Face of War* (Hart Davis, 1959)

Gellhorn, Martha: *Travels with Myself and Another* (Jeremy P. Tarcher, 1978)

Goodwin, Doris Kearns: *No Ordinary Time* (Simon & Schuster, 1994)

Hemingway, Ernest: *A Moveable Feast* (Scribner's, 1964)

Hemingway, Ernest: *The Fifth Column and the First Forty-nine Stories* (Jonathan Cape, 1939)

Hemingway, Ernest: *To Have and Have Not* (Scribner's, 1937)

Herbst, Josephine and Francis, Elizabeth: *The Starched Blue Sky of Spain and Other Memoirs* (Northeastern University Press, 1999)

Humes, Edward: *Over Here: How the G.I. Bill Transformed the American Dream* (Houghton Mifflin Hartcourt, 2006)

Ickes, Harold L.: *The Secret Diary of Harold L. Ickes: the First Thousand Days, 1933-1936* (Simon & Schuster, 1953)

Kennedy, David M.: *Freedom from Fear: the American People in Depression and War* (Oxford University Press, 1999)

Koch, Stephen: *The Breaking Point* by Stephen Koch (Counterpoint, 2006)

Ludington, Towsend: *John Dos Passos: a Twentieth-Century Odyssey* (Da Capo, 1998)

Lynn, Kenneth: *Hemingway* (Harvard University Press, 1995)

McIver, Stuart B.: *Hemingway's Key West* (Pineapple Press, 1993, 2002)

Mettler, Susan: *Soldiers to Citizens: the G.I. Bill and the Making of the Greatest Generation* (Oxford University Press, 2007)

Moorehead, Caroline: *Gellhorn: a Twentieth-Century Life* (Henry Holt, 2003)

Moreira, Peter: *Hemingway on the China Front* (Potomac Books, 2006)

Murphy, George: *The Key West Reader: the Best of Key West's Writers, 1830-1990* (Tortugas, 1989)

Olson, Keith W.: *The G.I. Bill, the Veterans, and the Colleges* (University Press of Kentucky, 1974)

Orwell, George: *Homage to Catalonia* (Benediction Classics, 2010)

Payne, Stanley G.: *The Spanish Civil War, the Soviet Union, and Communism* (Yale University Press, 2004)

Reynolds, Michael: *Hemingway: the Paris Years* (W.W. Norton, 1999)

Reynolds, Michael: *Hemingway: the Homecoming* (W.W. Norton, 1999)

Reynolds, Michael: *Hemingway: the Final Years* (W.W. Norton, 1999)

Reynolds, Michael: *Hemingway: the 1930s* (W.W. Norton, 1997)

Rollyson, Carl E.: *Beautiful Exile: the Life of Martha Gellhorn* (Backinprint, 2007)

Ross, Davis R.B.: *Preparing for Ulysses: Politics and Veterans during World War II* (Columbia University Press, 1969)

Schlesinger, Arthur M.: *The Age of Roosevelt: the Politics of Upheaval* (Houghton Mifflin, 1960)

Staten, Clifford L.: *The History of Cuba* (Palgrave MacMillan, 2003)

Suchlicki, Jaime: *Cuba: from Columbus to Castro and Beyond* (Potomac Books, 2002)

Tuccille, Jerome: *A Portrait of Hemingway as a Young Man: Romping through Paris in the 1920s* (Blue Mustang Press, 2010)

Tuchman, Barbara Wertheim: *Stillwell and the American Experience in China, 1911-45*, (Grove, 2001)

Voss, Frederick: *Picturing Hemingway: a Writer in His Time* (Yale University Press, 1999)

White, Theodore and Jacoby, Annalee: *Thunder Out Of China* (W. Sloane Associates, 1946)

Williams, Joy: *The Florida Keys: a History and Guide* (Random House, 1987)

In addition, the following articles and miscellaneous documents were invaluable:

"A Brief History of the Conch Republic" by Anonymous

"The Chase Brandon Espionage Series" by Sherri Bigbeen and Steve Hicok

"Gerardo Machado" by Jerry A. Sierra

"History of the Upper Keys: the Bridge That Never Was" by Jerry Wilkinson

"How Did Key West Become a Tourist Town" by Jerry Wilkinson

"Justice for Warriors" by Taylor Branch

"1935 Storm Swept Away All But Memories" by Associated Press

I would like to acknowledge a special debt of gratitude to my indefatigable agent, Linda D. Konner—no writer has ever been served better by his agent; and also to Xaviera Flores of the John F. Kennedy Presidential Library in Boston, MA; the Franklin D. Roosevelt Library in Hyde Park, NY; and the Hemingway Society in Winter Park, FL, all of whom have been extremely generous with their time and resources.

My wife Marie has been at my side for the past forty-six years and has long put up with my compulsive writing routine with infinite patience. Marie reviewed the manuscript prior to publication with a keen editorial sense and has been an irreplaceable asset throughout my career. Any errors contained herein are the fault of the author and no one else.

About the Author

Jerome Tuccille is the author of twenty-seven books, including highly acclaimed biographies of Donald Trump, Rupert Murdoch, Alan Greenspan, and the Hunts of Texas. *Trump* and *Kingdom* both hit best-seller lists. He has also written several novels. Tuccille's last in-depth biography was *Gallo Be Thy Name*, released by Phoenix Books in 2009, a history of the Gallo wine clan and its roots in organized crime. It was named one of the best books of 2009 by *Reason* magazine, and one of the best business books of 2009 by the University of California Library System. Two of the author's books—his true crime memoir, *Gallery of Fools*, and *Kingdom: The Story of the Hunts of* Texas—have been optioned for feature films.

The author is vice president/communications at T. Rowe Price, a major financial services firm. He previously taught at the New School for Social Research in New York City and is a former third-party candidate for Governor of New York. He is a member of Authors Guild and American Society of Journalists and Authors.

Check the author's website: www.jerometuccille.com
He can be reached via email at jtuccille@verizon.net

24657175R00159

Made in the USA
San Bernardino, CA
01 October 2015